CW00538602

All That Glitters

All That Glitters

A Story of Friendship,
Fraud and Fine Art

Orlando Whitfield

Profile

First published in Great Britain in 2024 by
Profile Books Ltd
29 Cloth Fair
London
EC1A 7JQ
www.profilebooks.com

1 3 5 7 9 10 8 6 4 2

Typeset in Sabon by MacGuru Ltd
Printed and bound in Great Britain by
Clays Ltd, Elcograf S.p.A.

An extract from *London Fields* by Martin Amis is reproduced
by kind permission from Penguin Random House UK.

A CIP catalogue record for this book is available from the British Library.

ISBN 978 1 78816 995 0
eISBN 978 1 78283 958 3

FSC
www.fsc.org
MIX
Paper | Supporting
responsible forestry
FSC® C018072

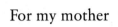

For my mother

'The art market is a fever chart. Its zigs and zags call less for explanation than for diagnosis'
— Peter Schjeldahl, *The New Yorker*

'No one seemed to have thought through the implications of a world in which everyone cheated'
— Martin Amis, *London Fields*

'All that glisters is not gold;
Often have you heard that told.
Many a man his life hath sold
But my outside to behold.
Gilded tombs do worms infold.
Had you been as wise as bold,
Young in limbs, in judgement old,
Your answer had not been enscrolled.
Fare you well; your suit is cold.'
Cold indeed, and labour lost.
Then farewell heat, and welcome frost.

      – William Shakespeare, *The Merchant of Venice*, II. vii.

1

In late February 2018 I woke up in the psychiatric ward of a hospital in west London. Outside, thick snow covered everything. I'd slept fitfully, waking every fifteen minutes throughout the night when a nurse or orderly would open the door to my room to check on me. I was on suicide watch.

Over the past year my life had started to unravel. I'd been drinking heavily, mixing alcohol with Xanax and tramadol. My relationship with my dying father was at a silent impasse and on Valentine's Day my girlfriend had broken up with me by phone. Beyond my crumbling personal life, I was struggling at work. It had been eleven years since I'd become an art dealer and the ensuing decade had had the feel of several lifetimes. The incessant travelling that a career as a dealer demands – to New York and LA several times a year, as well as frequent European trips and to art fairs in between – had ground me down; but the lies, one-upmanship, trophy-touting and greed that the industry runs on were the real poison. Duplicitousness had become my way of life, the constant demands of clients and artists leaving me nothing of myself. My friends and family could see what I couldn't: I was not only exhausted – I was having a breakdown.

By early May 2018 I had stopped working at the gallery I ran with a friend, and accepted an invitation to stay in Connecticut with a good friend who I knew would ask no questions, would ask nothing of me, and would offer just the type of quiet kindness I needed. I landed at JFK the week after the Frieze art fair had been held in New York – the time when galleries and museums put their best feet forward. The foreign dealers and collectors had all left, but the shows themselves would continue for a few weeks yet, open to the public. I spent two days walking through them, instinctively looking at the wall labels, looking for the lender's name – did I know that person; how could I contact them; would they sell? – before realising that I no longer needed to. Who owned what was no longer my concern. For the first time in years, I stood in front of an artwork and just looked.

But my story starts more than a decade before any of this – long before I started a gallery; before I learnt to lie as easily as I breathed air; long before art was reduced in my eyes to no more than numbers on a spreadsheet; before I had even thought of entering the art world at all. My story starts with a friendship; with a young man called Inigo Philbrick.

When you embark on something at twenty, which is when Inigo and I, inexperienced and wet behind the ears, started dealing art together, there's no telling where it will go, how boundless an opportunity it might reveal itself to be. It was the beginning of a friendship which, more and longer than any other, has shaped the way I experience and confront the world, and the whole direction of my adult life. At that age, you don't think about endings or contingencies. But of course, even in a world built on illusion, there's no escaping reality for long.

Sometimes a story is just a story. But there are some stories which, through an unexpected prism, tell us something about the world in which we live, about the people we are. Inigo's career in the upper echelons of the contemporary art market had been meteoric. Except meteors don't rise, they plummet. Radical bodies hurtling and tumbling through space, they become meteors only in the incandescent moment that they enter the Earth's atmosphere, trailing shimmering fire as they break apart, appearing to soar for a bright and fleeting moment, imprinted for ever on the memories of those who see them. The crash is devastating and destructive and final.

What Inigo did can inform us about a culture and world that no longer make sense. Though I was never more than a bottom-rung art dealer, I have lived most of my life either in or on the edges of the art world, and I am here to tell you that no depiction so far – be it cinematic or literary – comes close to capturing the gooey layers of absurdity and frivolous late capitalism that the international art scene now embodies. The reality, however, is absolutely buck wild. It is more opaque than words can muster and more preposterous than you can imagine; its denizens are by turns craven, lovely, ingenious, devious, supremely talented, completely amoral and utterly fascinating. It can exemplify everything bad about money and people and their avarice, as well as everything that is good about our capacity for beauty and curiosity and truth. It is precisely this bizarre mix – this heady, just-shy-of-toxic cocktail – that makes it so potent and engrossing, that sucked both Inigo and me in, and spat us out, broken, in our early thirties.

By the time Inigo turned thirty-two, he had navigated his way from an internship to a multi-million-dollar transatlantic empire. He was comfortable in the company of some of the richest and most private individuals in the world and they wanted, maybe even needed, his advice. And then, in October 2019, accused of defrauding collectors, investors and lenders of more than $20 million and in the face of a gathering storm of lawsuits and negative press, Inigo fled, shuttering his galleries in Miami and London. His phones were disconnected; emails to him and to his lawyers went unanswered. As dramatically and suddenly as he had appeared on the contemporary art scene a decade earlier, he vanished.

We live in dissonant times: the disparity between rich and poor has never been more acute, and yet it seems as if the popular obsession with great wealth – and especially its quick and easy acquisition – knows no bounds. Culturally, we seem to be in a golden age of scams and scammers, of get-rich-quick schemes and too-good-to-be-true opportunities. We gloated over Billy McFarland and his disastrous non-event festival, Fyre, and we delighted in the downfall of Elizabeth Holmes's blood-testing company Theranos, in a scam so ornate and far-reaching that it managed to con Henry Kissinger and Rupert Murdoch, among others. But first, we glorified them as visionaries, saw them as prophets of the future, representatives of the life we would all like to live, if only we were bold enough.

The art market has long been perceived as the bailiwick of cads and cheats, but the massive, years-long fraud that Inigo perpetrated came at a moment when a small number of people really were making vast sums of money in the market in a short time. What Inigo did was not a question of a fake Velasquez or a stolen Henry Moore; this was financial crime that perfectly exploited the shadowy aspects of the art market – the silent partners, the discretion, the handshake deals.

It is easy to see Inigo as a bad apple now excised from the barrel, but I believe what he did was emblematic of a wider malaise within the art market. It is sometimes said that both the best and the worst thing about the art market is that it's unregulated. The financial haziness which some buyers revel in, the ability to place money in moveable assets which can then be kept in temperature-controlled Swiss freeports, is often used to the advantage of dealers, unbeknownst to their clients. But Inigo was young and brash, and he got caught; sometimes I think it was simply the combination of all three which did for him.

One morning towards the end of October 2019, just weeks after he'd vanished, I woke to an email from British Airways which read: 'We want to let you know that Mr Inigo Philbrick has added you to their Family and Friends list. That means they can book reward flights for you with their Avios, which is the currency of the British Airways Executive Club frequent flyer programme.'

I sent him a screenshot of the email via the messaging app Telegram. 'Does this mean you're not coming back?' 'Not for a while,' he replied. 'But you'll like it here. The food's great.' I asked him where 'here' was. Underlying my curiosity was as much self-interest as friendly concern, since Inigo and I had worked together on and off for years and I had no idea if I might be implicated in the accusations against him. I could see he was online. The double tick appeared next to my message as he read my question. Then he was gone. Before that, I'd not heard from him in months. It was one thing to watch my friend's life unravelling in the pages of *The New York Times*; it was quite another to hear from him while the world was speculating as to his whereabouts. It was thrilling, like being invited into a secret society.

It's a daunting task to try to communicate the essence of someone one has known for a long time, so to begin with I will start where Inigo and I left off: on the phone. Inigo enjoys speaking on the phone. He has the kind of voice you expect to come dressed in a pastel polo shirt and accompanied by the rhythmic clinking of ice in Scotch. To the English he sounds American in the mid-Atlantic way that Cary Grant sounded American sometimes; to the Americans he sounds English in the mid-Atlantic way that Cary Grant also sounded English sometimes. He has a languid, inquisitive and encouraging conversational style that can make you feel like you're in the best job interview of your career. He listens deeply and peppers his speech with small, teacherly affirmations like 'Bingo!' or 'You've got it one' and 'When you know, you know'. Inigo will seldom correct you if he thinks you're wrong on a certain matter, but rather he uses conversational gambits like 'I see your point, but let me raise you one further'. He is unafraid of brief, mid-sentence silences as he gathers together his thoughts and he will indulge you comfortably if you do the same. Often he will signal that he wants to return to a topic briefly touched upon and as such the dialogue begins to take on the rhizomatic structure of a large and splendid tree. The overall effect is entirely seductive, and at the end of a wide-ranging, hours-long conversation you can hang up with little recollection of specific subjects discussed, but with the feeling of satisfaction you might have after a good dinner with life-long friends.

During those first few months we spoke infrequently – always shortly after I woke up, listening to the clatter of pots and pans on the other end of the line as I drank coffee at my desk – and texted more, often on the encrypted messaging app Telegram. Inigo had set it so that our conversations disappeared after an hour. Initially, I didn't know if he was alone or with his fiancée, who'd moved with him to Miami; rumours in London were that they had broken up before he fled. I didn't know what he was living on since a London court had frozen his assets. The press was giddy on its drug of choice, schadenfreude, with Bloomberg News claiming that he had made off with the best part of $150 million. I didn't know what to believe.

It went on like this for a month or so. We'd message back and forth exchanging easy generalities. I asked about what he was doing 'there' as I tried to deduce his whereabouts from the timings of the messages and photos he sent me. One was a photo of an ornate metal gate with a plaque bearing a painted Latin motto which sent me down a rabbit hole for most of an afternoon. The motto turned out to be meaningless. Another was an aerial photo of a beachside property with a Fuller-esque geodesic dome, but upon closer inspection on a bigger screen the photo turned out to be taken from a book. I could see the shadow formed by the gully of the pages.

He'd disappear for days, sometimes weeks, surfacing with explanations that seemed plausible: a storm on the island; they'd been moving house. Then again, plausibility was always Inigo's strong suit. I learned that what are called hurricanes in the northern hemisphere, are called typhoons in the south. When he told me there had been a typhoon where he was, I searched meteorological websites for storms in the southern hemisphere.

Speculation in London was rife. In the absence of actual information the art world press was full of rumour and gossip, worked into an indignant lather. One article – featuring fifteen-year-old Facebook photos of Inigo picking his way through a Bangkok street market – claimed that he was in Thailand. On 27 October 2019, Inigo sent me a link to a *Daily Mail* article. He'd long been impishly fascinated by the Mail Online, with its notorious 'sidebar of shame' and Z-list celebrity weight loss stories. But this story was about him. It claimed that Inigo had sold a sculpture by the Japanese artist Yayoi Kusama to Crown Prince Mohammed bin Salman of Saudi Arabia. The link Inigo sent me came accompanied by a caption that read: 'Finally made it into the *Daily Mail*!' The article went on to cast doubt on whether Inigo had had the right to sell the artwork. The thought of this terrified me. I replied to Inigo, 'Fucking hell, man! Look what happened to Khashoggi! MBS is not a guy you want to mess with!'

'It's all good, playboy,' came the reply, before he went offline again.

And that was that for a while. The lawsuits against him arrived with dizzying speed. He was accused of forging legal documents, double-dealing artworks priced in the millions of dollars, and refusing to pay enormous debts. Long queues of plutocrats formed behind their expensive lawyers, and yet Inigo's silence went unbroken. He was quiet for much of November and December 2019, but as the articles kept coming I would occasionally send him links. He had invariably read them, often telling me how wrong the coverage was. How much more there was still to come out. 'They don't even have ten per cent of what I did.'

It was difficult to say if he was enjoying it, or somehow relieved that it was out of his control now. In the spring of 2020, we talked about the past just as the present closed in on all of us. The British prime minister, Boris Johnson, that great unmade bed of a man, was gravely ill in hospital, struck down by the virus whose seriousness he had tried to minimise. Over a patchy phone line I heard Inigo clicking a cheap pen, propelling and retracting its nib rapidly, nervously, *click-clack, click-clack*. Outside my window, the stunted rush-hour grumble of the busy main road was drowned out by birdsong, intermittently punctured by ambulance sirens making their way to the large hospital near my flat, the oppressive existential tinnitus of life under Covid-19.

On Inigo's end, our conversations were occasionally interrupted by a new Dobermann puppy called Bacchus as he clambered over furniture or knocked over his water bowl. I heard the clatter of his claws on a linoleum floor. Inigo would sometimes stop to chastise him lightly. Longer pauses in the conversation gave me an auditory glimpse into the secret life of this wanted man. I listened for the ocean, anticipating wind chimes and wondering whether it would be possible to distinguish the murmur of a sea breeze moving through the fronds of a palm tree. I knew only that he was on an island, that it was remote. (The cellphone number he used to communicate with me was registered in Vanuatu, somewhere I'd never heard of. This didn't mean he was there, however; Inigo often used the app Hushed, which allows you to mask your true location, to hide in plain sight.) At one point, I googled the sound that a toucan makes in case I should overhear one when we were speaking. It was the most exotic thing I could think of.

Inigo was supposedly on the other side of the world, but somehow this global crisis made that distance seem less significant. If he was really where he told me, he was over 10,000 miles away. But it was the first time we had spoken properly in years. Some people found joy in the strangest places during the lockdown. I found it in having my friend back. He proposed writing an article together, one which might put his side of the story. To that end he sent me an enormous trove of documentation surrounding his actions, emails and spreadsheets and documents that encompassed years of his career, evidence that, along with my own memories, has formed the basis of this book. As Inigo told me his story he spoke in the passive and almost always in the present tense, as if these events hadn't happened to him but were somehow still happening somewhere, to someone else, some blameless other. And, he told me, he was in Vanuatu.

But this book isn't journalism, for there can be no objectivity where love has lived. I will try as best I can to give an accurate picture of the man I knew while also trying to reconcile that person with a different man, someone I have come to know since: a version of Inigo I have found it difficult to recognise. A man more desperate than I could have imagined, a man more ruthless than I dared believe. My role as Inigo's confessor frightened me as much as it excited me because I knew that the more I came to understand him, the more it would reveal about our friendship, and about myself.

Almost nine months after he had disappeared, on Friday, 12 June 2020, Inigo woke early in Vanuatu and made coffee using his 9Barista espresso machine, one of the few things he had taken with him when he had fled. On his phone, by force of habit, he checked Artnet News, *The New York Times* website and Bloomberg – mostly for the news but also to see if there had been anything published about him overnight. There hadn't. In fact, there had been few public developments in his case for weeks now.

Vanuatu had remained largely Covid-free, but a flu had been going around the island and he told me he felt exhausted all the time. 'Am just dead . . .' he wrote to me as he went to bed the night before. 'Hoping to be back on feet tomorrow.' We never did speak that morning, so I have had to piece together what follows from the media reports that came after his arrest, as well as what I already knew of Inigo's daily life there. It was a quiet, placid existence which seemed to me almost irreconcilable with the man I had known for so long.

Inigo had slept well and long, and had taken his coffee outside, his puppy leaping and bounding eagerly at his feet. He was starting to feel himself again. Gazing out at the ocean, at the hazy line above the horizon, he remembered that moment, not even a year ago, when he had done the same thing in his old life in Miami and felt dread rising with the tide. Now, the lapping waves were closer, calmer, bringing with them not fear but a gradual feeling of absolution. But no paradise lasts for ever.

After he'd fed Bacchus and given the scraps of last night's dinner to the pigs, Inigo showered and got into his Ford pickup truck. He'd never had a licence before moving to Vanuatu and he relished the feeling of power and control that driving can bring. As he manoeuvred through the village of Mele where he and his pregnant fiancée had recently bought a modest home, along a road spattered with potholes, the colourful, makeshift houses on either side seemed to grin widely in the morning light. On almost every porch the beach shoes and flip-flops of happy families exuded a contented torpor.

Inigo and his fiancée met for a late lunch in the garden of the Rossi restaurant in the capital, Port Vila, where the close-cropped grass lies flat like a carpet. The view over the bay to Iririki island, the sea dotted with tiny white boats like rabbits' tails, was as still and perfect as a theatrical backdrop. The place is frequented by visitors and a few expats and the food is mostly ordinary tourist fare – fried things served with fries – but it has a holiday feel and Inigo liked the sensation he had there of blending in.

That afternoon, the couple moved their way calmly through a busy street market. Around them, Bislama, the Creole language spoken by the locals, can for an English speaker sometimes effect the feeling of listening to a broken shortwave radio: familiar words stick like fish in a net, while others slip away, heard but not understood. All along the streets, men and women drank kava – a bitter, fermented drink made from a root – from coconut shells and ate 'washem maot', small bites of food designed to take away the taste of the drink before its relaxing effects take hold.

The day was hot and getting hotter and the market was thinning out as the couple left the street and entered a shop in Rue Carnot, known as the Chinatown of Port Vila. As they selected fruit and vegetables for their dinner that night, Inigo's face dropped, the blood draining from his features. A group of men, arms bulging in their polo shirts, had entered the shop and were barring the doorway. One of them said to him, 'Are you Inigo?' No sound came from his open mouth, but he sealed his fate with a single nod. Two of the men grabbed him by the arms and hurried him to a waiting SUV; another restrained his fiancée whose screaming shattered the slow quiet of the afternoon, waking the shopkeeper's baby who slept in an improvised cot beside the till. Before she reached the street, he was gone, the unmarked car driving off at speed with a siren howling. She, too, was pushed into a car: her mobile phone snatched from her hand, she was flanked on the back seat by two men who refused to speak to her. Neither Inigo nor his fiancée had any idea who had grabbed them or where they were going.

The cars sped through the gates of Bauerfield International Airport before screeching to a halt. Inigo, now in handcuffs, was led across the tarmac to a waiting Gulfstream jet as his fiancée watched on, powerless, from the car. Curious onlookers stopped to record the scene on their mobile phones. One photograph that captured this moment – and which made front page news the following week in the Vanuatu *Daily Post* – does not show a scuffle; rather, Inigo seems almost to be sauntering. His body, far from being tense or contorted in struggle as one might expect, appears relaxed, captured in an almost narcotic *contrapposto*.

It is easy to read this scene as something for which he had mentally prepared himself – an event long expected that had finally arrived. But from conversations Inigo and I had in the weeks leading up to his arrest he was feeling safe, even comfortable, in his new island life. Just prior to his arrest, we had been delayed in continuing our conversations, in fact, because he had been travelling, visiting different Vanuatuan islands where he told me he was unable to access sufficient internet to talk. Instead, he sent me a photograph of himself atop a beautiful green hill, smiling broadly into the wind, the sun beating down on his face, the deep, unguent blue of the Pacific stretching out behind him. He looked like a man without a care in the world.

2

Some friendships feel like they will go on for ever. Others are self-consciously fleeting, even conditional on their impermanence – the agreeable person you sit next to on a long-haul flight or a sympathetic bartender during your dark night of the soul. As for my friendship with Inigo, I sometimes find it hard to remember a time when he wasn't a part of my life.

The truth is we very nearly didn't become friends at all. We both started at Goldsmiths, University of London, in 2006, for very different reasons. I was there because I didn't know what I was going to do with my life. Inigo was there because he knew exactly what he was going to do with his. I wanted to find out why I liked art, what art I *should* like, and what to say about it. (Also, probably of paramount importance, how to argue about it with my father, who had been managing director of Christie's and whose expertise ranged from Renaissance bronzes to British post-war abstraction.) Inigo knew all these things already, as if pre-programmed as a connoisseur at birth. What he needed was a place to hone his skills, a place to get his patter down, before the business of his life could begin in earnest.

I'd taken up my place at Goldsmiths despite getting offers from what my teachers assured me were 'better' universities. But I wanted to move away from the art history I'd thus far encountered: classical architecture, depictions of drapery in Florentine frescoes and the infuriating dappled light of the Impression-ists. Most of all, though, I wanted to get away from the people who studied those kinds of things: red-trousered Tarquins and ample-bosomed Home Counties Camillas. Goldsmiths, then – urban, contemporary, iconoclastic – seemed to fit the bill perfectly and so I was thrilled, during my first lecture, to be treated to a compare and contrast between a sixteenth-century depiction of the flagellation of Christ with a Tom of Finland drawing. A quick text to a friend who had just started an art history degree at Cambridge underscored my sense of good fortune: his first lecture was on iconography in Byzantine coins.

But it would soon become clear that I had not escaped as cleanly as I thought. Our class comprised about forty or so stu-dents of whom Inigo and I were two of only five men. Among the female cohort were two minor European royals (Luxem-bourg and Germany) and a smattering of continental and homegrown nobility. In a lecture early in the first term we were discussing the feminist concept of the male gaze when one of the posh young ladies arrived late. The lecturer did the whole nice-of-you-to-join-us routine and told her what we were dis-cussing. 'Oh, I thought we weren't meant to call them that any more,' the young lady said flatly.

'Call who what?' asked the lecturer, puzzled.

'The gays,' the latecomer answered. 'The male gays.'

The room rippled with laughter and I remember catching Inigo's eye, sharing briefly in the general amusement. Neither of us at that point had spoken – to each other, or in class. I would be lying if I told you that we became friends in the lecture hall. In the coming months, however, Inigo suddenly became an intimidating presence in class. He spoke forthrightly and insouciantly, content to challenge professors and fellow students alike. Indeed, as term wore on he came to seem like an almost professorial presence; in lectures he never took notes, but instead made lengthy disquisitions – about the writings of Joseph Kosuth or Arthur Danto or the gender politics of Lee Lozano – things no one else in the class had ever heard of, let alone had defensible opinions on.

By the end of our first year, Inigo and I had hardly exchanged a word and he was seldom to be seen around Goldsmiths' south London campus outside of class. Indeed, it wasn't until the late spring of 2007 that we would first talk properly. This time, however, we were a world away from the linoleum corridors of the university. When we finally spoke, we were in Bloomsbury.

The name Bloomsbury conjures images of wide-eyed avenues and grinning squares, of pulmonary plane trees gently swaying, of publishers and academics. It is a place of ghostly literature and literary ghosts – in one passing man you may spot the pear-drop nose of T. S. Eliot or Dickens' crooked smile; in a woman seated on a bench you might see the sad middle-distance eyes of Woolf. In my mind's eye, Bloomsbury's skies are perpetually a wet grey, its streets always in recovery from an April dousing. It is a place of alleyways and secret courtyards, stuccoed houses and cloth awnings cloaking the facades of dusty second-hand bookshops, of jigsaw-paved streets with names like Emerald Court and Phoenix Place and Mount Pleasant.

At the arrhythmic heart of old Bloomsbury lies the British Museum. Created by an act of parliament in 1753 in order to house the enormous and eclectic collection that Sir Hans Soane had bequeathed to King George II, the museum still has posts whose job titles are like something out of *Game of Thrones*. One of these is the 'Keeper of Coins and Medals'. Along with custodianship over the museum's enormous numismatic collection, the role used to come with its very own grace and favour house, located just to the west of the museum, at number 89 Great Russell Street.

The last Keeper of Coins to live in the house was Sir Edward Robinson. He died in 1976, leaving the house vacant. At the time, Britain was embroiled in strikes. Refuse, shuddering with rats, was piled high in the streets and coal-fuelled power stations flickered on and off, intermittently returning large areas of the country to the darkness of the Blitz. The house's brickwork was stained bible-black by years of smog and its windows were rendered sleepy-eyed with grime. Still, its grandeur was unmistakable.

In 1979, the critic and curator Sacha Craddock saw an advert in the London *Evening Standard* reading 'Large House, Central London, To Let'. The house in question was 89 Great Russell Street, and she has held on to the lease ever since. Originally, she lived there with her mother, Sally, and the illustrator Corinne Pearlman, but over the ensuing years the house, known to all as GRS, has been home to – and a hub for – a great many members of the British contemporary art scene. The filmmaker Isaac Julien, for instance, lived there in the 1990s. Unsurprisingly, the annual Great Russell Street Christmas party is a bacchanal of the great, the good and the freeloading.

The house is a three-bay, four-storey affair which, with the windows diminishing incrementally in size with each floor, seems to get smaller towards the roof. If you look too closely at the brickwork you might fear that the whole building could come down on you, for the cement is eroding and the once-neat rows of bricks now undulate like a child's drawing of the sea. The ground floor of the building is clad in a whitewashed stucco crenellation that lends the house its pot-bellied hauteur, while its black front door is stern and heavy, scaly with decades of repainting; above it, a lantern window, emblazoned with a large gold '89', glows welcomingly at all hours.

In the hallway entrants must negotiate a scaffolding of bi-cycles – some in good working order, others rusted or gummy with oil – before reaching the sitting room. In the middle of the day there is seldom anyone there and the sagging sofas bask in the light of the two big sash windows. Tourists passing on their way to the British Museum look in eagerly through the glass, standing on tip-toes and gripping the cast-iron railings, craning their necks and camera phones to see this anachronistic version of English life, as if it were somehow a living exhibit escaped from the building next door. On the mantelpiece an Italianate marble bust of a man with hair like an octopus's tentacles peers down at the room; occasionally he is given a silly hat or a feather boa or a false moustache by a waggish late-night reveller. At the rear of the house a galley kitchen, its floor sandy with crumbs, looks out over an overgrown garden where various tables and chairs have been swallowed up by the vegetation.

Sacha Craddock is a ruddy, Chaucerian woman with a natural talent for consensus building – an ideal landlady for a house that is home to an ever-changing cast of artists, writers, curators and designers. That talent is also key for her role as committee chair of Bloomberg Young Contemporaries, one of the UK's most respected young artists' prizes. A rare example of a famous squatter, she once worked as a cleaning lady for the painter Howard Hodgkin, who lived on Coptic Street, just around the corner from GRS, until his death in 2017. In 1988, writing for *The Times*, Sacha was the only mainstream art critic to review the now legendary exhibition *Freeze*, a show which launched the careers of Damien Hirst (he also curated it) and Sarah Lucas, among other Young British Artists (YBAs). Outgoing

– even garrulous at times – and legendarily friend-rich, Sacha can nevertheless turn in an instant and a full showing of her ire is not something you easily forget. (Thankfully, she will likely not mention the matter again.)

When I was a frequent visitor to GRS, between 2007 and 2009, the house had six full-time residents. At the top, her apartment spread over two floors, lived Sacha and her daughter; on the first floor was a hirsute video artist called Steve Farrer who was often cross and seldom seen; in the basement lived Louise McKinney, who worked for the Serpentine Gallery and had mournful eyes which were often obscured by cigarette smoke; and at the rear in a small basement room of the house, really no more than a cupboard with space only for a single bed, lived a curator called Robert McPherson. The final occupant was Inigo.

Inigo lived in the basement at Great Russell Street in a room that contained a clothes rail, a sofabed and a small Formica table but no chair. Everything was from Ikea and everything was falling apart. Piles of art books sometimes functioned as bedside tables or even stools. The carpet was new but cheap, and balls of royal blue fluff would collect at the skirting boards and in corners, to be scurried away in the night by the mice for their nests.

In those days, Inigo had a wild mess of curly hair and was scrupulously clean-shaven. He dressed always in a shirt tucked into his jeans and a buttery leather jacket which I think had belonged to his father and which hung off his shoulders. I never saw him wear trainers. His bee-stung lips, to which he seemed constantly to be applying Chapstick, could make him look effete and he spoke openly about things like skincare and articles from *The New York Times*, which he read on his Black-Berry. At Goldsmiths, an art school in thrall to skinny jeans,

The Libertines and roll-up cigarettes, he stuck out like a Hollywood smile at a coal miners' strike.

He championed controversial opinions about artists or artworks, seemingly in order to test the limits of his knowledge or that of his fellow students or even that of the lecturers who were as bemused by him as the rest of us. I can't say he was popular. Then again, I wasn't either. I remember his defence of Damien Hirst, a Goldsmiths alumnus whose status as a market star somehow made him unworthy of serious discussion. (The nonchalant arrogance of art students knows few limits.) Inigo's speech was impassioned and convincing almost because of its languor, its I-couldn't-care-less-what-you-think attitude.

My father had been an auctioneer at both Christie's and Sotheby's and I had grown up in and around the art market. But I knew little of contemporary art and, what's more, I knew little of what I liked. Back then I couldn't understand how people could look at an artwork and proclaim it good or bad, one thing or another. I had always longed for the kind of conviction Inigo seemed already to possess and I figured that proximity to him would be a good way to go about getting it.

In the early summer of 2007, when all our essays had been turned in and the long break seemed to stretch out in front of us for ever, Inigo did a surprising thing: he invited us all to a party at his place – at 89 Great Russell Street. I went along with a couple of friends. We had some drinks at the nearby Museum Tavern before we got there and discussed the rumours surrounding Inigo. With his mid-Atlantic accent, some thought he was the black sheep son of WASP-y New Yorkers, banished to their London townhouse. Others speculated he was the orphaned child of Hollywood royalty. No one knew what to expect from the evening, but the promise of finding out more about Inigo – and about the surroundings that might have created this mysterious figure – was a powerful incentive to make the long crosstown journey from New Cross to Bloomsbury.

As I would later find out, Inigo had grown up in a family that was deeply rooted in the world of contemporary art. His mother was an artist and his father was director of the Aldrich Contemporary Art Museum, a well-respected regional institution in southern Connecticut; his grandfather ran a fine art foundry that worked with artists like Frank Stella and Joel Shapiro. Inigo himself had already interned at the prestigious White Cube gallery and continued to do odd jobs there. So while GRS felt like a very odd place for a young undergraduate to end up, in retrospect it feels now more like the logical conclusion of his upbringing and the springboard to the next chapter of his life.

In spite of the unexpected loucheness of the interior, the gathering was just the sort of thing you'd expect from first year art history students: regrettably attired young adults drinking cheap beer and saying things we didn't mean or didn't understand – frequently both. We rolled and smoked cigarettes and joints and poked around the house, which felt like the kind of place you might play hide-and-seek or sardines. Throughout the evening the other residents would sneer into the living room as they returned home. An older student, Nicola, who'd had a modelling career before starting her degree, came with her boyfriend, a thick-set property developer in his mid-thirties. At first he looked distraught at having been dragged along, but half an hour later was to be found deep in earnest conversation with Inigo about a recent *Economist* piece on global water shortages and advances in desalination technology. I, meanwhile, spent the evening trying to perfect a double high-five – front and back, you know, up top and down low as you pass each other – and lamenting the demise of The Libertines.

The whole evening felt like something Inigo had put on out of a sense of obligation. Something he *ought* to do.

Later, there was cocaine. We were down in Inigo's basement room by that stage, Sacha having ejected us from the communal areas of the house on account of noise. Mismatched socks hung drying on a rack like forlorn punctuation. Empty coffee cups sat on books and shelves and – as would become something of a domestic trademark for Inigo, no matter how sophisticated his surroundings – small plastic animals were scattered around, sheep and lions and dinosaurs poking out from behind and underneath the chaos of his room. I spotted a hotel notepad covered in a scratchy scrawl – words not joined up and letters of varying size – which I tried to read upside down until Inigo caught my eye. (I would always marvel at his handwriting. From that day to this it's startlingly puerile, uncertain, a marked contrast to the man he's become. Every time I saw him sign a contract or a letter, I would remember the Inigo – barely more than a boy – that I'd met that night.) Music leaked out of tinny laptop speakers and edgy greed filled everyone's eyes as the powder was passed around, claggy lines cut up on a paperback. That night I think we all felt it: the contrast of Inigo's home among this sophisticated bohemian clutter with all of ours, the flat-pack student experience, our flat-packed lives dusted with cigarette ash and the uric stains of dried-up beer.

When the book was passed to me, with its attendant baton of rolled-up banknote, I saw that it was *Mother's Milk* by Edward St Aubyn, a novel I had recently read and, along with the previous three in the series, loved. Inigo and I discussed these books for a long while that night – their damaged and acerbic narrator, his abusive father and the parade of repression and cruelty that characterises the English upper classes

– until the cocaine and everyone else had gone, and the sun was on the rise.

I walked towards home alone through early morning streets. I'd like to tell you that I felt something significant, something life-altering that morning. But I felt only the weight of my hangover and the discomfort of walking any distance in my too-tight jeans and ill-fitting Converse high-tops. I had no idea that I had begun a friendship that would so dramatically change the course of my life. But the easy intensity of our conversation that night, the alacrity of mutual openness, felt different somehow. I hadn't just made a new friend. I had found my tribe.

I was going to New York the following week for an internship at Christie's (this was the first thing I told Inigo which had visibly impressed him) and he was returning home to Connecticut for the summer. We agreed to meet in New York.

I've never known a heat like New York in summer. The janky pavements seem to melt underfoot and the air is sweet and wet like someone breathing too close to you. Without warning the rain comes down like fury, calling a brief time-out on the thermometrical onslaught. The only reliable places to find cold air out of office hours are the subway or the cinema. No one told me it would be that way.

In the three months I worked at Christie's in the early summer of 2007, I spent untold hours in taxis transporting frozen yoghurt between Koreatown and the offices, twenty blocks away at the Rockefeller Center. The specialists at Christie's had discovered Pinkberry frozen yoghurt and a new intern was the perfect way to keep them cool and refreshed without splashing out on the calories too much. The real problem I encountered as I strove to fulfil their desires was the taxi witching hour. At 4 p.m. every day, taxis all over Manhattan turn off their meters and lights and drive back to Queens for a shift change. (No one had told me about this before I arrived, either.) The avenues and cross streets, usually flecked with swarming black and yellow cabs, are suddenly empty. And if you're standing on a sidewalk holding eighty dollars-worth of fro-yo, it's a disaster.

It was after just such an excursion, having spent an aeon on the sidewalk begging the universe to send me a cab as I melted along with the yoghurt, that I returned to the offices, glazed in sweat and laden with cartons from Pinkberry. As everyone gathered around to eat, a man I hadn't seen before emerged from a corner office. This was the WASP-y department head, Josh Holdeman, who'd been away in London since my arrival a few weeks before. The main thing I remember about Josh was his hair, which he had cut in Paris every other month. It fell over his face like a wave and was always as clean as a razor. He dressed in suits which looked lived-in in that nonchalant, old-money way and expensive shoes which were polished by someone who really knew what they were doing. He had the kind of boyish eyes that would make you believe anything he told you.

Josh was telling everyone a story: during his trip to London he'd had to go to a black tie event, but he didn't have his tuxedo with him, nor did he have time to have it sent over from New York. This, Josh knew, was a problem that could be solved by having money – a lot of money – thrown at it, and so he'd gone around the corner from Christie's London office in St James's to Turnbull & Asser in Jermyn Street. Turnbull & Asser had recently provided the tux for Daniel Craig in whichever new Bond movie was out that year, and they were selling off-the-peg versions to customers who wanted to dress like a secret agent at charity events or the opera or wherever you wear a tuxedo to these days. So the man in the shop had fitted Josh for a James Bond tux and, as he was making minor adjustments to the trouser length, he'd asked if Josh would like a cummerbund to complete the look.

'And so I said to the guy, "What the fuck is a fucking cummerbund for?"' Just then, Josh looked at me. 'You, intern, you're British, right? What the fuck is a cummerbund?'

Now, I knew what a cummerbund looked like, but I had no idea what it was *for*. 'It was originally used by upper-class men to hold their opera ticket stubs,' I gambled. 'But all those guys were so fat that they became a kind of crumb-catcher as well.'

'Huh,' he said, unsatisfied, as he touched his hand to his midriff, seeking the silky ghost of his cummerbund. 'I guess I'll have to take your word for it.' He was unconvinced and I knew it. He opened his mouth again and I thought he was about to call me out, as if this had all been a ruse to faze the intern, but instead he turned to Stuart Alexander, the senior specialist, and gave him a quizzical look. Then he finished his story and his frozen yoghurt and returned to his corner office and closed the door.

A little while later, he came to the door and asked me to come in. His face told me nothing, but his flat tone of voice did not bode well. I stood up and straightened my tie, tucked in my shirt. I felt like I was back at school, being summoned, once again, to the headmaster's office for a dressing down. He turned his computer monitor round. He had the Wikipedia page on cummerbunds open.

'I can't see anything here about crumbs or ticket stubs.' I flushed red and shifted uncomfortably from foot to foot, preparing to be reprimanded. Some of us never leave the headmaster's study.

I tried one last gambit: 'Well, sure, if you want to believe Wikipedia . . .'

'Listen,' he stopped me just in time. 'That was total bullshit you just spun me.' Before I could reply, he continued: 'But it was some pretty good bullshit. When you're done with school, you should come see me about a job.'

I had no desire to work for an auction house; to do so would have been to play into my father's hands far too readily. The way I'd spoken to Josh was completely out of character and when he called me out on it, I felt engulfed in shame. But then I considered his offer. I knew it wasn't real, but I wondered if, at its root, was something truthful about what it took to make it in the art world. What had in reality been a panicky lie to cover up my ignorance had been taken for suave self-assuredness, a promising sign of future talent. At the time I remember thinking, Is that really all it takes? And then later, How do I do that on purpose? Consciously or not, we look for things in our friends that we lack, and I was already aware that Inigo was the most confident person I had ever met. If confidence was all I needed, maybe I could learn it from him.

Inigo and I always used to joke that we would write each other's biographies, that we knew each other well enough to be both Boswell and Johnson to each other. He was right, as usual, or at least half right: I wonder now if he ever really knew me in the way I felt I had come to know him. In those early days, I feel like I almost studied him, in the way a painter will study the brushstrokes of the Old Masters or a writer Hemingway's sentence structure. At nineteen, Inigo already seemed to have the assurance and poise of a man twice his age. With him, I felt somehow as if I were trespassing on a life, setting foot on foreign territory where at any moment I might be discovered as the rank imposter I knew myself to be.

I've had a lot of time to think about my friendship with

Inigo, the most formative of my life. To write about a friendship is an admission of an ending, perhaps not of the friendship itself, but, at the very least, a chapter of it. Over the past few years I have looked back in search of instances – tipping points, perhaps – trying to figure out when things started to go wrong. I don't know, really, but I do know the day that everything changed for me started when I met Inigo at Grand Central station in the summer of 2007.

Early on a Sunday morning, I took the subway from Newkirk Avenue in Brooklyn, where I was staying with family friends, to Grand Central. Waiting under the vast green and gold dome of the concourse, I didn't spot Inigo, he just appeared beside me and started speaking. 'Have you had coffee yet? I'll need one more before we catch the train. And you'll need a black and white cookie – have you ever had one? I've got the paper. Shall we go? We don't have long.' And with that he moved off quickly and with purpose. I almost lost him in the crowd before I jerked into action, following his mass of curly hair visible above the fray, downstairs to the food court where we bought coffee and the crucial black and white cookies and Inigo bought some green juice – a concoction of vegetables and fruits and what I presumed were rare mosses that turned my stomach just to look at.

This was only the second time I'd seen him since our coke-fuelled night in London six weeks before. A week before our meeting at Grand Central, he'd written to say that he was coming into the city from his mother's house in Connecticut to view the post-war and contemporary art sale at Christie's. Despite working a few floors above the viewing rooms, the thought of going myself hadn't even occurred to me. I took the elevator down to meet him at the appointed time and found him staring at a Carroll Dunham painting, his arms crossed behind his back. He was so absorbed – scouring the surface of the painting like a detective searching for clues – that he seemed not to notice me as I approached. When he finally realised I was there he seemed surprised, as if he'd forgotten our plan to meet. But soon we were walking through the galleries together. Inigo told me about the compulsive, repetitive work of the Japanese artist Yayoi Kusama who voluntarily lived in a mental hospital and who ate only tapioca pudding, and about Warhol's obsession with watching television adverts and his shooting in 1968 by Valerie Solanas, before segueing elegantly on to Jeff Koons, his porn star ex-wife and his preoccupation with breath and innocence lost; about Robert Irwin's love of fountain Coca-Cola and how, despite being from San Diego, he always wore a Yankees hat; about Donald Judd's Texas ranch and his collection of nineteenth-century Swedish furniture. In his telling, this trivia was far from trivial. He spoke fluently, easily. There didn't seem to be an artist or artwork he couldn't talk about. I listened enviously.

As we were nearing the end of the galleries, I turned a corner to see Brett Gorvy, then the company's international chair of post-war and contemporary art (Christie's has a lot of chairs), talking to what I would later come to recognise as a typical art-collecting couple: a tall man, elegantly dressed, with a froth of grey hair and the blasé lassitude that can only be mustered by a man with a black Amex waiting in his pocket; and his younger wife, pairing athleisure wear with vintage couture and nursing an aggressive-looking armpit dog. I felt Inigo's hand pull at my elbow. 'I know them,' he said. 'Let's walk out the other way.' Much later he told me that the man was on the board of the museum where his father worked, but he never gave a reason as to why he'd wanted to avoid him. I didn't mind. Soon I'd be used to Inigo, who seemed already to know everyone worth knowing in this new world of beauty and money, pulling me away from people he wanted to avoid. The reasons why he needed to avoid them were rarely expressed, and something about his manner meant I could never ask. There was a characteristic play of intimacy and distance inherent in this, the first of countless mysteries surrounding Inigo – you were allowed close enough to know that there *was* a secret, but exactly what it was, he kept to himself. I would later come to see this character trait as an integral part of Inigo's personality. He had a tendency to compartmentalise people, seldom encouraging different groups of friends or associates to encounter each other on his watch. Back then it confused me: he was so suave, so confident and yet there were these sudden real-life curtain drops which seemed born of shame or fear; it didn't fit. Now, though, I suspect it had less to do with emotions like those and more to do with a transactional way of seeing the world, of guarding your advantage and waiting for the exact right moment to play your hand.

We took the train along the Hudson river from Grand Central to Dia Beacon, the museum for the Dia Art Foundation's collection of modern and contemporary art. The journey is almost a work of art in its own right. Your Metro-North carriage – its seats girthy and uncertain with their whack-a-mole springs and mouthy heating vents – emerges from the city's girdled underbelly into Harlem before joining the river, which it then clings to all the way to Poughkeepsie in upstate New York. The view is the sort of thing you'd pay good money for: fifteen minutes out of Grand Central the granite cliffs erupt through the greenery and the trees are bushy with a capital 'USH'. There's a good chance that you won't want to get off the train at all when the conductor calls, 'Next stop, Beacon!' but trust me, you should.

The building that houses the collection used to be the

biscuit box factory for Nabisco (NAtional BIScuit COmpany), the company that makes Oreos and Ritz crackers. Enormous and low-slung, the riverside building is a red-brick leviathan with a white roof of zigzag skylights like the raised heckles of an angry beast. Inside is one of the finest collections of minimalist art in the world – work by Richard Serra, Carl Andre, Mel Bochner, Donald Judd, Agnes Martin and more. The vast bright space is tranquil, almost religious in its silence, and the long, warped wooden floorboards have a playful springiness to them that's at odds with the stark brutality of many of the artworks.

I knew of these artists – Andre in particular, who was famous for selling an artwork that comprised of nothing more than two layers of bricks to the Tate and was famously cleared of the murder of his wife, the Cuban-American artist Ana Mendieta (Andre told the 911 operator that his wife had 'somehow gone out the window'). I knew these artists mostly from textbooks or exhibition catalogues. I had seen so little of their work in the flesh that to be suddenly confronted with so much of it all at once was something of a sensory overload. As we walked through the galleries, Inigo did his talking thing. I tried to listen, but couldn't. At that moment I didn't care about where the artists lived or how they made their work. The pulsing silence – the aggressive quiddity of it all – was so pleasurable that I had, for hours afterwards, the warm feeling of being slightly drunk. What I loved about that day – what I continue to love – is the way works by these artists stay with you. Not just in the form of visual memories, but how they change the way you see the world around you. Serra's abysses and looming, rusted slabs; Andre's bricks; Warhol's jagged shadows; Irwin's windows – all these changed the way I saw, pushed me to see the potential beauty inherent in the everyday.

To my mind, that's what great art can do. It's about more than soothing you, or giving you joy in the moment you see it; rather, it has the power subtly to change everything else, to make you see the world anew.

In the museum cafeteria afterwards, we sat eating Reuben sandwiches and drinking seltzer in the sun. I felt like I was in a Woody Allen movie – *Hannah and Her Sisters*, perhaps, or *Annie Hall* – intoxicated by all this intellectual East Coast Americana. I'd never had a friend like Inigo, someone to discuss books and films and art and music with in an unabashedly earnest fashion. My few friends before him had been outdoor types – a fisherman, a rugby player, a car enthusiast – who held no truck with libraries and art galleries. With Inigo, however, I was able to speak without fear of ridicule. With him – because of him – I was able to shed the shame of my teenage enthusiasms and to embrace a wholly new life. I had found my tribe.

Conversation turned to Goldsmiths and the classes we would both be taking the following year. Inigo asked me how I was finding the course.

'I like it,' I conceded, 'but there's not as much work as I was expecting. In a way I don't mind – I see shows, and I take pictures and I read. But I could be busier, that's for sure.'

He looked at me over his tortoiseshell Ray Bans (Inigo would wear sunglasses at the slightest opportunity) and sighed deeply. 'I feel the same,' he said. 'And I'm a little bored, frankly. I came to London and did the internship at White Cube and they're still giving me a few research jobs, but I want to be doing more.' He shuffled in his seat and moved food around his plate, his mind suddenly far away, transported to a future of which I knew nothing.

I'd been harbouring fantasies of becoming a photographer or a filmmaker, having spent much of my abundant free time

working for something called the Archive of Modern Conflict –
a war photography archive owned by the Canadian billionaire
David Thomson – and the rest assisting a photographer called
Matt Stuart.

I asked what he thought he might do and he told me that
he was thinking about curating, but within a commercial
gallery setting. In his father, he said, he had seen the struggles
of working in museums – the interminable committee meetings and the schmoozing of self-serving donors, the inclusivity
quotas, the health and safety measures and the marketing cam-
paigns, and all before you got anywhere near an artwork or an
artist. Inigo didn't want to end up in all of that. He preferred
the immediacy of the commercial art world.

'The commercial gallery world is, as I see it, where the really
exciting stuff happens. When you're a gallerist talking to an
artist, you can help shape their body of work, you can contrib-
ute something to their practice, to their career. When you sell
the work, though, when it goes to a big collector who then gives
it to a museum – then you're changing art history.' He stopped,
almost as impressed as I was with his impassioned eloquence.
'Plus,' he said, grinning, 'I don't want to live in a basement next
to Robert for the rest of my life. I want to make some fucking
money.'

Inigo knew that, though by this point retired, my father had
worked his whole career in the art market and asked if I had
ever considered doing the same. The truth was I hadn't, but
when Inigo soon followed up by asking if I would like to work
with him on 'putting together a few deals', I said yes without
hesitation. Despite spending my childhood on the fringes of
the art world, I had no real idea what went into dealing, but I
knew that this offer – this opportunity – was far too exciting
to give up.

*

Robert McPherson is a very tall, very quiet man. Standing well over six foot, he has a soft, hesitant voice, making him sound as if he's always unsuccessfully interjecting into someone else's conversation. His wit is as quick as a knife, and he can deploy it to devastating effect, but for the most part he's just funny. I first met Robert in Inigo's company in the late summer of 2007, just after my return from New York. He'd been living in his basement room at Great Russell Street for at least a year, although, as he was at frequent pains to remind anyone who would listen, this was not a permanent set-up. Just one of temporary – though indefinite – convenience. Indeed, Robert did spend much of his time elsewhere, housesitting for friends with smart addresses, like the historian and Cuba expert Richard Gott, who lived in Ledbury Road, Notting Hill; or a high court judge with a house on Doughty Street opposite where Charles Dickens used to live. During these stays, Robert would put on lavish lunch parties for his many friends. He's an excellent cook, with a wide repertoire, but his preference was for the kind of fare found in British boarding schools or the so-called gentlemen's clubs of St James's – greying roast lamb with potatoes and carrots and mint sauce and lumpy gravy covering the multitudinous sins, followed by apple crumble and custard, for instance. But in Robert's hands classic English dishes seemed always to have a novel levity, a deliciousness that would convert even the most sceptical Frenchman. The real treat, though, was always the dessert: cake, along with gossip, were Robert's twin vices.

Along with the other oddballs and curios who lived at GRS, Robert was an early lesson in art world stratification. Theirs was – still is, for all I know – a dusty, bohemian world of doughty partygoers and committee-sitters, a static and avowedly not-for-profit enclave in the midst of a world which has become all about upward momentum and money. Like the remora fish who live symbiotically with sharks, cleaning their skin of parasites and eating the scraps that fall from their jaws, this stratum of the contemporary art world exists by a process of bottom-feeding and legitimising. They are the people who will turn up to a gallery opening on a rainy Thursday evening in January; they will raise funds and write catalogue essays for too little money; they will selflessly arrange artist talks and in-conversations; they will engage in 'discourse' (the thing that supposedly elevates artworks above the status of mere luxury goods). But these people exist because of the market, not for it. With no expectation or desire to climb the financial ladder, they are in it for the artists, for the difficult-to-sell performance and video works, the stuff that still convinces the outside world that the art market isn't merely a playground for plutocrats and oligarchs. In other words, they really care about art.

Inigo had known people like this his whole life. Both his parents had worked in this non-profit art world. But when he was still a young boy, he told me, he'd been at an event packed with just these kinds of people when suddenly a small, elderly man with an aquiline nose arrived. He moved with a stately grace, like an ageing monarch. A hush went over the room as the man was helped out of his long fur coat, revealing a thread-perfect three-piecer. He took off his hat and surveyed the assembled crowd with an ambassadorial smile.

The man was Leo Castelli, the first truly great contemporary art dealer, who had represented Andy Warhol, Jasper Johns and Robert Rauschenberg, to name but a few. When Inigo told me this story about Castelli (a story he was to tell me multiple times over the years), his eyes and his whole manner would soften as if its very recollection were some form of palliative drug. That was the moment Inigo decided that when he grew up he wanted to be a great art dealer.

Robert had worked as a curator for much of his time in the art world. In the 1970s, he was head of Gainsborough House in Sudbury, Suffolk, the former home of Thomas Gainsborough, a much-revered eighteenth-century painter of Arcadian land-scapes, dainty women and wealthy men whose chins had been eroded by generations of inbreeding. More recently he had curated exhibitions for the British Council, the cultural arm of Britain's diplomatic missions. In the 1980s, however, he had run AIR Gallery, on Rosebery Avenue, where, in 1981, he gave the Portuguese artist Paula Rego her first London show. Rego's early career had been overshadowed by that of her husband, Victor Willing, but Robert's show was significant in raising her profile. By 1985 she was showing at London's prestigious Ser-pentine Gallery – a not-for-profit venue that has helped launch the career of many a young artist. The show at AIR Gallery was also a commercial success, with the majority of the works on paper selling early in the exhibition's run. Some were sold to Robert's friends and Robert, naturally, bought a small gem-like work for himself.

Inigo and Robert were an unlikely duo but the friendship was mutually beneficial: Inigo was given a legitimate in into the cliquey London art world by Robert and Robert had a clever young man for company. After the time Inigo and I spent together in New York I soon became part of their little set. The three of us began to spend a great deal of time together, going to exhibitions and openings and, wherever feasible, stop-ping for tea and cake. An unmistakable and much-loved figure on the London art scene, Robert introduced us to many of its stalwarts, often with a fabulously bitchy aside thrown in after-wards: 'He'd go to the opening of an envelope!'; 'That dress fit her better in the eighties!' When we told him that we had decided to become dealers, Robert was wildly amused. A few weeks later, after we'd decided on a name, I & O Fine Art, and had had some business cards printed, he lovingly drew us a card of his own. It read: 'Idiot & Oaf Fine Art'.

Around this time, in late 2007, Robert had taken his Rego – a small watercolour – to her London dealers, Marlborough Gallery, and asked them if they might buy it from him. They offered him a paltry £4000 and Robert asked us if we could do better. As luck would have it, Gloria, a Spanish girl on our course, had invited us to meet her boyfriend, Enrique, the son of a prominent Spanish art dealer. (This was much to Inigo's chagrin, since he was besotted by Gloria.) Despite the fact that Rego lived and worked in London, she was an art world rock star in her native Portugal, with an entire museum dedicated to her work just outside Lisbon. We believed that we might achieve a higher price for Robert's piece if we were to find a Portuguese buyer.

It all happened in a blur. Within weeks we had, via Enrique, agreed a deal in principle with a dealer called João Nunes from Lisbon: €15,000 cash for the Rego. €12,000 for Robert and €3000 left for us – our first slice of commission. Was this really *work*? I remember thinking. Is this what art dealers do? By the time we were on a 6 a.m. flight to Lisbon a few weeks later, sleepy-eyed and aching in our cramped seats, my anxiety was at fever pitch. The Rego rested on the empty seat between us in its portfolio. Every time I looked at it, I could feel a rush of panic. Inigo meanwhile was sleeping peacefully, his head resting against the plane's window. As long as I've known him, Inigo has always slept like the dead.

We'd taken a twin room at the Sheraton Lisbon and arrived shortly before check-in. The lobby was all sharp edges and lines, the kind of corporate chic that makes you feel like you are anywhere and nowhere all at once. We waited in the bar where Inigo ordered a club sandwich and I drank a double whisky.

'Why are you so nervous?' he asked me, spreading mustard on his sandwich.

'Why aren't you?' I retorted.

At lunchtime we took a taxi to Galeria João Nunes. Our driver was a man on the downward slopes of decrepitude. His posture was like wet cardboard and a cigarette smouldered in his mis-shaven mouth. He squeezed his car down the narrow cobbled streets giving no indication that he had any idea where he was going or where his brake pedal was located. When he swerved to avoid hitting two nuns leading a group of children, he merely coughed and lit another cigarette. As we arrived – finally – at the gallery, Inigo and I thrust a twenty-euro note at him and leapt out without waiting for our change.

The gallery was large and sparsely hung with a few pictures by a local artist. As we entered no one came to the door, but we could hear voices coming from a back office. We stood around looking at the art and coughed loudly a few times. I wanted a cigarette but I looked at my phone instead. Eventually a man in a grey suit came out of the office and cheerfully shouted something at us in Portuguese. We both recognised the crucial word: 'Rego'.

João Nunes was a man in the prime of early middle age. Under his grey suit jacket, his white shirt strained slightly against his flesh, like the sails of a yacht in a strong wind. He wasn't wearing any shoes.

As he removed his jacket with a matador's flare, João beckoned us into his back office, where his assistant did her assisting by translating in much the same way that Brits abroad like to communicate: as we opened the portfolio and explained a little of the work's provenance, she diligently and slowly repeated exactly what we said, but in a thick Portuguese accent. Amazingly, this seemed to do the trick and João, having inspected the work, leaned back in his chair, his socked feet knocking auction catalogues and an empty espresso cup off his desk. He lit a cigarette and offered the pack around.

'The price €13,000, yes?' he said.

'We agreed €15,000 with Enrique,' said Inigo, as he leaned gingerly forwards to take back the portfolio from next to João's foot. 'We won't take anything less.'

'And cash, yes?' asked João.

'Yes. That's fine.'

João shouted something in Portuguese and his assistant came into the room with his shoes and his jacket.

'I have lunch now,' he said. 'You come back tonight. Eight o'clock. I have money for you then.'

We returned at eight to find the gallery dark and shuttered. Inigo pulled out his phone and tried in vain to call Enrique in Madrid; neither of us even had João's number. But after half an hour or so, just as we were about to leave, we heard the choking sound of a car's engine careening up the steep street that ran perpendicular to the gallery. A silver Mercedes crested the hill and jerked to a stop next to us, Yanni's *Live at the Acropolis* blaring from the speakers. João leaned out of the driver's side window and opened the rear door, beckoning us in.

'You like fish?' his ever-present assistant asked as João hammered the throttle.

'We like cash better,' replied Inigo.

João and his assistant were steaming. You could see the booze coming off them like heat on a desert road. João's seatbelt was buckled behind him, allowing him freedom of movement without the alert going off. He smoked without stopping, throwing each butt out of the window until I yelped as one flew back in and hit me in the ear. He laughed so hard that his foot must have slipped off the throttle, and for a brief moment the car slowed as he wound up his window and used the car ashtray instead. Soon enough we were on a motorway. The music and the engine seemed to have reached a catastrophic agreement with one another. His assistant's finger was tracing figures of eight on João's thigh as he drove and smoked, and in the mirror I could see him grinning with the thrill of the speed. Her skirt was creased like a concertina.

We arrived at a large restaurant on the seafront and followed João in, Inigo gripping the portfolio under one arm like a life preserver. João clearly knew the manager: they joked and backslapped their way to a table at the rear of the restaurant, just next to the fish tanks where lobsters and crabs mounted each other despondently.

For the next couple of hours João and his assistant paid us almost no notice as they ate turbot drowning in butter and capers and drank vinho verde by the quart. Cold, blue light leaked out from the tanks and for a while I watched as a sucker fish cleaned the inside of the glass, its hungry mouth feeding on slime I couldn't see. Dishes arrived at the table without anyone having ordered them and occasionally João would eat something from one of these new plates – a bright oily gobbet of tomato or a mouthful of roe, shovelled up with a crust of bread – and exclaim to his friend the manager, rising slightly from his seat to shout above our heads.

Inigo and I remained more or less silent, knowing no Portuguese but aware that they likely knew more English than they let on. When either of us went to the bathroom, we would pass the portfolio to the other for safekeeping until Inigo came back and didn't sit down.

'I think we should go,' he said to me. João removed his nose from his assistant's ear.

'Yeah. Let's go,' I said.

As I rose João suddenly turned to us both and beamed a wide smile. 'But why?' he asked. 'The food is not good? The wine?'

'We've got an early flight,' I replied.

João put his head in his hands and drew his fingers through his thick grey hair. He stood up, his movements exaggerated like a mime. From inside the suit jacket which hung on the chair behind him, he removed an envelope and handed it to me. Inside was a rainbow wedge of euro notes.

'Count it,' he said, sitting down and lighting another cigarette. I did, and then handed it to Inigo. We both agreed: it was all there; €15,000.

By the time we turned back to the table, João and his assistant had gone back to canoodling. I put the portfolio on the table and we made a swift exit, both of us trying to contain the strange mixture of joy and relief that was boiling up within us.

That night we were too tired to celebrate much, although we did count the money several more times. (I also did that thing you see in hip-hop videos of throwing a pile of cash into the air and letting it fall where it may, which in reality didn't look that cool and was a total nightmare to get back together.) We ordered champagne from room service, and I felt like Macaulay Culkin ordering up ice cream in *Home Alone 2*; the waiter arrived as we were still clearing up the cash and he gave me a disapproving glare. I handed him a five-euro tip as he uncorked the bottle. We drank it fast, the sugar and the alcohol and the coldness of it soothing our jangled nerves. The booze had unmasked a great hunger in us both and we phoned down for club sandwiches and more champagne, but I fell asleep before they arrived, only waking again at dawn, wracked with hangover. I devoured my sandwich cold in the bathroom.

As we boarded the plane later that morning, eyes blood-shot, palms sweating, I think we both imagined it would be like this for the rest of our lives. We were art dealers now, no question about it. I can't ever recall being so excited.

3

Thierry Lopes contacted me by text one evening in the spring of 2008, a few months after Inigo and I had sold Robert's Rego in Lisbon. Inigo and I had been scrabbling around for more artworks to sell, with no success. We'd earned a little more than £1500 each (a princely sum for two students, to be sure), but add to this the fun we'd had and the relative ease with which we'd pulled it off and we were both eager for more deals – bigger deals. I had a sense that if I stuck with Inigo there would be no stopping us, that I could learn not only how to ape his weapons-grade confidence, but learn to mimic the instinctive sense he had for dealmaking. Thinking about it now, I feel a modicum of guilt for the shamelessly self-interested way in which I regarded our friendship. Perhaps, though, it is really only with the benefit of hindsight that I see my own motivations with such clarity. It all channels into a confusion that I have long harboured: I was clear why I wanted to be friends with Inigo. But why did Inigo want to be friends with me? What was in it for him?

Thierry's message was long and in French. In it, he explained that he was a Portuguese art dealer, but that he lived in France. He understood (from whom we never found out; Thierry was discreet to the point of spycraft) that neither of us spoke Portuguese, but that we had access to artworks by Paula Rego.

I quickly called Inigo and told him about the message.

'God, that's too funny,' he laughed. 'Who is he? Have you googled him? I wonder who gave him your number.'

'It's a pretty common name,' I replied. 'I think it's unlikely we'll find him.'

'What have you said to him?'

'I haven't yet. I mean, we haven't technically got anything to sell him, do we?'

'That's not important,' Inigo said flatly. 'Find out what he wants. Tell him we have several different works by Rego. Try to get him on the phone. I'll go and talk to Robert, see what he can rustle up from those west London friends of his. At least one of them will have a church roof to fix or a horse that needs new shoes.'

'Uh, OK. But what if he wants to see images? What if he asks for prices? I'm not even sure my French is up to this.'

'Dude,' Inigo said, exasperated, 'just get the man on the phone. Tell him we have Rego works and find out his budget. Figure out where he is. We can work it out from there.'

Back then I was terrified of making phone calls, both of us were. Whenever we had to make a call like this, we would pass the phone back and forth, arguing about who had made the last one. If that failed, we'd resort to rock, paper, scissors. A couple of years later, when I had my first office job, I would sit and wait out the phone on my desk as it rang, silently daring whoever was calling to hang up. After a couple of days a passing colleague picked up my phone and held it to my ear, leaving me no option.

I rang Thierry the following morning and did my best to extract information without giving away my inexperience or the fact that we had nothing to sell him. His rasping voice had a squishy quality to it and I could hear the papery crackle of one of his one-after-another cigarettes as the hot tip made its steady march towards the mouthpiece of his phone. He was blunt and cagey, not telling me who had given him my number; he had many clients for Rego works, he told me. He called me 'Monsieur Orlando' and kept asking me, '*Mais, qu'est-ce que vous pouvez m'offrir*? [But what can you offer me?]'

I managed to get off the phone with a modicum of dignity intact and the promise that I would send him images later that day. Because he hadn't told me what he was looking for, I was unable to pin down his spending power: he could have been a tyre-kicker who had no idea what Rego works sold for or he could have been a major private dealer – we were flying blind.

Inigo for his part had managed to get himself invited to a Holland Park dinner party with Robert later that week, where he hoped to be introduced to a Rego collector. 'It'll be all tepid salmon and vegetables with the vitamins boiled out of them and I bet you they'll serve butter with the supermarket cheese,' Inigo told me on the phone as he walked from the tube station to the dinner. 'Jesus, I'll never understand these posh fucking English people.'

A few hours later Inigo called me again, this time walking back to the tube with Robert. 'It's on, playboy,' he said as soon as I picked up. 'The old fucker has some school fees to pay so he's going to give us a big Rego to sell. And get this – he wants to be paid in cash, the tax-dodging bastard!' Back then, Inigo hardly drank, certainly no more than a beer or two, and even that would get him tipsy. That night, though, I could hear the booze in his voice. I imagined him at the Holland Park dinner party, surrounded by corpse-like upper-crust Londoners, wrapped up in their ageing velvet and frayed tweed, exchanging raised eyebrows between the flower arrangements as this young American, emboldened by wine, held forth on matters dangerously close to that English conversational third rail: money.

'He told me he's got a couple of big works on paper and he'll give us one to sell,' Inigo told me excitedly. 'Robert told him we were "ruthless" with his Rego. That seemed to impress the old boy. Maybe we'll become friends and he'll take me fox murdering at the weekend.'

Inigo went back to Holland Park the next day and returned in a taxi with an artwork about the size of a small coffee table. We laid it out on the floor of his basement room, making a clearing in the socks and piles of books scattered about. It was a work in the same style as the one we had sold before – a bright, folkloric scene in brushy watercolour on white paper; women and monsters and children all crammed together in a bustling and colourful dance. We took photographs of it with a hot pink digital camera borrowed from my younger sister and I composed an email to Thierry in my best schoolboy French.

We priced the work by its surface area, multiplying what we'd sold the previous work for by the size of the new one, although when Thierry and I spoke the following morning and he readily accepted the price, we wondered whether we'd undercut ourselves. Still, the owner was happy with the deal even minus our 10 per cent and we set about working out how to get the work to Thierry. We had agreed to meet Thierry in Lisbon at the end of the following week, which meant that, even as we struggled to finish end-of-term essays for Goldsmiths, we needed to work out how to move the Rego. And we needed to avoid the prying eyes of any customs officials at either border. Moving artworks of that value was definitely something that needed paperwork.

Arranging professional art shippers to transport it would not only have demolished our commission and taken too long but we would have been obliged to declare the Rego's value to customs and face a hefty levy. Thankfully, however, Inigo discovered that certain airlines offered a dispensation which meant that you could book an empty seat for a wedding dress. On the phone to someone at Ryanair (miracles do happen), I overheard Inigo ask languidly, 'Oh, that's fascinating. So, what if I weren't planning to get married in a dress, but instead I wanted to bring my favourite artwork with me to Lisbon? Could I book it a seat next to me?'

Amazingly, after some more back and forth with the airline, Inigo had booked seats for the Rego and both of us on a dawn flight to Lisbon the following week; it was only fair, then, that I should be in charge of the packing solution. Having made a number of rather haphazard attempts at fashioning a case for the painting (all of which were properly rejected out of hand by Inigo and a cackling Robert) I was stumped until, coming back from class a few days before we were due to fly, I spotted from the top of a bus a shop specialising in board games and puzzles. Dragging Inigo off the bus with me, disgruntled to be pulled away from his copy of *The New Yorker*, 'Come on,' I said, 'I know what we can use to pack the Rego.'

As we got off the bus and walked back towards the shop, I explained. 'When we were kids my younger sister and I were keen on jigsaw puzzles – it was one of the few shared activities that wouldn't result in sibling bloodshed.' When the great schism occurred (Inigo and I were both, as we liked to joke, children of divorce and this was for years how I referred to my parents' separation) my sister and I would sometimes be halfway through a jigsaw at one parent's house when we were due to go back to the other's. This not only left us dissatisfied, but also annoyed our father, who then had to rebox the puzzles. Eventually, though, he bought us a jigsaw puzzle folder so that we could safely move our works-in-progress between parents.

'A jigsaw puzzle folder? You had a weird childhood, man,' Inigo retorted.

'Trust me,' I said, 'this will work.'

And it did. Later that week we were boarding our flight with the painting secured in an enormous case with a toothy, bespectacled cartoon squirrel emblazoned on the back and a speech bubble that read 'I'M JUST NUTS ABOUT PUZZLES!' Despite the terrifying moment when we were asked to put the case through the X-ray scanner for over-size luggage, no one at either airport asked us to open the case and a helpful flight attendant even offered to store the folder in the crew's area.

We were due to meet Thierry that afternoon at our hotel, the trusty Sheraton Lisbon. As we were checking in, I recognised a man from our flight who seemed to nod at Inigo as he walked past us and went into the bar. We took the Rego up to the room and left the case on the bed ready for the viewing. The whole thing suddenly felt rather seedy, preparing to meet a stranger in a foreign hotel room to receive a large amount of cash.

'I need a drink,' I said. 'Shall we go down to the bar? Thierry isn't due for another few hours and I want to steady my nerves.'

'Let's go out,' Inigo said. 'The bar here is fucking awful.' The remark struck me as odd since it was Inigo who'd so enjoyed the bar's club sandwiches during our last stay at the Sheraton, but I was in no mood to argue. As we walked through the lobby I looked into the bar and saw the man from the flight sitting with his back to us reading an English newspaper.

We spent a tense hour or so wandering around downtown Lisbon disagreeing about where to eat. Eventually we settled on a sushi restaurant whose chef looked like a Japanese Gary Cooper and who wore heavy eyeliner that had spread like the roots of a tree either side of his wrinkled eyes. No sooner had our food come, however, than Thierry sent me a message to say that he had arrived at the hotel early.

'Shit,' I said, showing Inigo the message. 'We're at least fifteen minutes away, what do we do?' I started to inhale my dragon roll.

'Relax,' Inigo told me. 'Take a beat. Then send him a message telling him you're in a meeting but that you'll meet him at the time we arranged.'

'But what if he's in the lobby when we get back . . . '

'He's never seen you before. Just walk quickly and tell him the room number when you get back to the room. I'll wait for you in the bar. Just let me know when it's done or if there are any problems.'

'Wait, why won't you be there?'

'Dude, come on, I don't speak French. And he doesn't know about me, does he? Trust me, it'll only complicate matters if there's someone there he doesn't know. This way there are no tricky questions.'

We took a cab back to the hotel and I speed-walked through the lobby trying to scan the space casually, like someone trying not to get caught shoplifting. The man from the plane was still in the bar, but among the faces in the lobby I saw no one that looked like an international art dealer.

Ten minutes later, at the appointed time, I answered the hotel room door and was taken aback. Thierry wore a beige fleece over a dirty white polo shirt, chinos and old boat shoes. He had the physique of a flotation device and bulging, blood-shot eyes surrounded by a rough, pouchy face. His skin was translucent and his front teeth were stained almost sepia with nicotine; I could smell the cigarettes coming off him like smoulder on a battlefield.

'Monsieur Orlando?'

'Yep, that's me,' I said without thinking. '*Pardon. Oui, c'est moi.*'

Theirry shuffled into the room. '*Voilà!*' I said, quickly opening the puzzle case before he could see the squirrel. The Rego was yanked out of place by my too-forceful opening of the case but I managed to get it flat without too much hassle. '*Desolé,*' I said. Thierry grunted as he leant over the work.

'I can touch it?' he asked me in heavily accented English.

'*Bien sûr,*' I replied. I felt ridiculous, like a waiter in a Monty Python sketch.

Thierry notified me of his satisfaction with another grunt and reached into the pillowy recesses of his fleece to produce a tatty padded envelope stuffed with Euros. I took it from him and looked inside.

'Please, you must count it,' he said. I sat down at the small desk and began to count. 'I can smoke?' he asked. '*Ça vous derange?* [Does that bother you?]'

'I don't think it's allowed in here.' Another grunt. I went back to counting and Thierry went into the bathroom. Just as I was finishing the count I smelled smoke coming from under the bathroom door and then thirty seconds later Thierry came out.

'You have counted?' he asked. Smoke was seeping into the room behind him. I looked up at the smoke alarm above me.

'Yes, all here.'

'You have more works by Paula Rego?' he asked me as he closed the Velcro straps on the case.

'Not just now, but soon, *j'espère*,' I said, holding the door open for him and willing the smoke to dissipate. He grunted one last time as he left the room and I texted Inigo to say it was all done. I separated our commission and left the rest in the envelope.

Inigo came into the room almost bent double with laughter. 'Was that the guy?' he asked. 'The funny little man by the lift. Jesus, what a weird-looking dude.'

'I know. He kept grunting and then he locked himself in the bathroom to smoke when I told him he couldn't smoke in the room. Anyway, the money's all there. I kept our commission separate; the rest is in the envelope. Now I really do need that drink. I'm just going to the bathroom. I'll meet you in the bar? Then we can go out, I don't care.'

'OK, fine,' he said. 'I'll see you down there.'

From the bathroom I heard the door of the room close, but when I came out not only was Inigo gone but so too was the envelope of money. I rang him. He didn't pick up. I ran down the corridor to the lifts and press the down button frantically. As I waited for the lift to come my brain spun through the possibilities: someone (Thierry? We knew nothing about him, after all) had forced their way into the room and taken the money – or had Inigo done a runner with the cash? And if so, why?

As the lift doors opened into the lobby I saw the man from the plane walking through the main doors of the hotel. He was holding the envelope. Inigo stood a little off to the side looking placidly in my direction.

'Who was that guy?' I asked him. 'Why has he got the money?'

'That was my client. The seller.'

'What? Wait, I don't get it. Why was he here? Why didn't you tell me he was coming?'

'It wasn't important. You had your side of the deal and I had mine.' He held my gaze for a moment longer than I could stand. That look hit me like a fist.

Thinking about it now, it wasn't deceit – not exactly – but rather an economy of truth that left me bemused and hurt. I can understand that the buyer might have wanted control of his money as soon as possible (and frankly it was a relief not to have to think of new ways to smuggle cash through customs). But it was also the first example of an instinct I would only much later come to recognise in Inigo – an odd desire on his part always to be in possession of one trump card, a demonstration, perhaps, of his control, his prowess.

What Inigo seemed to understand almost innately was that secrecy meant control. The art market is like a stock market where all the shares and their owners are secret. Holding something back, however small, is therefore a potential source of leverage, of power. This, though, was secrecy as meaning, as both barrier and invitation. I see now that it was a way for Inigo to shift the balance of the partnership, to take possession of a needless amount of power. At the time, however, it felt to me like a form of violence. It filled me with fear, but as usual I did nothing, said nothing. But from that moment we were never equals again. He won because he knew how. I let him because I didn't.

These early deals – these escapades – were few and far between. While we spent an inordinate amount of time *talking* about being art dealers (and what we would do with our newfound wealth and cultural capital), our glittering careers were at that time firmly in the realm of fantasy. In those days, Inigo and I would spend long hours, too, holed up in my student digs or in Inigo's room at GRS discussing art and books, film and theatre, politics, even opera. It was from those conversations, often fuelled as much by cocaine as mutual curiosity, that my real education came about. It wasn't necessarily that Inigo knew more than I did (though his knowledge of contemporary art, even then, was astonishing), but rather that the conversations were so challenging, so richly wide-ranging, that I can still trace many of the opinions I hold today back to those long nights. Afterwards, we would often take dawn walks around Bloomsbury in an attempt to shake off the jarring effects of the drugs. Those mornings, in the coppery dawn light that pricked its way through the leavings of the night, I saw the world anew, its cultural possibilities boundless and infinitely fascinating. Life seemed so clear to me in those days; it was a clarity born of a friendship the like of which I hadn't imagined to exist outside of books.

At the time, Inigo was supplementing his studies with frequent and absorbing work for Tim Marlow, head of exhibitions at White Cube, and between infrequent lectures and an undemanding workload, I found myself with time to fill. I began looking around for opportunity, for some path in the art world which would be distinct from I & O Fine Art and from Inigo.

So, in the early summer of 2008, while Inigo was occupied with some special project for White Cube, I spent week after week in a basement room in Fulham sorting through the archive of a documentary maker. The Gili 'collection' – assemblage might have been more accurate – was enormous, part of a photography archive financed by the Canadian billionaire David Thomson called the Archive of Modern Conflict, where I'd been working on and off for a year. It was our job to go through all forty trunks of photographs, objects and ephemera, sorting the items by category and then describing, measuring and photographing them.

Jonathan Gili had worked mostly for the BBC. In a long career he had travelled widely but the things that he had collected – or at least those things that together formed this collection – were of the most prosaic nature imaginable. As well as train tickets – hundreds of them – there were countless boarding card stubs and menus (mainly from Sally Clarke's eponymous restaurant in Kensington); postcards, unwritten and unsent; movie tie-in toys from kids' meals; a complete set of Looney Tunes Pez dispensers; business cards for people and businesses that no longer existed; limited edition Tic Tacs, the ovate candies stuck together like cells under a microscope in their clear plastic cases; and so much else besides, all of it the rightful jetsam of a life in the twentieth century.

As soon as we had dealt with one trunk it would be taken away and another brought in to replace it. Day after day, week after week, we combed through the detritus of one lifetime's obsession. Had the collection been the work of a poor unknown it would likely have been written off as hoarding, the whole lot thrown away when he died. It's the difference, as my father used to say, between an oddball and an eccentric: an eccentric is just an oddball with money. The power of money – and its infrequent bedfellow, class – has the ability to change something worthless into something with pretensions towards cultural importance. The notion of quality is sometimes no more than a whim.

I loved the work, although I recognise now that my fascination with archives was a product of anxiety: any taxonomic system is an attempt to make sense of the world and I was bewildered by life, desperate for a way to order it, for someone to say, 'Start here, learn this, and everything will be all right.' Even today, a lifetime's worth of insecurity masquerades as a desperate need to know everything and these mental images of archives act as a soothing balm against the frustration of an impossible task.

But I came to see the collection's merit on its own terms,

too. In its vastness, its omnivorous scope, it captured something of the essence of the late twentieth century, the poignancy of consumption and its inevitable corollary, waste; the way things that touch our lives only briefly can in time take on the aura of relics. The Gili collection wasn't art per se, but I began to realise that the cultural caprices of just a few people could be extrapolated to the wider market, and indeed to an entire culture. Sometimes all it takes is someone like Timothy, the man who ran the archive (a cultural gatekeeper), and a wealthy patron like Thomson (whose collection also boasts works by Raphael and John Constable, among many others) and something that might otherwise have been ignored, even jettisoned, becomes noteworthy and valuable. Beginning that summer, what I gradually came to see was that the world of culture reflects the tastes and predilections of a tiny few. What the wider public considers good or worthy, bad or irrelevant, is actually contingent on the convictions of a small cadre of loud voices. Almost by definition, there are no right answers when it comes to cultural quality; there is only the persuasiveness of the loudest voice – and that's how you make a market.

Later that summer, I would have my second lesson in the insularity and power dynamics of the art world. Inigo had asked me to join him and his father, Harry, for what Inigo had hazily described as an 'all-expenses-paid art world retreat' and in late June I flew to Bangor, Maine, to meet them. The trip started badly – the airline lost my baggage – but soon after I'd filled in the forms at the lost property desk I climbed into the back seat of Harry's battered Subaru station wagon and quickly forgot all about it.

Soon, the landscape of Mount Desert Island and Acadia National Park unfurled before us like a VistaVision dream. The hills were covered with thick forest and bright lakes flashed between the trees as we drove. Seeing this landscape for the first time, I readily understood why the pilgrims had thought America was the Promised Land.

As we turned off the highway I saw a sign that warned of moose crossing and as we drove down a dappled track I scanned the woods nervously. We were staying next to a lake called Long Pond, in a log cabin, a one-floor affair with bare wooden walls and shiny wooden floors and a smell of pine so strong that at first I thought it must be piped in. The sofa was the fiery orange that red cloth takes on when it has been beaten by the sun for a long time and the kitchen table was scattered with last night's empty beer bottles and this morning's discarded coffee cups.

We were in Maine to attend ASAP (the Acadia Summer Arts Program), affectionately known as 'Kamp Kippy' after its founder and benefactor, Kippy Stroud. The programme, so Inigo told me, had been set up by Stroud as a way for impoverished art world folk to have a free holiday among like-minded people ('impoverished' here being a distinctly relative term). The only obligation was to attend dinner every other night at Deer Acres, the programme's campus, and to give a talk once during your stay. No art dealers were allowed.

Harry was a big, square-shouldered man with a blowsy face and beery breath. Earlier that year Inigo and I had flown to San Diego to meet him and catch the last days of the Robert Irwin exhibition at the contemporary art museum there, and I'd taken an instant liking to him then. He was unlike my own father in nearly every way: he drank beer instead of wine; he listened to Neil Young instead of Bach; he loved sport and could talk about baseball as if it were poetry he'd learned at school. He came from a WASP-y New England family; his father, Charles, had been a legendary professor of English at Brown

University. As the first male Philbrick for several generations not to attend Brown, Inigo told me that Harry was something of a black sheep, choosing instead to move to London and go to Goldsmiths. He later worked as head of art education at London's Hayward Gallery before returning to the US. He was the first bona fide contemporary art curator I'd ever met, a role I'd only heard spoken of in reverent terms. Best of all, though, he seemed willing to help Inigo and me in our quest to become art dealers.

When we arrived at Deer Acres for our first dinner I felt dazzled and shy. The airline still hadn't found my bag and I'd bought what I could afford from the L.L. Bean outlet in the nearby town. As we arrived, I caught my reflection in a car window: in my oversize blue sweatshirt and green corduroy cut-offs I looked like I was wearing a WASP-y hobo's hand-me-downs.

As soon as we entered the barn where the dinner was to be held, Inigo and Harry both fell into conversations with people they knew. For a while I stood off to the side and watched the room. A glamorous, preppy crowd stood around in the large whitewashed barn converted especially for such gatherings, while young waiters moved unseen between them. The day had been warm but the temperature was dropping; I overheard someone say that cool air was coming in from the Atlantic. The men wore pastel-coloured sweaters around their shoulders and the women wore shawls. There was an air of nervous expectation, as if there were a mosquito close at hand in a dark room.

Inigo seemed, as ever, to take everything in his stride. Both of his parents were keyed into the American contemporary art scene and he'd been rolling with this kind of crowd since he was a child; the painter Frank Stella had been his occasional babysitter. From my vantage point just to the side of the bar,

I could see Inigo in conversation with a man in a wheelchair. Though they both had their backs turned to me, I watched as Inigo leant down to catch what the man was saying. Their conversation was jocular and intense, but eventually it became clear that dinner was ready and Inigo shook the man by the hand and sidled over to me.

'Who was that guy?' I asked.

'Arthur Danto,' he replied. 'The philosopher.'

'You're kidding?' I said. Danto wasn't just any old philosophy professor. He was one of the most celebrated art philosophers alive, someone Inigo and I had read at Goldsmiths. He was a legend. I remember feeling hurt that Inigo didn't think to introduce me to him, too; he must have known how much of a thrill it would have been for me. I don't know if this was another example of Inigo compartmentalising, or whether he sensed my profound awkwardness at the wider situation – a room full of confident high-achievers not dressed in clothes they'd bought at a discount outlet. Inigo had presumably spent much of his childhood in rooms like this (certainly he had attended ASAP before), around people just like this. The closest my father ever let me get to his world was the back of an auction room, where I was forbidden to make a sound or move a muscle lest someone think I was bidding. Closer than most, of course, but very much face-pressed-against-the-window.

'Yeah, he's here most years,' Inigo told me, looking back over his shoulder at Danto. 'He and Kippy are pretty close, apparently.'

'And you know him? You never said.'

'I don't know him, know him. But we've met here a few times and I've been to his apartment in New York. He's a great guy. Funny as hell.'

Over the next week I would meet many such people: senior

curators at major museums; brand name artists; and writers whose names were familiar from the pages of *October*, *frieze* and *Artforum* – people whose texts we were reading at university. If Inigo didn't already know them personally, Harry almost certainly did, and I was casually introduced to some serious people. They asked me questions about my studies, even seeming interested in my opinions of various exhibitions I'd seen in London out of what I can only assume was kindness. It all felt heady and vertiginous; while our fellow students were in dreary London reading stuffy texts and listening to dreary lectures, we were playing truant, out in the world meeting real artists and thinkers.

What was clear, even then, was that Inigo knew instinctively how to translate one lot of connections into another. Crucially, he realised very early on that people like to have a protégé, so as to be in touch, even tangentially, with the next batch of bright young things. In the art world, that's an invaluable currency. Continued relevance is a war which can last a lifetime; it's much easier to have someone to fight your battles by proxy. Many people were eager to introduce this impressive young man to others, to be the person responsible for a new partnership.

It may also have crossed my mind at the time that I might benefit from my association with Inigo. But the one thing I could never ape, however long I was in his orbit, was Inigo's ambition. Even then, with the thrill of the few small deals I & O Fine Art had brokered still raising the hairs on my neck, I had no sense of the scale that it was possible to achieve in the art market. I knew names like Larry Gagosian and Sadie Coles, Marian Goodman and Jay Jopling, but had no real idea of the money and power they commanded. (I was yet to learn about people like Ivor Braka or Dominique Lévy, discreet secondary market dealers whose deep pockets were matched only by their

Rolodexes and good taste.) Inigo, however, knew all about these people. He knew their galleries and their programmes, he knew who bought from them and sold through them. Inigo was studying them for one reason: he wanted to be one of them. This, he knew, was a world where enormous fortunes could be made and you could have fun doing it. Back then, all I knew about was the fun. I wanted to keep this most exciting of new friends close by me.

To be a good art dealer you need to be both prescient and manipulative. The mere ability to spot a trend or an artist is not enough. You have to know how to get what you want from the situation, to buy early and hold your nerve. That I never had this instinct can be evidenced by the fact that when I went to the British street artist Banksy's Christmas pop-up, Santa's Ghetto, in December 2004, I bought two prints for about £100 each. I took them home and stuck one on my wall with drawing pins in the full glare of a south-facing window; the other I promptly lost to the murky gods of the underbed. Today, in good condition, those prints would be worth upwards of £150,000. *Each.*

When I told Inigo this story he almost fell off his chair laughing. Banksy has aways occupied an odd place in the contemporary market, a nether region of mutual disdain and avarice. Back then, Banksy still existed mostly in the world of street art and tabloid speculation about his identity. His work peppered the walls of east London and he showed at the gaudy Lazarides Gallery in Soho. The art world at the time cared little for Banksy and I suspect the feeling was mutual. Inigo, however, sensed opportunity.

The art market boom that had started with the YBAs in the 1990s was driven by four main factors: an influx of money from the former Soviet Union and then, later, the first dot. com boom; the public relations know-how of dealers like Jay Jopling; and the opportunism of collectors like Charles Saatchi. Many of the new players in the market made their first purchases through the auction houses: Christie's, Sotheby's – and to a lesser extent Bonhams and Phillips – are globally recognised luxury brand names and many new collectors, wary of being ripped off by unknown galleries or sharky dealers, chose to begin their collecting through the auction houses, with their veneer of international trustworthiness. Banksy, and other street artists like Kaws and Mr. Brainwash, with their easy visual punchlines and uncomplicated politics, were a perfect gateway drug for a new generation of wealthy potential art buyers. Auction houses will hold entry-level sales (Sotheby's jingoistic, cashing-in-on-Brexit-sentiment sale, 'Made in Britain', for example) to lure in new clients with Banksy prints and the like, only later to persuade them that they need to get a little more serious about their collecting (i.e. spend more). Once those auction guys get their teeth into you, they'd sooner leave their dentures in your leg than set you free.

One afternoon in the autumn of 2007 Inigo emailed me an image of a pair of metal doors. The email contained no text but the subject line read 'Call me when you've seen this'. At first I was confused. The doors looked ordinary, grubby; I could see litter strewn about on the pavement to either side. The photo was blurry but when I zoomed in I noticed at the bottom of the door on the left what appeared to be a Banksy rat wearing a baseball cap and holding a beatbox on its shoulder. I called Inigo immediately.

'That's quite a find,' I said. 'How did you come across that?'

'Walking home from Hoxton Square. I got stuck on the phone so I went round the block a few times.' (This compulsive habit of walking while he was on the phone would stick with Inigo for as long as I knew him. Now, when I remember him pacing back and forth in the gallery at Mount Street with his phone glued to his ear, it seems to me an eerie prognostic of him in some prison exercise yard.)

'It's great,' I said. 'The doors are filthy but the rat itself looks in good condition.'

'I've already sent it to a guy I know at Phillips,' he told me. 'What are you doing now?'

'Nothing special.'

'Want to come and meet me here? Maybe we can find out more.'

When I arrived about half an hour later it was dark and raining. I found Inigo sitting on a low wall, huddled under an umbrella and glued to his BlackBerry. As I approached him, he started talking without looking up. 'I've found the owner on the Land Registry,' he said flatly, 'but I don't think that's the way to do this. Really what we want to do is find whoever's in charge of the building – the super, I guess. Is that what you call them here?' (The only 'super' I'd ever seen was that rotund fellow on *Friends* so I kept quiet.) 'Anyway, we find the guy and offer to replace the doors and bang him some cash. Say five grand for the door and ten for the super? We want him to feel incentivised.'

'Where are we going to get £15,000 from?' Whatever our dubious early promise as art dealers, our bona fides as spenders were well established; all the proceeds from both Rego deals were gone. 'We'll figure all that out,' said Inigo dismissively. 'The important thing is to get in with our offer quickly and keep the building guy quiet. We don't want him finding out what it could be worth.'

'How much do you think it's worth?'

'I won't know until we hear back from my guy at Phillips, but I would guess upwards of £50k.'

'You're kidding?!'

'No, sir. People go crazy for this shit. No idea why. I assume it's a bubble.'

We walked back together in the rain, Inigo still glued to his phone, attempting to look up Banksy prices on Artnet. He muttered under his breath as he toggled the parameters for his search.

The next morning Inigo called me early. 'My guy from Phillips emailed me overnight.' His tone was breathy, rushed. 'They'll take the piece. They want the Banksy. And, dude, the estimate . . .'

'Don't leave me hanging.'

'Eighty to ninety thousand pounds fucking sterling! This could really set us up, big boy.'

'Christ! What's our next move?' I asked, trying to convey unfelt enthusiasm. The whole idea seemed to me an odd mix of fantastical and simple. Buy a door, bribe a building manager? How hard could that be? But where do you start? A fucking door shop? How do you approach the building manager? And how would we raise the money? In Inigo's mind, the deal was halfway done; in mine it was dead on arrival.

'Are you up? Let's go and see if we can find the building guy,' Inigo said.

'Give me half an hour.'

It had rained all night but the sun shone that morning and everything looked as if it had been hosed down for a film shoot or a visiting dignitary. Inigo was outside my door drinking an espresso from a paper cup when I came out. Whereas it never occurred to me to wear sunglasses except on holiday, Inigo would put his on at the slightest ray, and that day he wore his father's enormous old leather car coat, too. With the collar turned up and his free hand stuffed down in a pocket, he looked like he was going to an audition for a private detective role, with me his squinty sidekick.

'So I think you should do the talking,' Inigo said as the building came into view a little while later. 'If he's English he'll hate Americans. Frankly, wherever he's from, if he's ended up here, he'll probably hate Americans.'

'I'm not sure a Brit named Orlando is going to do much better, but I'll see what I can do.'

'Our names are ridiculously impractical,' Inigo sighed.

It was still early on a Saturday and the building, which housed offices and design studios, was quiet. Through the plate glass windows we could see a cleaner at work and a security guard dozing off, his hand holding his cheek like a clam in its shell. He shuddered awake as I pushed at the locked glass doors. I smiled broadly. He levered himself out of his chair, all six foot six of him.

Opening the door a crack he looked down at me and said, 'Hello?'

'Hi,' I replied cheerily. 'Are you . . .' – I hadn't thought through what I was going to say – '. . . the super?' He looked confused. 'The building manager?' His expression morphed to one of decision-making.

'Yes.' And then after some consideration he said, 'Sometimes.' That was good enough for me.

'We're interested in your doors.' He opened the glass door further and looked at it as if seeing it for the first time. With the sleeve of his jacket he polished away some greasy hand prints and a mark that looked like it might have been left by someone's forehead. 'Ah, no,' I said quickly, 'not these doors. The ones around the back. The metal ones.'

63

'Show me,' he said, opening the door fully and locking it behind him from the street before giving a five-minute hand gesture to the cleaner.

We walked around to the back of the building, Inigo keeping a few paces behind us, failing to suppress a grin. When we reached the doors I froze. The man looked at them and then back at me. 'So what do you want? Is there something wrong?' he asked.

'We collect street art,' I told him grandiloquently. 'We want to buy the doors for that rat.' He looked at me like I had suddenly broken into song.

Inigo stepped forward and interjected. 'We'd like to buy these doors. We're happy to pay for them to be replaced. And we'd be happy to give you some cash if you could help us make this happen.' The man stared at Inigo and then back at me before he crouched down in front of the door and inspected the Banksy rat.

'You really want *this*?' he asked, looking up at us both. 'I'll have to talk to the building manager,' he said.

'I thought you were the building manager?' I said.

'I'm just the night manager. Sometimes cover for the main man when he's away. But stuff like this,' he said, pointing to the rat, 'has to go through him. Must be worth something to you, all this effort . . .' he trailed off.

'Do you have his contact details?' Inigo asked.

'Can't go around giving people's numbers out just like that,' he said, standing up. 'You'll have to come back on Monday.'

'And there's no possibility we could just do this through you without involving your boss?' I asked.

'He's not my boss. Did I say he was my boss?'

'We would certainly want to pay you for your help and your time,' Inigo said smoothly. 'Is there a number that would make you reconsider? How much would a new set of doors cost, for example? We'd be happy to pay you the same amount in cash for your help. Double, even?'

'Like I said, you'll have to talk to Steve on Monday.'

'Could we leave you our contact details?' Inigo stretched out a hand with his card.

'I'll pass it on,' he said, sneering at the card in his massive palm.

'Well, it was never going to be easy,' I said to Inigo in an attempt to break the mutual silence as we walked away from the building.

'We've got to somehow do this without alerting them to what they have.'

'Maybe if we damaged the other door somehow they'd have to replace them both and we could buy them as scrap. Do we know anyone who could accidentally on purpose reverse into it?'

'Not a terrible idea,' Inigo replied, 'but too risky. Plus the only person we know in London with a car is your mother and I wouldn't trust her accuracy in reverse! Let's see what Steve says on Monday. I'm going to have breakfast with Robert. Want to join?'

The following Monday I went to Goldsmiths to attend lectures as usual while Inigo said he had a meeting at White Cube. Despite his consistently high grades, Inigo's attendance at Goldsmiths was, at best, minimalist. Towards the end of the afternoon, he called me to say that he'd not heard from Steve but that he was going to walk by the building on his way home. I wasn't surprised at Steve's silence; I imagined that the surly night manager had thrown away Inigo's card the moment we were out of sight.

Half an hour later, Inigo called me in the middle of a lecture on the French philosopher Maurice Merleau-Ponty. When I called him back at the end of the lecture the phone barely rang before he picked up. 'They fucked us!' he yelled. 'The fuckers. They fucking fucked us, dude. The door. It's fucking gone. I went past just now and there are some guys finishing off putting in the new doors.'

'Did you speak to them? What happened? Was this Steve guy there?'

'They don't know anything. They'd just been called this morning to replace the doors. They said that one of the doors was gone when they got there. It was already boarded up.' Moments after this call I received a photo from Inigo. It showed two workmen fitting the new doors. Beside them, leaning against the wall, was a door-sized sheet of plywood. It was already riddled with graffiti.

As I made my way home on the bus that evening, I felt utterly deflated. It had been a long while since the Rego deals and I felt sure that Inigo would soon lose interest in I & O Fine Art and in turn in our friendship. I was coming to see that he was a strange mix of fierce determination and an easy-come-easy-go attitude. It wasn't until years later that I realised that this was the perfect way for an art dealer to be. So many potential sales come to nothing – after all, you're selling something that no one *needs* – that disappointment is an inevitable aspect of the job. You have to chase every deal with the same intensity, and when nine out of ten just don't work out, you have to brush yourself off, forget all the effort and expense, forget the late nights spent with people you'd happily watch drown, and wake up the next day ready to push hard all over again. I took defeats too personally – I still do – and setbacks stick in my skin like thorns; for Inigo, they seemed only to spur him on.

*

Weeks went by. I buried myself in essays and reading and for a little while I saw less of my friend. Inigo was spending more and more time at White Cube, working, so he told me, on an upcoming Gilbert & George exhibition. When our fellow students asked me about Inigo's absences they were incredulous that a mere student should be working with world-famous artists. They didn't know the Inigo I had come to know.

One wet and brooding Thursday afternoon in November, however, Inigo joined me on the bus down to Goldsmiths. 'I got a crazy email from the department administrator,' he told me by way of explanation. 'They were threatening to cancel my student visa unless I started showing up to class more. Which would obviously have been incredibly dull. I can't keep on at White Cube if I don't have a visa.'

We sat together at the back of the lecture hall, Inigo's laptop screen alternating between Bloomberg, *The New York Times* and his inbox. I saw emails from Tim Marlow, Director of Exhibitions at White Cube, come in and watched him reply with quick, confident key strokes. I leaned over at one point and asked, 'Do Gilbert & George email you, too?'

'No chance, dude. They only have a fax machine and a landline. White Cube had to install a fax machine just to communicate with them!' he whispered back with a grin. 'Have you got plans after this?'

'Not especially,' I lied. I had an essay to finish and I guessed he did, too, but I was keen to distract myself; an evening with Inigo was just what I needed.

'I'm going to check out some openings on Vyner Street,' Inigo said. 'Not sure there'll be anything good, but I told Tim I'd go and see if there was anything worth his time. We could check out Vilma Gold and Herald Street, too. Maureen Paley has a new show opening, I think.'

'I'm game,' I replied. I was thrilled.

An hour or so later we were on a train with some fellow Goldsmiths students rumbling its way north towards Bethnal Green. We all disgorged at Cambridge Heath Road where the cobbled side streets and railway arches shimmered with a distinctly old London glow. When we reached Vyner Street, there were people spilling out into the road despite the downpour. Mutual congratulations were thick in the air.

Today devoid of galleries, Vyner Street was in those days the Mecca of London's contemporary art scene, albeit a Mecca with a pub. At the first gallery we came to, Modern Art (a gallery name with a chutzpah I found impossible not to admire), Inigo and I both grabbed beers from the bucket by the door and pushed our way in through the crowd. The exhibition was a show of photomontages by the artist Linder. Torn-up and cut-out images of pornographic models were juxtaposed with domestic interiors and appliances. There was a tension in those works – a feeling at once of oppression and rage, beauty and underlying violence, entwined in a punk aesthetic – that seemed to capture something intrinsic about the art scene itself and the way it was gentrifying places like Vyner Street. Linder was an artist we had studied at Goldsmiths, a legend of radical feminism, and it was a thrill to see her new work. It was and remains one of the reasons I love seeing primary market gallery shows: you're seeing an artist's work before the market has had a chance to intervene, before curators and critics try to make up your mind for you. It's the next best thing to visiting their studio.

We saw a few other shows that night, each of them less interesting than the last. Indeed, were it not for the Linder show at Modern Art, there is only one reason why I recall anything of that evening. That was the night I met Keith.

Inigo and I were pretty buzzed from all the free beer but I could see his face scowling at the artworks. It was nearly 8.30 p.m.; openings typically run from 6 p.m. to 9 p.m. The crowds were thinning out and the beer buckets were empty. Just as we were about to leave, Louise-with-the-mournful-eyes, Inigo's housemate from Great Russell Street, came into the gallery. She was accompanied by a short, skinny man with rodent-y features and an air of furtive exhaustion. He wore an expensive-looking overcoat with a velvet collar that was several sizes too large for him, corduroy trousers and threadbare plimsolls. He stayed rooted to the spot as Louise crossed the gallery to greet us.

'Inigo!' cried Louise. 'Didn't expect to see you here! We were just doing the rounds. Did you see the Linder show?'

'Only thing worth coming here for,' Inigo replied.

'Do you know Keith?' Louise asked, beckoning the man over. With a quizzical look on his face, he shuffled towards us. 'You guys have met at GRS surely? The Christmas party last year?' Louise said to Keith and Inigo.

'Good to see you again,' Inigo said, extending his hand. Keith shook it wordlessly, his lips tensing into a cautious smile, the only acknowledgement that he might recognise Inigo.

'This lot is fuckin' terrible,' Louise said, casting her eye around the quickly emptying gallery. 'We're going across the road to the Victory. Come for a drink?'

The Victory is in a squat building on a corner whose exterior approximates the mock Tudor style so poorly that it feels like it's making a mockery of mock Tudor. Its interior that evening was a sticky mess of swirling carpet, horse brasses, animosity and off-target darts. The air was thick with cigarette smoke, despite the recent ban, as the art crowd muscled in around the bar. I joined their ranks to buy a round.

Ten minutes later I was still waiting to be served when Inigo sidled up to the bar. 'I thought I'd help you carry the drinks,' he said, 'but you don't seem to be having much luck.' He took a twenty from his wallet and, holding it between his first two fingers, leaned over the bar. A barman materialised and while the drinks were being poured he turned to me and said, 'You know that's Keith Coventry, right? The painter. I think he and Louise have a thing. Maybe. I don't know. He's at GRS a lot.'

'Ah, no, I didn't.' I looked over at the table beside which Keith was slumped in a chair, his downtrodden gaze fixed on nothing in particular. He looked a far cry from the wild YBA I'd read about.

Keith became more animated as the evening wore on, however, regaling us with stories of the art world of the 1980s and 1990s. Debauchery and skullduggery featured heavily, as did the founding of City Racing, the renowned artist-run space in a former south London betting shop. I was totally starstruck. I'd read Andrew Wilson's book about City Racing, full of baby-faced photos of the artists whose work I had come to love as a young adult.

When the Victory rang last orders at 11 p.m. Keith invited us to his studio around the corner, where he doled out whisky in chipped, tea-stained mugs. The place was absolutely crammed with paintings, all in Keith's distinctive white frames, all greying with dust. An enormous bronze structure like a lattice lay on the central table.

'What's that?' I asked Keith.

'Oh, that,' he replied. 'That's my broken window piece. Part of it anyway. I need to figure out getting it sent to Moscow. I'm not terribly organised. I need to hire an assistant really.'

'I could help?' I was shocked to hear the words come out of my mouth. It was as much a question for me as it was for him.

'Yeah, get Whitebread to help you!' Inigo chimed in, laughing on the other side of the room. I think Keith and I were as confused as each other, but he nevertheless wrote his email address down on a scrap of paper and handed it to me. 'Drop me a line. I won't need much help really. At the weekends, I reckon.'

Inigo and I walked home that night in the after-rain cold. As we came to Clerkenwell, Inigo's pace quickened. 'I almost forgot,' he said, turning back to where I lagged behind. 'I found something you *need* to see. It's just up here.' We quickly reached a scooter shop with an empty lot beside it and Inigo turned to show me the shop's side wall. The render on the wall was a patchy white and a large area of it had been haphazardly rollered with grey paint. On top of the grey were four stencilled black and white figures – old people's faces atop bodies dressed in youthful streetwear. One, who had the face of an old woman complete with hairnet and pearl necklace, sat on a 1980s-style beatbox. Above this, sprayed in hot pink paint, were the words 'OLD SKOOL'.

'I'm not a hundred per cent it's a Banksy yet,' Inigo said after letting the impact of the reveal land; even drunk on a wet street late at night, Inigo instinctively knew how to show an artwork. 'I've sent an image to David O'Connell. He ought to know.' (David was a fellow student at Goldsmiths and Banksy obsessive who managed to write almost all his essays, no matter the question, about Banksy.)

'I mean, this is great,' I said hesitantly, 'but it's on a fucking wall. A door was one thing, but this is different.'

'I know. But it has to be doable, right? *Has* to be. Think of all those frescoes they move in Italy. And those things are fucking ancient.' In the mustardy light of the street lamps I couldn't read his expression. Surely he was joking, I thought. 'We'd need to get a financial backer,' he continued. 'I have someone in mind. The father of a high school friend. It'll be expensive, but it could be very lucrative.' These last two words he spoke with obvious delight, slowly turning them over in his mouth, as if somehow the syllables themselves might have financial value that could be exploited and enjoyed.

Of all the things Inigo and I did (or attempted) together in the time we ran I & O Fine Art, this now seems like the very peak of our madness. We were green-as-they-come art history students with silly names in our second year at university. We had no real world experience and yet we were trying to raise tens of thousands of pounds, pull off a major feat of delicate buildings conservation, followed by a massive art deal. We didn't even have a company bank account. At the time I remember a plunging feeling of doubt, certain only that this would fail. I don't think failure ever even occurred to Inigo. In all the years I knew him, he never had any use for uncertainty.

The next few weeks were a roiling mix of anxiety and excitement. Inigo came to class seldom but we were constantly in touch as he researched the work and arranged a phone call with his friend's father. The street art specialist Inigo had spoken to at Phillips hadn't known how to value the Banksy – nothing of the kind had ever come up at auction – but assured us that there would be buyers for such a piece through their private sales division. Collectors in China were going crazy for Banksy's room-temperature political posturing and were busy building and filling private museums with it. Though we had no idea what we could sell the work for, we knew it would be significantly more than what we might have made from selling the door. The only problem was getting it off in one piece.

At this point, I really didn't know much about the

contemporary art market. My father had been an auctioneer, yes, but his expertise was in antique furniture and Renaissance bronzes. His was a fusty world of men with privet-hedge eyebrows and bad breath. These men had narrow and exacting enthusiasms; mention Damien Hirst or Tracey Emin and you would be greeted with a headmasterly sneer.

Until Inigo and I sold that first Rego, I hadn't even known that art deals happened without the involvement of galleries. Like many people I've met since, I believed the art market was a world of simple if extravagant transactions. Artists made artworks, gallerists showed those artworks and, in a very passive way, sometimes sold those artworks to collectors who would hang them on their walls or place them on plinths ready for the admiration of their cultured friends. Occasionally (mainly once the artist and collector had died), the paintings and sculptures would make their way to auction and, even less frequently, into museums. What I had in mind was a sort of trickle-up economics. It was wholly naive. What Inigo was showing me, however, is that the art market was a far more complex ecosystem of organisms feeding into and off each other. Symbiotic might be a polite word for it; incestuous is nearer the mark.

I was right about one thing, though: it all starts with an artist making an artwork. By hook *and* by crook, that artist then finds somewhere to show said work, preferably a gallery run by a gallerist. The work is shown, people come to an opening (these people are mainly the artist's friends) and hopefully some of the works sell over the course of the exhibition's run (typically four to six weeks). This is what's known as the primary market, the phrase used to describe works of art being sold for the first time, whether for £500 by a recent art school graduate or £500,000 for a new painting by an established market star in her eighties.

Everything after this point is known as the secondary market. The term encompasses the second time the £500 art school painting is sold (as well as the third, fourth, fifth, and so on) as well as every other sale of an artwork that has previously been sold. People who operate mainly in the primary market are known as gallerists; secondary market operators are called dealers.

Even though the Banksy clearly hadn't been sold before, what Inigo and I were attempting was nevertheless dealing, straight-up hustle. We didn't have any clients so we were going to try again to work with the auction house, Phillips. The auction houses, or 'the rooms' if you want to sound in the know, are sort of like Switzerland: they know where everything is and what everyone owns; and they pretend to be impartial while making money from both sides. If you don't have a buyer for something, the chances are they will.

To begin with, just like in a Greek tragedy, all the action seemed to be taking place off-stage, with Inigo masterminding things. Generally I only learned what had happened after the fact. One day Inigo called to tell me that his potential Banksy backer was coming to London and so, with just hours to spare, we were holed up in his room, compiling I & O Fine Art-branded PDFs comprising surreptitiously taken photographs of the mural along with auction results and impressive visuals and testimonials from websites of companies who'd undertaken mural removal and preservation.

At the same time, I had started working for Keith on Saturdays. We would convene at his studio on Cambridge Heath Road in the late morning and then go for breakfast, afterwards returning to the studio to hem and haw about what to do, how to ship his enormous bronze sculpture to Moscow where Dasha Zhukova, the then-partner of Roman Abramovich, had just opened her contemporary art museum, the Garage.

Despite having been included in the seminal 1997 *Sensation* exhibition at the Royal Academy (RA), Keith was not at that time represented by a gallery, hence the need for him to arrange the shipping of his own artworks. In the mid-1990s he'd been represented by the YBA-studded Karsten Schubert gallery but his career had since floundered in a limbo of group shows and directionless exhibiting which meant he missed the great upward career thrust of his peers, many far less talented than him.

It was frequently unclear to me what Keith had done between one visit and the next but certainly we made little progress those Saturdays I was there. Often, after a certain amount of in-studio procrastination, Keith would suggest that we go for a drink, a suggestion he always made as if it were a wholly novel and surprising thought, one that had never occurred to anyone ever before. He was a member of seemingly every exclusive drinking club in London, memberships for which he didn't pay, he was careful to tell me, but rather had exchanged for artworks. Credit was added to his account to the value of a painting. He belonged to the Groucho Club, both Soho and Shoreditch Houses and many others I'd never even heard of, let alone been to.

It was during one such Saturday afternoon drinking session that Inigo joined us after his meeting with his friend's father. We were at the Ivy Club, situated above the eponymous restaurant by then so festooned with *Daily Mail* celebrities that the management must have figured that real rich people needed somewhere to escape. Much of the club, as I recall, felt like being in a gold-plated attic where overly attentive staff moved softly between bar and tables, hovering like hummingbirds as they set down their orders. Keith and I were drinking Twinkles – a lethally sweet cocktail made from vodka, champagne and elderflower liqueur which has the astringent smell and mouth-feel of a hair removal cream – and Keith ordered another round as Inigo sat down. I could see from Inigo's face that he had something he wanted to tell me, but when I leaned in at what I thought was an opportune moment, he just smiled and said, 'Later.'

There was a football match showing on a nearby television which had been requested by another table of members, and Keith, although less interested in the match than he was in the discovery of mutual friends with one of the watchers, had temporarily decamped to drink with them. Inigo was several Twinkles down when he leant back triumphantly in his chair and said, 'Looks like we got the backing we need. He's agreed to thirty thousand with the possibility of an additional twenty if we need it. We just need to get the thing off the wall and sell it. Then we split the upside.'

'That's incredible,' I said, scarcely able to comprehend what he was saying. I was a few drinks ahead of Inigo and the numbers were swimming in my mind. At this stage, I was genu-inely puzzled by Inigo's desire to include me. He was across all aspects of the deal, whereas I had had almost no involvement or input whatsoever. Inigo's ambition and confidence seemed to exist – through no fault of his – in an inverse correlation with my reluctance and anxiety. Where he saw opportunity and promise, I saw obstacles and defeat.

'That's all you got for me?' Inigo said, sensing my reticence.

'No, of course, it's fantastic. I just don't know how exactly we go about doing this.'

'Nor do I! That's the fun of it, no? We'll figure it out. But it would really set us up financially.'

'For a gallery, you mean?'

'Sure, a gallery,' said Inigo, finishing his drink. 'Or maybe something more private, a nice office somewhere we can deal from. It's all to play for, my friend.'

The following Monday we hit the phones in the kitchen at GRS. Robert hovered, pretending to make tea and sniggering openly at 'Idiot & Oaf'. While Inigo tried to set up a company bank account I cold-called structural engineers and building restoration companies. Nervous of a repeat of what happened with the last Banksy we'd tried to procure, I described what we wanted to do in the vaguest terminology I could muster.

'We've got this wall,' I would start out. 'It's a brick wall, made from London bricks. Probably Victorian? Then there's a layer of concrete on top of that' (I felt like I was describing a cake) 'and on the concrete is a painting. Can you remove the painting?' This was usually met with silence, sometimes more vocal consternation, and other times just the dead-end of a dial tone. Those few people I could keep on the phone for long enough to explain what we were trying to do soon hung up when I told them we didn't own or even have access to the building in question. Soon I was just calling builders out of the phone book trying my utmost not to sound like an art history student with a ridiculous name. ('How are you spelling that?' 'Orlando, you know, like Florida, like Disney World.')

Eventually, I called a builder I knew called Joe who'd done some work on my mother's house a few years previously. I'd been revising for my A-levels at the time he was working there, and we'd become friendly. While, as Joe told me, it was not his area of expertise (strictly speaking he is a cabinet maker), I felt able to trust him with the bare bones of our plan and he agreed to come and look at the Banksy with us.

Inigo and I arranged to meet Joe in Clerkenwell after the scooter shop's business hours, and at just before 7 p.m. on a

December week night, the three of us stood on the pavement in the cold London air. The empty lot next to the shop was used as a kind of holding-pen-cum-car-park for second-hand and broken-down motorcycles and was guarded only by a heavy chain cordon. We all stepped over the chain and, for the first time, came face to face with the Banksy.

'Well, there's your first problem,' Joe told us, patting the middle of the mural.

'What is?' I asked.

'It's not level, is it? It's painted over the chimney jamb, look.' We looked. The back of the building's chimney protruded over the middle of the mural, something neither of us had noticed before. 'That'll make it a lot trickier to remove,' Joe continued. 'You'd have to do it in stages and then stick it back together. Five chunks. Not straightforward at all.'

'But it can be done?' Inigo asked.

'No reason why not,' Joe said, 'but it'll be pricey. You boys must really want this thing.'

At that moment we heard a clattering sound close at hand and a tall, meaty man poked his head round the corner. He held a set of keys in one hand and a motorcycle helmet in the other.

'Can I help you guys?' The three of us froze, caught in the act. Inigo stepped forward.

'Hi,' he said trenchantly. 'We were admiring your mural. What are our chances of buying it?'

'You're too late, I'm afraid,' the man said. 'Oddly enough someone bought it just last week. Funny. It's been there for years and no one's ever even asked about it, then two people inside a week. German fella bought it. Going to have it removed first thing in the New Year.'

'Would you mind me asking what he paid you for it?' Inigo asked, his voice smooth and assured. The man was unlocking his scooter and didn't look up from the task in hand. Inigo stepped forward. 'We might be able to make you a better offer.'

At this, the man stood up slowly and seemed to grow taller, wider. 'He paid the owner of the building a thousand pounds. Far as I'm concerned that's the end of it.' He had started to put on his helmet when Inigo interjected.

'We could pay the owner five thousand, and there'd be something for you, too, of course. Cash?'

'Look, mate,' he said, starting his scooter with what he must have hoped would be mechanical menace, 'the deal's already been done. I just run the bike shop, but the owner of the building isn't the kind of man to go back on a deal. It's not going to happen, all right?' And with that he fastened his helmet and sat down heavily on his scooter, driving it slowly in Inigo's direction. For the briefest of moments there was a stand-off, but then Inigo stepped out of the way and the man rode off into the evening.

Inigo turned to me and rolled his eyes. 'Fuck,' I said by way of reply. It was all I could muster without giving away the relief I really felt.

When the Banksy deal fell apart (though, in reality, it wasn't ever even a deal *in utero*), the very vivid realisation that this was not what I wanted to do – at least not then, not like that – became suddenly apparent. I thought perhaps this setback would deter Inigo, too; that he might also feel the art world wasn't for him and that we could just go back to being friends in an ordinary way. But that wasn't how he operated. The failure that for me seemed final was for Inigo a jockey's whip.

A month or so later we were into our last term at Goldsmiths. As we both wrestled with dissertation writing and voluminous final essays, we continued to try to pull off art deals together.

These attempts were desperate: we tried to sell, on behalf of a New York-based dealer, a painting by Arshile Gorky called *Pirate II* which later became the subject of a lawsuit when John McEnroe sued Larry Salander; and we attempted, unsuccessfully, to represent the estate of the photographer Bruce Bernard. By now I had given up on my hope that Inigo, too, might have been discouraged, and in my mind the business – such as it was – and our friendship were inextricably linked. If one failed, I was convinced the other would perish with it.

In the moment, this period felt enormously difficult and weighty. Inigo and I had been spending so much of our time together that I had largely neglected my other friendships. I was torn between desperately wanting to do well in my studies and continuing to work with Inigo. I was afraid that if I were honest with Inigo – that if I told him I wanted out – the friendship would end. It would have devastated me.

In the end, I did what all cowards do: nothing. I sat tight and allowed reticence to accrue between us like cobwebs just out of reach. By the end of our final year at Goldsmiths, I simply could not find the capacity for both university work and the business of our friendship; for his part, I think Inigo realised this without my ever having to say so directly. We quietly dissolved I & O Fine Art.

On a few occasions in early 2009 we walked past the scooter shop in order to check on the Banksy, both of us probably hoping to see very different things. Soon after our attempt to buy it, a makeshift structure was erected around it made from corrugated metal, held together with chains and padlocks. It looked a bit like a treasure chest in a children's cartoon. Early in the New Year the protective structure swelled considerably and for a month or so after that workmen could be heard inside.

And then one day it was gone, and the broken-down scooters were back in place as if nothing had ever happened.

Months later, just after we graduated, I found myself alone not far from Clerkenwell with nothing to do. It was spring turning to summer and I walked up the hill from Farringdon station towards the scooter shop feeling buoyant and carefree. It had been a wet few weeks, but in the warm sun that morning everything seemed to be breathing again. Moss and buddleia were sprouting richly green between the concrete cracks. As I passed the shop and turned to face the wall where the Banksy had been I was surprised to see something had replaced it. Around the edge of the space where the mural had been was painted a dotted line with a scissor symbol. And in the middle, as if stencilled on the side of a vast crate, the word 'COLLECTED' in large capital letters.

4

The origin stories of great art dealers are as various as the men and women who tell them. Larry Gagosian got his start flogging posters on the streets of Los Angeles; Danny Katz discovered a forgotten nineteenth-century sculpture in a Swedish museum's storage facility and sold it to the Getty; David Zwirner took his father's business model and transposed it from cold war Cologne to twenty-first-century New York. Had we pulled off our Banksy deal, Inigo and I were planning to say we'd won big at the greyhound track. Jay Jopling's origin story stands unique among contemporary art's big-hitters.

Some people are born to sell and Jay Jopling is just such a person. His career as a door-to-door salesman of fire extinguishers was short-lived (complaints were made about his unusual methods, which, it is said, included setting his own trousers on fire on the doorstep before dramatically dousing the flames), but in the forty years following Jopling has risen to become one of the most prominent – and powerful – contemporary art dealers in the world. His name is synonymous with the Young British Artists, many of whose careers he helped to launch. This was a group of artists who, with their public shenanigans and boozy, brawling ways, brought the contemporary art market to public media prominence. They, the work they made and their prices became notorious far beyond those of their predecessors: they were literally front page news and marked a long-awaited tipping point. The (contemporary) art market has always been the preserve of the much-too-wealthy, but it wasn't until the 1990s and the public rise of the YBAs that art collecting speculation became a recognised way for people to make big money. The YBAs' eye-catching and polarising artworks were some of the first to be featured in regular contemporary art auctions (previously most contemporary art prices had been secret) and the tabloids did the rest. And while many dealers remained in the shadows of their artists, Jopling stepped discreetly forward into the limelight, where he remained for some time, like a slow-moving predator gliding through the shallows of Cool Britannia. Though these days he's much less public-facing, he still represents Damien Hirst, Tracey Emin and Antony Gormley and, as Emin liked to say of him, he is a 'great dealer and a great deal more'.

Jopling, whose given name is Jeremy but whom everyone calls Jay, came from the kind of background that you can't just brush off anymore. He went to Eton with Boris Johnson and his father, Lord Jopling of Ainderby Quernhow, was Chief Whip and subsequently Agriculture Minister under Margaret Thatcher. (Jopling senior is also credited, in Alan Clark's *Diaries: In Power 1983–1992*, with perhaps the most succinctly snobbish putdown in the history of English, saying of his colleague Michael Heseltine, 'The trouble with Michael is that he had to buy all his furniture.')

In 1993, Jopling opened White Cube gallery on the first floor of 44 Duke Street, St James's, in a building owned by Christie's. It had previously been used by the auction house as a photocopying room back when photocopiers were so big they needed their own rooms. The gallery's name alludes to a 1986 book of essays by the late art critic Brian O'Doherty called *Inside the White Cube* that highlights the importance of white-walled gallery spaces in the history of modern art and makes a case for the white cube as an ideal – quasi-sacred – arena for twentieth-century art and beyond. For Jopling, who was working hard to lure working-class artists to his stable, the name brought the armour of intellectual heft just at the moment when his privileged upbringing might have caused him to fall flat on his face.

The space is so small and Jopling – at well over six foot – so large that when the gallery was showing installations or sculptures he would apparently hover in the doorway while clients viewed the exhibition. But it was there, in 1995, that Damien Hirst had his first show with the gallery. And it was there, in 2000, that Lucian Freud exhibited a single painting, *Naked Portrait*. In it, the woman's gaze is elsewhere, refusing to meet ours or that of the painter; instead, the fact of her ageing body confronts us – her bony knees and bunioned foot, her sagging breasts. There's something sorrowful, even morbid, about the painting – a sense of resignation in the face of the inevitable. It was the last commercial gallery show in which Freud would ever participate, in the city he had called home for seventy years – an extraordinary coup for such a young dealer, and one that elevated Jopling above his peers. Jopling was already at the forefront of a culturally resurgent Britain. Hoxton, where he had just opened his second space, was rapidly gentrifying; Damien Hirst was directing music videos for Blur; Tate Modern was being opened by a rather baffled-looking Queen Elizabeth II; and Tracey Emin's bed was causing outrage from the provinces to the auction rooms. Britain was cool, albeit briefly, for the first time since the miniskirt, and Jopling was right there in the thick of it, pulling strings and cashing in.

Despite the economic downturns of the early noughties,

Jopling's empire continued to expand and he rode the YBA wave all the way to the bank. At his Hoxton Square gallery – now the epicentre of London's trendy East End – he continued to build his roster of artists with new blood as well as more established artists like Gilbert & George and Anselm Kiefer. In 2006, after six years in east London, Jopling returned to St James's, opening a flagship gallery in Mason's Yard, just off Duke Street. A sepulchral monolith, it was the first new free-standing building the area had seen in almost forty years.

Back in 2005, White Cube staged its first show with the German neo-expressionist Anselm Kiefer. Wildly ambitious, the exhibition comprised installation, painting and sculpture, and ran in two parts: Part I (painting) for six weeks and then Part II (sculpture) for a further six weeks after that. For the duration of the show, Hoxton Square played host to an enormous corrugated steel pavilion which had the forbidding look of a slaughterhouse and contained about thirty paintings. For any dealer – even one as prosperous and ambitious as Jopling – this represented a massive outlay of time, real estate and money. 'It's like a collision between painting and sculpture,' Jopling told *The New York Times*. It was a bold, risky bet.

As Inigo later told me, Jopling sold the entire body of work to Andy Hall, the billionaire oil trader, on one condition: that Jopling arrange for the pavilion and the paintings to be shown at a US institution. One Harry Philbrick, director of the Aldrich Contemporary Art Museum in Ridgefield, Connecticut (a museum also supported financially by Hall), agreed to be that institution and came to London to see the pavilion for himself.

A good deal in any market is one in which both buyer and seller are happy. But in the art market, where your customer pool tends to be small (and ideally full of repeat buyers), this is especially important. This deal worked out well for everyone. Kiefer was happy with his new dealer for selling a large and difficult group of paintings (all of Kiefer's work is large and difficult); Jopling was happy because Kiefer was – is – a major European artist who lent his gallery heft, repositioning Jay from being merely the YBA guy to giving him more of an international presence. (As a bonus, he didn't have to store the art, which would have been a nightmare, frankly.) Hall, meanwhile, was happy because he got some new art and a museum in which to show it, giving the works institutional blessing and therefore value were he ever to want to sell – unlikely, as he was already a multi-billionaire. And Harry was happy, too, because one of his biggest donors was happy, because he could boast an Anselm Kiefer show at his little museum and not least because he managed to wangle his son Inigo – directionless having just finished high school and angry about his parents' ongoing divorce – an internship at White Cube, which made Inigo happy, too. Everyone's a winner, baby.

So, a few weeks later, in early 2006, the teenage Inigo started in the publications department at White Cube, reporting to Susan May and Tim Marlow. Marlow, who at the time was working with Gilbert & George on their exhibition, *SONOFAGOD PICTURES: Was Jesus Heterosexual?* started to give Inigo the kind of research jobs that would normally be the purview of junior staffers with master's degrees, not interns with high school diplomas. More importantly, however, Inigo impressed Gilbert & George.

The duo have been central figures in the British art world – and on the wider international contemporary art scene – since the late 1960s. In London, they had been represented by Anthony d'Offay Gallery for much of their career. But when d'Offay closed his gallery in 2001 he did a King Lear, splitting up his empire between Matthew Marks and Larry Gagosian in New York and Sadie Coles and Jay Jopling in London. For Jopling, representing Gilbert & George was another savvy move, pivoting him away from being a single-focus dealer and opening his remit up to a more established collector base both in Europe and the USA. The artists are among the few figures in the contemporary art world to have achieved public notoriety and an almost (inter)national treasure status. It was, all round, a coup for Jopling and his gallery. But Gilbert & George are infamously tricky to work with: they communicate by telephone or fax only and, according to Inigo, are so prickly that when a senior White Cube staffer named his first-born son George in tribute, they never spoke to him again. So when Gilbert & George responded well to Inigo, his fellow White Cubers, many of whom had written him off as an obsequious young know-it-all, had to sit up and pay attention.

Throughout our time at Goldsmiths and during the early days of I & O Fine Art, Inigo continued to work for White Cube, taking on research projects and assisting on the writing and compilation of catalogue copy. (Years later he told me that the gallery was paying his tuition.) He had been quick to recognise how the art market was shaped by a select few figures – people who effectively decided what art mattered and what didn't. Now, he was almost obsessed by it, fascinated by, as he put it, 'how, in the art market – which is very different from the art world – a star is made, prices are achieved, and a career is built'.

While we were still studying, Inigo managed to get himself a place on the White Cube committee for artist acquisition and development. Tasked with identifying new artists that the gallery should be recruiting, the committee was chaired by

Susan May, White Cube's Global Artistic Director, and was made up of some of the gallery's more junior staffers, plus, as Inigo put it, 'a couple of young salespeople who didn't have enough clients to fill their day'. Jopling also sat in on the meetings from time to time, and that was where Inigo started to gain more access to him.

On one such occasion, Inigo told me, Jopling himself was presenting an artist – a friend, really – he was keen for the gallery to work with. He showed a video work by this friend of his, Marco Brambilla. The video was, Inigo said, 'this weird druggy, LSD pixellation of gargoyles turning into people on fire turning into zombies fellating each other . . . And I cannot stop laughing. Literally so hard that I fall out of my chair . . . And Jay says, "That's enough, Inigo." But I can't stop laughing. I can't get over the fact that he's showing this to us.'

After the meeting Inigo was worried that he might have offended Jopling – that he might have jettisoned the good will he had spent so long building up. That fear only intensified the next morning when he received a call from Jopling's assistant asking Inigo to come and see him.

'I go along and he offers me an actual proper job,' Inigo told me. 'And that's Jay in a nutshell. He's a strong guy who responds to people being strong. And in truth I wasn't being strong, I just thought it was really funny. Jay spent so much time with so many people – this museum director, this top curator, this art advisor – and everyone had an opinion but kept their cards so close to their chest that I think he was so glad to have someone who was willing to speak their mind.'

For a while after Goldsmiths – after Inigo and I disbanded the business – we went from spending almost all of our time together to seeing each other only once or twice a week. We remained friends, albeit at something of a digital remove, emailing links to articles we each thought the other might find amusing or interesting, typically pieces from *The New York Times* or *The Onion* or tidbits from *Artforum*'s gratuitously gossipy 'Scene and Herd' art world diary.

But the intensity of the friendship that had consumed the past three years of my life was now heavily diluted; my degree ended just as I was starting to enjoy it; and I felt I had no place in the art world – I wasn't smart enough to be a curator and I clearly didn't have what it took to be a dealer. Lost and bewildered, I retreated into myself, spending six days a week at the London Library, situated in St James's Square, very near to White Cube. I waded through long, difficult books, understanding little, looking for nothing and finding even less. I made abortive attempts to write fiction and essays and applied for jobs and postgraduate programmes with unthinking abandon. After the previous three years of certainty – of thrusting, forward momentum and purpose – the sudden shock of stasis was salutary. Slowly, inexorably, Inigo became the adult in our relationship, a dismissive older brother whom I couldn't help but want to please.

In this period, just after we closed down I & O Fine Art and had finished studying, Inigo lived almost monastically, working late into the night in his basement room, scouring online gallery archives, reading the catalogue essays in those big coffee table art books, the essays no one really reads. He approached the art market like a quantitative analyst, subscribing to Artnet, the auction price database, and buying old magazines to track the careers of artists who hadn't made it, always seeking to understand why some artists succeeded and others failed. He was already a man possessed by the market.

'A big part of being an art dealer and art dealing is numbers,' he later told me bluntly. 'If you're going to send someone an invoice, it has to have a number on it.' During the days of I & O Fine Art, Inigo and I spent long evenings talking all this through, analysing and trying to understand how we could make our way in the art world. We idolised Jopling and his gallery, even jokingly transforming the What Would Jesus Do? (WWJD) slogan of the evangelical Christian youth movement into WWJJD – What Would Jay Jopling Do?

In fact, Inigo was flourishing. Almost immediately after we'd finished our degrees he went back to working part-time for White Cube. The gallery, although unable or unwilling to sponsor him for a full visa, were keen enough to keep him around that they apparently agreed to partially pay for him to do a masters at the Courtauld Institute of Art so that he could remain on a student visa. Since his application was late, the only option available was a course called 'The Male Nude'. Needless to say, Inigo's attendance was threadbare and he did not complete the course. From my desk at the back of the London Library, with its view over Mason's Yard, I sometimes glimpsed Inigo as he crossed back and forth between White Cube and the overflow offices nearby in Ormond Yard, often talking seriously into his phone, carrying hefty piles of auction catalogues, Post-it stickies poking out in all directions. He had begun to dress differently, too: gone were the jeans, the Chelsea boots and the leather jacket, replaced by highly polished brown brogues, grey flannel trousers and crisp white shirts open wide at the neck. It amused me to think of him in his basement room at Great Russell Street, furtively ironing his shirt each morning. But despite this overt and faintly laughable newfound serious-ness, Inigo was – unbeknownst to me – making big moves.

We saw each other only occasionally during this time. I remember being surprised when we met for coffee one Saturday morning and Inigo put two BlackBerry phones down side by side on the table between us. Despite it being the weekend, one of the phones buzzed and flashed throughout our meeting and he got up from the table several times to take calls. 'It's auction week next week,' he said, by way of explanation, 'and Jay has no conception of weekends,' he added with a weary, knowing eye-roll. Little more than a year previously, we'd sat in the same café discussing Jay Jopling in excited, reverential terms. Now, here was Inigo displaying mild irritation that he was calling him on a Saturday to discuss auction strategy.

In December 2009 I started work as an editorial assistant for a small independent publishing house in Bloomsbury. The work was challenging, the hours long and the pay desultory, but for a while I thought I'd found something I loved. By day I worked principally on non-fiction titles – political memoir, history, journalism – and in the evenings, when I wasn't reading manuscripts, I made attempts to write a novel about a German photographer working between the wars, banging my head against a brick wall of florid but unfeeling prose. It was a brief period of time unencumbered by money (I had very little) and a welcome respite from the professional disappointments I had experienced in the art market. I didn't have to deal with sales figures or profit margins; all there was were books and that suited me just fine.

I had several kind and extraordinary colleagues who eventually drew me out of myself; bright, intelligent men and women whose generous erudition, it seemed to me at the time, knew no bounds. Over long evenings in crowded pubs my eyes were opened to a vast world of knowledge and writing that felt apart from commerce, and to the fact that it might exist almost for its own sake. This was naive, of course, but it went some way towards justifying the long hours and bad pay with something approaching nobility of purpose. I suppose this is the Faustian pact that any young worker in the culture industries makes, and I can tell you, it's intoxicating, at least for a while.

Whenever I saw Inigo I would bring him books from the publishing house, pre-publication copies of things I'd worked on or thought he might like. He had always been an avid reader and received them with apparent gratitude, but admitted he had little time for such things any more. When he wasn't elbow-deep in auction catalogues or insurance valuations or arranging the lending of artworks to museums, Inigo still had to produce essays for his MFA.

As well as the work he was doing for White Cube and for Jopling directly, Inigo was inveigling himself into the upper echelons of the London art crowd. He attended meetings of the Brutally Early Club – 'a breakfast salon for the 21st century where art meets science meets architecture meets literature', according to its founder, another art world taste-maker, the Serpentine Gallery's Artistic Director, Hans Ulrich Obrist – where, as far as I can tell, people gathered in cafés at 6.30 a.m. and ingested as much coffee as possible in the name of intellectualism. His acquaintanceship with Gilbert & George blossomed into a close friendship and Inigo also started to befriend Sir Norman Rosenthal, who had just stepped down from thirty years at the helm of the Royal Academy. This friendship was an important behind-the-scenes relationship for Inigo and went on for over a decade.

To begin with, these friendships lent Inigo a veneer of institutional respectability and intellectual weight. The art world is funny like that: you can be a shit-hot young dealer making big sales, doing what you do with panache and verve, but people will always want something else from you – not more, but other. Stop being so commercial. Give back a little more. Engage in the discourse. And most people kowtow, most of the time, but Inigo called the bullshit and rode it out. He never felt the need to sit on panels about the state of the culture or support young artists or do studio visits in the back end of beyond. This was business, not work, and there's a big difference. His association with Rosenthal and people like him helped him maintain a facade of arty respectability in the eyes of zealous onlookers, and it worked for a good long time. And it was also from Rosenthal that Inigo had confirmed what he had long suspected about the art world: that it is an arena where strong opinions, loudly and widely expressed, are what make a market move.

Like Jopling, Rosenthal had been a vital part of the rise to market prominence of the YBAs when, in 1997, he staged the controversial *Sensation* exhibition at the RA. Rosenthal's endorsement – and by implication, that of the RA – helped many of the artists included in the show (Damien Hirst, Tracey Emin, Chris Ofili and Sarah Lucas, to name but a few) achieve international fame, and there was criticism at the time that the show would raise the value of the works, many of which belonged to Charles Saatchi, and that many of the artists were represented by White Cube. The show also toured to Berlin and New York, though a planned show in Sydney was called off when the National Gallery of Australia's director decided the show was 'too close to the market'; the show was sponsored by Christie's, who already saw secondary market opportunities on the horizon and such an exhibition as a great way of flushing out collectors. There is, after all, little reason other than forceful and clamorous opinion for the value of these artefacts.

Just as Rosenthal had been helpful to Jopling in the 1990s (*Sensation* put many of Jopling's artists on the map), so he was an important part of Inigo's rise, introducing him around, the visible fact of their friendship a seal of approval. Years later, however, a resentful Inigo would regale me with stories of Rosenthal's unrestrained relish when Inigo took him for expensive lunches at the Mayfair restaurant, Scott's. It was one of many relationships I saw go sour. It seemed like Inigo eventually outgrew everybody, though I could never be quite sure that his account of how the relationship ended was the whole truth.

Despite the uptick in his fortunes, Inigo was still living at Great Russell Street and I was living at home with my mother and sister – situations neither of us were keen to perpetuate. And so, about a year after I started work in publishing, in December 2009, Inigo and I found a flat to share in south London, not far from Goldsmiths. Having dropped out of the Courtauld but still needing to maintain a student visa, Inigo was in fact back at Goldsmiths doing a Master of Fine Arts in curating. Our friendship remained cooler than it had been at the beginning, but Inigo wanted finally to get out of GRS and I wanted to live with someone I knew I could tolerate in close proximity for long periods of time. But I also nursed a hope that something of our pre-art-dealing friendship might still be salvageable. The flat was in an area which might then have been generously described as 'up and coming' – the kind of neighbourhood where the white tent set up on a street corner might equally have been a bloody crime scene or an organic farmers market. (I still live in the same flat and have written the majority of this book in the room that used to serve as Inigo's bedroom. At times it's given me an unsettled feeling, like walking on a grave.)

Between us we had an almost laughable lack of possessions, but a few days after we'd moved in I heard a loud noise coming from Inigo's room. When I went in, I found Inigo, drill in hand, hanging three small artworks.

'What are those?' I asked him.

'Wade Guyton works on paper,' he replied. 'Bought them a few months ago and just got them back from the framer.' I looked at them. Pages cut out from art books had been printed over, a bold black 'X' on one, thick horizontals on the next, and a translucent image of flames on another: banishment, redaction, destruction. I liked them instantly.

'These are great,' I said.

'Tell me about it,' Inigo shot back. 'He's going to be a *big* deal, mark my words. You should buy one if you can. They're only a few thousand dollars now. I can get you a good deal if you like. Prices are gonna explode soon.' I'd just come back from the petrol station across the road where I'd taken out cash with my credit card. I declined his offer.

Apart from using his room as a repository for his growing art collection, Inigo wasn't in residence much, spending most of his time at his then girlfriend's place in central London. They had met on the Goldsmiths MFA and would often stay at the flat only on days when they needed to attend class. We joked that it was Inigo's country place. On one of the rare occasions that they were there overnight, I recall waking up early in the morning. The air in the flat was dense with silence and I had that prickly sense that I was alone. I heard voices from the street outside. Out of curiosity, I went to the window and saw them both walking towards a large black Mercedes town car. Inigo opened the door for his girlfriend and waited while she got in before walking around the back of the car and getting in himself. All this he did with a kind of dynamic lethargy, as if he'd been born to limousines, as if the whole rigmarole were a dull necessity to be endured. Only weeks before, he'd been running for the bus.

*

At the time, Jopling's reputation in the art world both preceded him and exceeded the reality. Clever dealing, savvy PR and his easy access to London high society meant that his name became synonymous with the art market boom that continues, largely unchecked, to this day. But there was one glaring difference between Jopling and Gagosian *et al.*: he was, when Inigo started working for him, mainly a primary market gallerist with little to no secondary market business; they were massive secondary market dealers whose primary market galleries gave a presentable front end to their enterprises. Whereas Jopling's nominal peers were selling primary market works for hundreds of thousands, they were also able to sell a Picasso for $50 million. Jopling wanted in on the action.

Except the thing is that the art market is not unlike the aristocracy: there are hidden rules, impossible to discover until one has fallen foul of them. One of these clandestine rules is that you don't want to *seem* like you're making money. (The appearance that a dealer is richer than his clients is the kiss of death, except for Larry Gagosian, who is a) richer than almost everyone, and b) seemingly an exception to most rules.) With no established secondary market operation, Jopling still had what Inigo later called his 'innocence'. He may have done a few secondary market deals here and there, but this was far from being an integral part of his business model. Jopling was still perceived by artists, collectors and curators alike as being primary market-focussed – a somehow honourable man in amongst a line-up of commercial rascals. Jopling wanted to find a way to have the prestige and the profits that came with having a secondary market operation, without the potential negative PR impact.

The job Jopling offered Inigo pretty much as soon as he'd graduated was Assistant Collection Manager for his company,

Modern Collections. By way of context, almost all dealers are collectors, too, and their collections are essentially extensions of their gallery's inventory. Jopling's collection was huge and unwieldy. Traditionally the role was given to a promising young staffer, but soon after Inigo joined, his manager, Carol Cohen, left to start a gallery in New York. So Inigo, twenty-three years old, just out of university, was promoted to running the operation. He now reported directly to Jay Jopling.

According to Inigo, the principal function of Modern Collections had been to hold Jopling's personal collection in a limited company. He also apparently used it, however, to trade discreetly on the secondary market. When Inigo joined, he saw that the collection contained some real gems. But the more he looked, the more he saw that there was a lot of inferior work in there, too. So he began to sell large numbers of works from the collection at auction and, with the proceeds, he pitched new opportunities – upcoming works coming to auction which Inigo saw as undervalued – to Jopling. All that time Inigo had spent combing through auction results on Artnet was finally, and literally, paying off. He went from making £35k a year to £35k a month.

As Inigo told me, before the opening of a gallery exhibition, Jopling would go through lists of available works, frequently purchasing one or two of the best works for Modern Collections, i.e. himself. It is not uncommon for gallerists to buy artworks by their own artists before the opening of a gallery exhibition (I should know; I did it myself), especially if the artist's career looked like it was going in the right direction. Typically, the gallerist would only pay the artists' share (generally 50 per cent of the price) and nothing to the gallery. Essentially, you're buying the works at half price and so your profit margin is already high, but the hope is that you hang on to the work until all your hard work pays off and/or the artist leaves the gallery. At bigger galleries, this not only takes money directly out of the sales team's pockets but it means that they are often unable to offer the best works to good clients of the gallery.

Inigo was also beginning to learn other intricacies of the art market and starting to see that the public image of any success-ful large gallery is likely very far from the reality. A gallery like White Cube has a stable of artists (like a team of racehorses; the association with gambling should be noted). These artists – if they and the gallery are doing their jobs right – will have fairly frequent selling exhibitions, say, every couple of years at the outside. The gallery may sell things direct from the studio between times, or the artist may have shows elsewhere, be they commercial or institutional.

In general terms, once an artist has become established, her work may start to come up at auction. The estimate – the price range that the auction house attributes to the artwork – may have little or nothing to do with what the work originally sold for. This is totally reasonable since the auction house doesn't *owe* the artist or the gallery anything, only the vendor. They'll be guided by what they think the market will pay. The problem arises if, for example, an artwork that sold from the gallery for £50,000 comes up for sale at Phillips or Bonhams with an esti-mate of, say, £25,000–£35,000. If this happens, and the work sells for a number in that range (or worse, doesn't sell at all), the dealer is likely going to wake up to some angry emails from collectors whose artworks, bought at full retail, are suddenly looking overpriced. Collectors like that might rush to consign their pieces for fear that the market is in terminal decline, and the flood of artworks on to the market will further depress the price.

In order to prevent this, dealers may choose to work to

protect their artist's market at auction. The first port of call would always be the auction house itself which might – *might* – refuse to consign a work from a really young artist, on the basis that it's not fair to hamstring their career before anyone's had a chance to see where it might go. But you only have one or two chances at that; sooner or later, if the artist is hot, someone's going to want to see just how hot by putting something into auction and that's the moment the dealer needs to be prepared to step up.

Now, obviously, a dealer isn't going to want to do this all the time (all buying and no selling does not an art dealer make) and so sometimes galleries from different countries who represent the same artist will band together to protect the market by bidding up the price of the work at auction, or even purchasing it back. Sometimes even the artists themselves will get involved. Damien Hirst is well known to be a deft trader in his own market. Other big-ticket artists might have an informal arrangement where they would exchange a fresh-to-market piece with one that their dealer buys in at auction. That way the artist's market is protected and the dealer gets a new artwork to sell.

Inigo also began to tag artworks that he thought Jopling should look at – pieces by artists he collected or wanted to collect – as well as works that Inigo considered a good buy in the estimate range. This was outside his brief and a bold move for someone at his level of experience. It had not been something that previous collection managers had done and Jopling was impressed. Inigo had seen an opportunity to step up. This wasn't gallery business; this was just straight business.

In conversations with Inigo, Jopling began tentatively to offer his young protégé a percentage of Modern Collections, telling him that if and when he came to sell the business Inigo would take a share of the proceeds. The problem, as Inigo knew, is that art galleries don't work like that; you can't sell a gallery in the way that you might a café or a barbershop or a social networking company. As a business, a gallery is not much more than the sum of its parts and its parts are the artworks it owns and the reputation of the owner; very few artists have contracts to work with their galleries, the art world being one of the last bastions of the handshake agreement, and they make frequent, unpredictable moves between galleries, or are represented by multiple galleries. When Inigo pointed out that any putative sale of the business would essentially be just a stock sale, Jopling apparently countered that any such agreement would have to come with caveats – that certain works be ring-fenced where the profit that might be achieved would be above a certain level; if, for example, Jopling had bought a work for £5000, which was now worth £3 million, Inigo's share would be capped.

These conversations went back and forth for a while and all the time Inigo was gaining in confidence, experience and connections. Then Jopling had an idea – he would open a secondary market gallery of which no one would know he was the backer. Such businesses – places that openly sold contemporary art on the secondary market – existed in the US but hadn't yet taken root in the London art market. Jopling's original intention was that he would bring in a heavy-hitter to run this new gallery, someone whom Inigo would work alongside.

The two of them discussed this potential gallery for about a year. Meanwhile Inigo continued to impress his mentor so much that eventually the idea of another, more senior dealer's involvement was quietly dropped. They continued to get on well, too, establishing an avuncular, matey rapport, but Inigo was beginning to see that, despite his public persona, Jopling could be circumvented.

Inigo had begun to buy aggressively on Modern Collections' behalf, taking positions in the market for artists like Christopher Wool, Wade Guyton, Rudolf Stingel and Danh Vō. Sometimes the negotiations for these art works would go on for weeks until Inigo had got the seller down to the number he and Jopling had agreed upon as a good price. In a number of instances, however, Inigo told me he would negotiate an artwork that he and Jopling had agreed was a good buy at, say, $700k down to $625k, only for Jopling to do an about-face, saying that he wanted to buy it for $600k and telling Inigo to walk away from the deal. As Inigo later told me, he would wait a few days and write to Jopling to tell him he'd bought the work for the lower number and just needed authorisation in order to make payment. When Jopling replied with his approval, Inigo would then alter the number in the email chain below and forward it on to the accounts team. The artwork would then be entered into the stock book at the price that they'd paid.

These early instances of commercial subterfuge taught Inigo a valuable art dealing lesson, one that stemmed from Jopling's apparent capriciousness. Since artworks seldom have any intrinsic worth, the monetary value attributable to an artwork often emerges emotionally from the buyer and can accrue or diminish in perceived value for the buyer even during the negotiating process. The art market may be free of most regulation, but it is still subject to the same emotional irrationality as any other market. This insight would serve Inigo very well indeed.

On the rare occasions I did see Inigo in the flat we were nominally sharing, he was often tired but debonaire, describing his role and his relationship with Jopling with a completely straight face, coyly withholding key details despite my persistent questioning and evident fascination. What I had always thought of as a tendency to exaggeration in my friend now seemed to be pushing new limits, as he told me of multi-million-dollar art deals, private jet flights and warehouse viewings of astonishing treasures. When he told me matter of factly that Jopling planned to stake him in a Mayfair gallery I simply didn't believe him at first.

By comparison, my career in publishing was making a slow, indecorous start. I had grown up with a certain fantasy of the editorial life – of long, wine-stained lunches with authors, and of the slow, lathe-like process of helping to hone a manuscript into perfect shape. In reality, after the initial gloss of free books and the company of Very Clever People wore off, mine was a world of spreadsheets (so many that I coined the collective noun 'a Kafka of spreadsheets' to encompass them) and meeting minutes and the interminable business of clearing quotation permissions.

For all that I didn't enjoy these more mundane parts of the job, I was also pitifully bad at the more conventionally editorial aspects. In my brief time as an editorial assistant – and then later, after I was mysteriously promoted to assistant editor – I presided over an amazing array of fuck-ups. I was twice the direct cause of massive book-pulpings. Once, when I didn't know the difference between the country Colombia and the District of Columbia on the back cover of a book about a drug lord; and again when I sent the wrong files to the printers – files riddled with errors I'd been tasked with correcting – for a book about ancient Rome. I was feckless in the face of detail and morose when confronted with hard work. I have no idea why I wasn't fired.

In late September of 2011, Inigo called and asked me to dinner. He'd moved out of the flat at the beginning of the year and into an apartment in an upmarket area of central London with his girlfriend. It seemed to me a gulf of maturity was opening up between us, as if he were growing up at a faster rate than me.

As I was making my way across town from my office to the restaurant, he sent me a text message with an address: 89 Mount Street. 'Come meet me here before we go to dinner.' I soon arrived at a white-painted shopfront on a Mayfair street overrun with Lamborghinis. The air was hazy with cigar smoke from the restaurant terrace next door. All around me people spoke in heavily accented English; but these were not the kinds of polyglots whom nationalists bemoan. These people were the wealth creators, the patron saints of economic turbocharging. I felt out of place as I fastened my bicycle to a black- and gold-painted lamppost.

The large windows were papered over and there was a rectangular hole next to the door where the bell was meant to be. I knocked on the window and waited. I was about to knock again when I heard a voice from far behind the door coming slowly closer, like the sound of water draining out of a bath. Inigo opened the door and ushered me in as he continued his phone conversation.

I put my bag down by the door and he sauntered away from me with his cock-of-the-walk saunter. His footsteps reverberated expensively in the large empty room vying in volume with his phone call. The gallery was long and thin with pristine white walls. A shadow gap at the bottom gave the space the floaty feel of a hotel spa. The floor was aged parquet, a herringbone expanse of rich, coppery browns. The whole thing was so sophisticated – so far beyond what I might have imagined – that when Inigo eventually got off the phone, I was still dumbstruck.

'What do you think?' he asked me.

'It's incredible,' I stammered back. 'This floor is beautiful. Is it original?'

'I think we got it from an old school gym. It's pretty great, no? Will look fantastic in the install shots. And the paintings are arriving tomorrow, thank God. Come see the viewing room downstairs.' We walked down a set of poured concrete steps. To the left at the bottom was a room about a third the size of the gallery above. There were wet paint signs still on the walls. I'd never been in a gallery viewing room before that moment; they are the purely commercial inner sanctums of an art gallery, a place where a prospective buyer can go to look at an artwork away from the prying eyes of the art-loving public. 'This is where the magic will happen,' Inigo told me with a grin.

We went to dinner that night at a pizza place down the street and as I cycled home later that night, tipsily dodging the buses on Park Lane, I felt a rancorous envy rising up in me. Inigo seemed like he had it made. We'd left university only two years previously and already he was opening his own gallery in Mayfair with backing from a world-renowned art dealer. In comparison my life felt static, pedestrian. A growing part of me began to think, 'I want back in.'

Soon, though, those jealous feelings would turn to pride. The gallery opened with no private view; they did no advertising, issued no press release. One day it was just . . . there. A little while after it opened Inigo sent me a photo of the front page of the Frieze edition of the *Art Newspaper*. The headline read 'Too Much Too Young?'; Inigo's caption simply read 'Too funny!' Without reading the article, I wondered if they were right.

I had assumed the article was about Inigo and it wasn't until months later that I actually read it. In the piece, the author bemoans the burgeoning trend for younger artists being traded on the secondary market. Inigo had opened with a show of Wade Guyton and Kelley Walker, two young-ish art market stars whose works had, up until a few years previously, been selling in the region of $30–40k. But demand had pushed their prices way, way up, and paintings by Guyton and Walker were now trading for almost $1million on the secondary market.

The controversy was not just about the money. This was somehow also about propriety, about decorum and politesse. Art dealers and art advisors were quoted as saying that shows like this were 'irresponsible', 'totally inappropriate' and 'confusing'. They thought it would lead to market speculation and the early ruination of these artists' careers. Others, including David Zwirner, pointed out that the art market had remained largely unchanged for decades and that new ventures like Modern Collections were 'pioneering different business models'. Inigo himself pointed out that his gallery had precedence in New York, that it would be 'doing the things you would expect of an Upper East Side gallery'.

Dealers and auction houses had long been making big money doing just what Inigo was planning to do with his new gallery. Was it perhaps his brazenness that was so irksome? As always, the art world reaction boiled down to taste. But, in any case, it was perfect PR. Reading the article, I could just see Inigo's face light up mischievously. It was exactly the sort of controversy he enjoyed, and soon would come to court. In this, as in many things, Inigo was ahead of the game.

Like Norman Rosenthal, Gilbert & George were central to Inigo's career right from the get-go and, even when he'd ostensibly moved on from White Cube, they maintained a close friendship. In the early summer of 2012, Inigo put on a show of Gilbert & George's 1975 body of work, *Bad Thoughts*. The series, which comprises nine works (each of which is made up of grids of between four and sixteen individually framed photographs), had originally been shown at Galerie M.T.L. in Brussels back in the year it was made. However, the series was shown incompletely; *Bad Thoughts No. 6* and *Bad Thoughts No. 7* were inexplicably excluded and, indeed, neither work had ever left Gilbert & George's East End studio and were framed for the first time for the Modern Collections exhibition.

This exhibition served many purposes for Inigo and his new gallery. It distanced him from the impression that the enterprise was a purely commercial venture (only two of the works were for sale) and shifted the gallery into the Upper East Side mould of galleries like Skarstedt, an impossibly chic and exclusive-feeling New York gallery that pulls together selling exhibitions of museum-grade artworks. It was also a tacit announcement of his friendship with Gilbert & George; no one would dare try to mount an historic, commercial show like this without their approval.

Gilbert & George have always been prolific (in 1975, the *Bad Thoughts* show at Galerie M.T.L. was just one of three international exhibitions they did that year), but they recognised early on that their rallying call of 'Art for All' was in conflict with the fact that their works were being bought by wealthy private individuals. In order to rectify this, they have always produced (and subsidised the price of) lavish catalogues of their art. Inigo therefore knew that to stage his *Bad Thoughts* exhibition he would also have to produce a catalogue – especially since there existed no original photographs of the series displayed together.

I went to see the show after work one day in June 2012. It was a warm evening and London was in the sweaty grip of Olympics mania. Inigo wasn't at the gallery when I got there but his assistant let me in before scurrying quickly downstairs and I was left on my own. They were good pictures to be left alone with. In black and white and dyed, rage-red photographs, the two men stand alone in panelled rooms. Windows that might otherwise be sources of light – both literally and met-aphorically – instead offer up a conspiracy of diagonals and looming, silhouetted tree branches; in *Bad Thoughts No. 2* interior architectural details crowd around them in a perverted Union Jack; and in *Bad Thoughts No. 7* Gilbert & George, still separated and alone, are surrounded by their own glower-ing, reddened faces. In contrast to the jingoistic furore that had overcome London during the Olympics, these works were a dark reminder of the city's capacity for isolation and division. Mayfair, with its international boutiques and Filipina maids walking their employers' expensively coiffured dogs, felt like the perfect setting for such works to be reshown.

After a while, Inigo appeared at the front door and jolted me out of my reverie, striding into the gallery in sunglasses and a hot breath of aftershave. 'What's up, what's up,' he said in playful greeting.

'This show's amazing, man,' I said. 'Hats off, seriously. I'd never seen any of these before in the flesh.'

'Bro, no one has. It took for *ever* to get them all together.'

'I bet. Have G & G been in to seen it?'

'Yeah, they came in before it opened.'

'What did they think? What did they say?'

'Hard to tell. I think they liked it? You never know with those boys. Listen, I have a quick email to send, but do you have time for a drink afterwards?'

'Of course,' I said.

A little while later Inigo came back upstairs and we walked down the street to the Connaught hotel. As we walked in, I saw him reach into his back pocket and then finger a note from a thick roll of twenties and pass it, without acknowledgement, to the waiter who seated us. It felt like a move out of time – something you'd expect from Robert DeNiro in a mob movie. Before I had time to say anything about it, however, Inigo started speaking.

'How's work?' he asked. 'How's . . . what's the place you work called again?'

'So so,' I said. 'It's not at all what I thought it would be. I can't tell if it's publishing, or the company specifically, or if it's just offices.' (It was all three.) What I didn't say was that the publishing company I worked for was on its knees financially and that members of staff were sometimes reduced to tears in meetings. I wanted out of there almost as much as I wanted back into the art world.

'Because,' he said, pausing as the twenty-pounds-richer waiter put down our drinks, 'I need to do a book for the *Bad Thoughts* show. And you know how G & G are about their books, it's got to be good, like, *really* good. And so I'm thinking: I really don't have the time to do it justice. Plus, you know, I want to do more shows like this one and catalogues for all of those, too. We're going to do a Keith Coventry show next year. Your old pal Keith. All Estate Paintings. Try and make a market for them. I want to call it *Twentieth Century Estates*. Has a nice ring to it. Anyway, what do you think?'

'What do I think about what?'

'Bro,' he said, disappointed I hadn't been following his thinking. 'I mean about coming on board to do the books. The catalogues, I mean. As, I don't know . . . we could call you Publications Manager.'

'I mean, yeah. Wow. That sounds great. It doesn't sound like there'd be a *huge* amount for me to do, though. How many catalogues would you plan on doing per year?'

'Two, maybe three,' he said.

'Sounds like it's not a real job. Not a full-time one anyway.' What the fuck was I doing? What was this aptitude I had developed for looking into gift horses' mouths?

'You may be right. We could throw in exhibitions, too, I suppose. I really should be focussing on sales. That's the name of my game.'

'Is this something you've talked to Jay about?'

For the briefest of moments I saw his eyes flash with anger and embarrassment, like a child caught out in a lie. He rallied quickly. 'My gallery, my staff,' he said curtly. 'Jay couldn't care less so long as I make him money – and there are no worries on that front.' He drained his glass and signalled to the waiter for the bill, taking out yet another twenty as he did so.

'Think it over,' he told me on the pavement outside the hotel. 'And let's keep talking. It could be fun!' And with that he stepped into a cab and was gone.

It took us a few weeks to hammer out the details and then a long silence when I thought it might all have been an unfunny joke. But by the time August came around and I was about to give up, he sent me a contract. The salary was more than I was earning in publishing – not much, but enough to make a difference – but it wasn't that which made me sign it. It was the prospect of working with my friend again, of that old dream we'd cooked up all those years ago finally coming good. True, it would doubtless feel strange to be working *for* Inigo rather than with him but I told myself that it had, in reality, been ever thus.

5

Inigo is a brilliant raconteur. It's one of the many things that can make him such fun to spend time with. He tells stories with a fluid and irreverent rhythm that can have the improvisational feel of a great jazz track. At once astonishing in their moments of heightened virtuosity and bewildering for their elasticity of narrative, Inigo's stories became part and parcel of his legend.

If you knew Inigo well, as I felt I did for almost fifteen years, the more outlandish of his stories could have a ring of truth to them precisely because of who was doing the telling. To know Inigo was to know that his life was indeed a litany of outlandish luxuries and absurd encounters; the madder his tales the more indistinguishably credible they became. But, as with anyone who tells a lot of stories – especially someone you know well and speak to often, inconsistencies began to arise between repeated tellings: embellishments, the shifting sands of granular detail. The elements of the story he told me about buying and selling a watch one late summer afternoon, however, never changed.

It is a truth universally acknowledged that a young man in possession of a new fortune must be in want of a Swiss watch and, like many young men on the rise, when Inigo started making good money he bought himself a Rolex. And for a while that was fine – who wouldn't be happy to own a Rolex? – but it is the nature of our world to create dissatisfaction at every economic level. Soon the question 'What next?' was playing on his mind and on his wrist.

When you *start* with a Rolex, the question of where to go from there is a tricky one. You could go vintage and pretend you like the scratches and the discolouration of something you hunted down for months and paid some bloke in Utrecht an exorbitant sum for; or you could simply build your collection, adding in watches that you somehow have come to need: a diver for your annual dip in the sea at Cap d'Antibes; a pilot's watch for your next business class flight to Mustique; and, of course, something dressy for all those many gala dinners you attend.

Or you could do what Inigo did and cut the crap. Sell it all and buy a Patek Philippe Nautilus – one of the most iconic watches by the world's most respected maker. It's the equivalent of going from driving your parents' twenty-year-old Volvo around your neighbourhood to getting into a new Ferrari the day you get your licence.

As you might expect, Inigo didn't just fall in love with watches – he learned how to read the watch market as well. One Saturday in the late summer of 2011 Inigo had lunch at Chucs, a Mayfair restaurant that is home to the kind of room service-inspired food beloved by the sort of people who spend a lot of time in high-end hotels. That afternoon, London – though more specifically the London art world – was coming slowly back to life. Dealers were returning from warmer climes and collectors were ruefully swapping their beach houses for their town houses.

Inigo's mood that day was pretty great. As usual, he'd had a profitable summer; where many other dealers stopped working in favour of a supine August of fresh fish and rosé-pink flesh, Inigo always doubled down. All summer long he would buy and sell with furious abandon, catering to the needs of clients whose fear of losing money was exceeded only by their fear of financial inaction. As he sauntered down Dover Street he looked every inch the carefree man about town, a modern day Beau Brummel in his bespoke shirt and Prada jeans. Both his phones (by this time Inigo was carrying a BlackBerry just for emails and an iPhone for everything else) were vibrating regularly in his hand and he had a pleasant buzz-on from the wine at lunch.

As he turned east on Stafford Street and then south on to Albermarle Street Inigo switched from one call to another more important one. He entered the Royal Arcade, a glossy snicket that runs from Albermarle into Old Bond Street. Here the air was cooler and smelled of leather and brass polish. Inigo was tiring of his caller's conversation as he looked at the shoes in the window of George Cleverley, all scalloped calf skin and effete toes; a few years before these shoes would have been everything he wanted, but he'd moved on in the world, moved up.

A little further along, he stopped in front of a shop called the Watch Club. The man inside the shop looked like the type to call you 'sir' and his wares 'time-pieces'. A shiny array of watches was arranged over two velvety levels beneath the convex window. Inigo's eye ran over them: metal and leather and crystal and price tag and all their slyly moving parts. Still his caller droned on.

Opposite him was the Burlington Arcade. In for a penny. He walked past windows stuffed with cashmere and windows stacked with shiny black pens. Halfway down he stopped in front of another watch shop: more of the same. Vintage Rolexes and Omegas in serried rows, buffed to perfection like guardsmen outside a palace. And then, if you'd been there, you might have noticed a brief moment, a firework burst of something like inspiration or sudden recognition flash across Inigo's face. His phone disconnected with his ear as he leaned forward to press his face to the glass. He stared, his face quizzical, hardening to certainty.

Inigo turned on his heel and retraced his steps. By the time he'd left the Burlington Arcade the same way he entered it, he'd ended his phone call. Enough was enough and besides, he had the scent of something else, something more immediate, in his nostrils now. He walked quickly, almost trotting, all the while maintaining the dignity of a Mayfair man. Once back inside the cool, shadowy recess of the Royal Arcade, he slowed his pace and took a beat. Then he holstered both his phones and walked into the Watch Club.

Ten minutes later, he left the shop with a Rolex Explorer from the 1970s boxed in a stiff paper bag. Walking again in the direction of the Burlington Arcade, Inigo removed the watch box from the bag before pocketing the receipt and throwing the bag away in a bin on the corner of Old Bond Street. With the box under his arm, he walked into the second watch shop. He showed his new watch to the man behind the counter. Some conversation ensued and the man took the watch into a cupboard-y back room and handed it to another man wearing a loupe in one eye. A quarter of an hour passed and eventually Inigo came out of the shop minus the watch but holding an envelope containing a cheque. It was made out for £500 more than he'd bought the watch for a little less than an hour previously.

When Inigo told me this, I laughed. Sitting opposite him, I remember expecting him to start laughing, too. But instead he smiled, slowly. His story stretched belief as much as it amused. But it was amusing precisely because it was also completely believable – at least to me. To this day I have no idea whether it was really true, but everything I subsequently saw in my time working for Inigo makes me feel sure that it happened just the way he described it. Because to be a great dealer rather than just a good one you have to be totally ruthless, able not only to spot opportunity but to exploit weakness, to pounce on missteps. You need to be willing to prod wounds like Doubting Thomas, to push and harangue and to withstand the same. It's a business done really well by real bastards.

Inigo had an eye, not just for good art but for good deals, and right from the get-go Modern Collections was a commercial success. This was all the more remarkable for the fact that Inigo was the only person making sales. So far as I know, most of this early success was the product of work as honest as that of any art dealer; Inigo really did have the instincts of a great dealer and he worked incessantly. The rest of us – Inigo's assistant, me, two guys who were based in a warehouse in south London and basically ran the logistics side of the business (shipping, installation, database, etc.) – were there essentially as touchline support for Inigo's one-man selling operation.

At first I was thrilled with my new job. Instead of the dowdy, tumbledown environment I had been used to at the publishing house, I now shared a shiny, architect-designed basement office with Inigo's assistant. Our chairs were vintage Eames and instead of the endless droning of the photocopier, there was only the muted click-clack of expensive shoes on the pavement above our heads.

I enjoyed having a job title that didn't include the word 'assistant' and took pleasure in telling people what I did and the glamour that they (incorrectly) inferred from it. I would tell people that I'd always been an art dealer, that Inigo and I had cut our teeth together as students; I told them publishing had just been a bookish sabbatical. The art world was where

I belonged, I told myself. I read books by and about famous curators – people like Harald Szeemann – and convinced myself that I too could do good things, that I could use Modern Collections as a launch pad to greatness. But delusion has always been a strong suit of mine and in this instance it was also a survival tactic. Deep down, the pride I felt sat uneasily alongside shame: I knew that I was totally unqualified to do the job I'd been given and that I had literally been *given* it by a friend rather than earned it. Still, I was determined to make a success of the opportunity.

If it was good for me professionally, the move didn't herald a return to the closeness of the I & O Fine Art days. The dynamic between us in the gallery was quietly tetchy. I found it difficult to treat Inigo with the deference an employer naturally expects from an employee and he seemed to me to exist behind a scrim of self-importance and perpetual busyness. (I really didn't help matters when, in what I thought was a totally hilarious move, I gave him a 'WORLD'S BEST BOSS' mug for his birthday.) He was always on the move, seldom in the gallery for longer than a few hours. In contrast, I went nowhere. I shuffled back and forth between gallery and the flat we'd once shared, a place that had come to serve as a marker of how far Inigo had gone – he was living in Mayfair by this point – and how non-existent my own progress was by comparison.

As Inigo's fortunes buoyed, so, too, did his ostensible sophistication. Suddenly he was known by the maître d's at some of the toniest restaurants in town; he began to talk knowledgeably about wine; and his clothes, which had always been good, became refined and declaratively bespoke. In those in-between days of our friendship, I came to feel like a parvenu around him, a Nick Carraway to his Jay Gatsby. His suits were tailored in Milan; I wore my keys on a clip on my belt.

The job itself started well, however, and I felt proud of the first show I put together. As I would soon realise, my role at the gallery consisted principally of making an exhibition based on whatever Inigo had for sale at any given moment. I would often get emails from him in the middle of the night with an image of something he'd just bought and an accompanying message that read 'Let's put this in a show ASAP' or 'We should do a whole exhibition around this!' What I was tasked with doing was trying to conjure up a theme that would connect the artworks. These proposed exhibitions were often a moveable feast; there could be great excitement about an idea for a few days and then without warning Inigo would change his mind and it would be on to the next, leaving me scrabbling to keep up. But, like a child making a necklace out of pasta shapes, I knew that what I was doing wasn't real. I was a glorified window dresser.

I keenly remember the work around which the first exhibition was to be based. Inigo's email came late as usual (he was seldom in the same time zone as his gallery), but there was no image attached. Instead, there was a scan of a certificate which read 'This is to certify that the Sol LeWitt wall drawing number 62 evidenced by this certificate is authentic'. Below this were a set of instructions: 'Vertical and horizontal lines intersecting, drawn as long as the drafter can reach with one stroke (standing in one place). Black pencil.' That was it: those instructions, which were also the work's title, *were* the latent artwork. Inigo told me no one knew what it looked like; no photograph of it drawn on a wall existed and it had only been drawn once, by LeWitt himself.

I knew a little about LeWitt and had seen some of his wall drawings installed on the trip that Inigo and I had taken up to Dia Beacon a few years previously, but I had no real idea how they worked. They seemed to exist in a strange nether region, coming alive only when coaxed into existence by a technician. And yet the certificate – or rather, the instructions on it – *were* the artwork.

The work was on loan from a client who had bought it, so Inigo told me, on something of a whim (people in the art world think nothing of seven-figure whims). He wanted to see what it looked like when it was installed – when it was drawn on a wall – and Inigo was happy to facilitate this. This wouldn't be a big money move, but it was a favour to the client and Inigo just straight-up loved LeWitt's work. For my part, it felt like something I could really get my teeth into, though I had no idea where to begin.

LeWitt had died in 2007 and I spent a fruitless week politely cold-emailing people connected with his estate. Eventually someone from the Paula Cooper Gallery in New York got back to me and put me in touch with a man named Anthony Sansotta who had been LeWitt's long-time assistant and subsequently the artistic director of the artist's estate.

Now, of course, you could just go and make the drawing yourself. *You* could do it now; you have the instructions, all you need is a pencil and a wall. And once I realised this, I was pretty keen to give it a go myself, but Inigo was understandably hesitant and so Sansotta put me in touch with Nicolai Angelov, an estate-sanctioned Sol LeWitt wall drawing installer.

Nicolai arrived from Berlin one Friday morning a few weeks later. He was a burly man in his forties with a shaved head and a near-perpetual half smile. He wore a dark shirt and trousers that seemed more suited to an office worker than an international conceptual art technician. The gallery was closed that week and the space was littered with crates and paintings on blocks. (Leaving artworks that are for sale casually resting on foam blocks and leaning against the wall is a tried and tested art-dealer trick. It can give a prospective client the feeling that the work is so fresh to market that no one else has seen it yet; or that it's so recherché that it'll be sold so quickly as to make hanging it a waste of time.) Inigo was away and the show was due to open the following week.

We got to work almost immediately; Nicolai was flying home on the Sunday. 'We'll need all the time between now and then to make the drawing,' he told me solemnly. I showed him the spot I had selected for the drawing – a west-facing wall on the left of the gallery that was about fifteen feet long. Nicolai approached the wall and inspected it, his nose almost pressed against it. He seemed to breathe it in as he ran his hands over its surface, almost caressing it.

Together we chose the place that he would stand and the point which would mark the centre of the drawing. Nicolai placed a piece of yellow masking tape on the floor about a foot and half from the wall and stood just behind it, like a runner toeing a starting line. He produced a long, wide ruler, an eraser ('Just in case,' he said with his half smile) and a propelling pencil, the kind where the lead is as thick as a regular pencil and is gripped by something that looks like a fairground grabber.

From his spot on the floor, standing in his socks and using both hands, Nicolai first marked the limits of his reach on the wall with the masking tape and then the approximate centre of the site. What emerged was a circular, cordoned-off area of white wall, the dashes of yellow tape like road markings on a drive that went nowhere. We stopped for coffee. As he drained his cup, Nicolai stretched, as if he were getting ready for strenuous exercise. 'Let's begin,' he said.

All that day and into the afternoon of the next, I stood by in silence as Nicolai worked. As he drew, the drawing seemed to me to be emerging *from* the wall, as if disclosing itself – as if it had been there all along. Unseen softnesses in the wall revealed themselves as Nicolai's pencil swept across them. They were the spots where artworks had hung before – holes filled and painted over – ghostly palimpsests of paintings been and gone. Points of hesitation or discomfort were visible in Nicolai's lines, too; a tremor in a line which might have been anxiety or cramp or a brief distraction. When it was done we both stood back and faced it together. It seemed to pulse, as if the wall had come alive or were at least displaying the remnants of the life it had taken to make it.

A few weeks after the show opened I was at the gallery on a Saturday morning. It was a beautiful, crisp day outside and I was feeling out of sorts – probably hungover. We seldom had visitors during the week, but we almost never had visitors on Saturdays. Occasionally some feckless item of minor European aristocracy would press the buzzer and ask if Inigo was in. He never was.

Just as I was preparing to shut the gallery so I could go out to find myself some lunch, Inigo called me. 'Jay's on his way over to the gallery,' he said. 'I'm in Paris so you'll have to take him around the show, OK?'

'Right. But, like, does he want to be talked through all the works and that sort of thing? What's the vibe here?' I was panicking. I had never met Jopling before and my teenage reverence for him was still deeply engrained.

'You'll be fine,' Inigo replied. In the background I could hear laughter and the unmistakable clatter of a busy restaurant. 'Call me afterwards,' he said before hanging up.

I didn't want to loiter up in the gallery – how uncool would that be? – so I waited downstairs by the intercom in the office nervously watching the small black and white screen. I waited for five minutes, ten. Maybe he'd gone off the idea, I wondered hopefully. This was Mayfair, after all. He could have popped into Purdey's the gunmakers to buy himself a new twelve-bore or bumped into his second-favourite oligarch outside Harry's Bar. The thought even flashed through my mind that Inigo had set this up on purpose, had told Jopling to come in and grill me. I could envisage them having a laugh about it over drinks at the Connaught as they prepared to fire me.

And then suddenly there he was on the screen in monotone miniature. He was here. His unmistakable trademark Buddy Holly glasses hove into view and then away again, like a shark assessing its prey. He paced in front of the gallery talking into his handsfree. Then the bell went and I very quickly buzzed him in.

I climbed the stairs from my basement office two at a time, trying to take deep breaths but actually only causing myself to become more flustered. When I reached the ground floor he was still by the door reading the press release. He was regally tall – even taller than I'd imagined – and was wearing a fur coat, long and lustrous and brown like an antique dining-room table. I strode forward with my hand outstretched. 'Hi,' I said in a voice I should really have reserved for outdoor use. 'I'm Orlando, the Exhibitions Manager.' From his great height he surveyed my hand. He seemed unsure what to do with it at first. In the end, however, he shook it briefly and dismissively, the way he might dispense with an insect.

'I'm Jay,' he said.

Yuh, I know, I didn't say. 'Inigo asked me to show you around the exhibition,' I did say.

'Great. I'm having lunch with my mother up the street so I can't be too long.'

I thought we'd save the best for last and so I started off opposite the LeWitt, working my way anti-clockwise round the gallery. Nothing else in the show was of real interest, frankly, and many of the works were the kind of high-octane market stars that were Inigo's stock in trade at the time but who have since faded from view as their gimmicks became tired and collectors moved on to the next shiny new thing. We walked quickly round the gallery and each time he slowed to inspect a work more closely, I dreaded him asking for more information.

His demeanour was cool, almost frosty at first, but as we reached the LeWitt he seemed to thaw. 'Inigo tells me this is one of the very early wall drawings?' he asked.

'Yes, it's from the first few years of the series, I think. Late 1960s and first installed by LeWitt himself in '71. We don't think it's been installed since.'

'That *is* special,' he said, leaning in to look at it closely. 'Did you install it yourself, or did you have an installer from the estate?'

'We had an installer. I worked with him over a couple of days. It was an amazing experience. It had a sort of priestly feel to it, like being inducted into a cult. It was the closest thing I've ever had to a religious experience, I think.'

He looked at me, perplexed, and started walking towards the door. He opened it and turned back to half face me. 'Ritualistic,' he said with a slick grin. Then he was gone and that was the only time I ever met Jay Jopling.

The thing that had always confounded me when Inigo and I were first working together was how art dealers went about finding and building their client bases. With such a crowded marketplace, the build-it-and-they-will-come attitude seldom bears fruit. Aside from those outliers who are simply gifted with an innate talent for the art of the deal, many dealers and gallerists will have cut their teeth at bigger or more established galleries before going out on their own; others are connected to money from birth and need only rifle through their parents' address book to drum up business. But while Inigo's background was relatively privileged, he hadn't come from great wealth. He had grown up on the tatty fringes of the art world and worked for White Cube where he had access to a vast array of collectors, but most of the deals he did in those days were strictly trade: dealer to dealer or dealer to auction house.

By the time I went to work for Inigo at Modern Collections, he seemed almost to have a surfeit of clients. He could become comically exasperated when his phone rang for the tenth time that hour as he was pestered by the indolent children of wealthy collectors. Many of them, I suspect, believed that proximity to Inigo would reveal the secret to his success and Inigo was slow to disabuse them while being quick to get them to do his bidding. From those early days, though, one client stood out: Andre Sakhai.

Inigo had met Andre – who was the owner of the Sol LeWitt – through a woman on his Goldsmiths MFA course. She and Andre had grown up together on Long Island and had remained friends as the two of them had made their ways in the art world. Andre had grown up around art and art dealing; his father, Ely Sakhai, had been a successful Impressionists dealer until, on 9 March 2000, he was arrested by the FBI.

Ely, who is Iranian by birth, had come over to the USA in the late 1970s. He had had initial success as an antiquities dealer, but by the late 1980s he was dealing exclusively in Impressionist and Post-Impressionist works. This shift coincided with a boom in the market for such paintings in cash-rich Japan. Married to a Japanese woman, Ely spoke the language fluently and was therefore perfectly placed to sell to this new breed of Japanese collectors.

New wealth is often an easy mark for hucksters and

carpetbaggers and the Japanese businessmen that Sakhai was selling to were accordingly wary buyers. They insisted that any works they bought should come with a certificate of authenticity. In the contemporary art market, authenticity is seldom an issue since the artist is generally alive; for older art, panels of experts and scholars are convened to certify artworks, often for a hefty fee. As such, many buyers prefer not to have their works authenticated for fear of the charge, and perhaps lest they get some bad news (authorities will often destroy paintings they deem to be fake).

Sakhai's scheme was a clever one. At auction he would buy up middle market paintings by famous artists like Chagall or Renoir or Gauguin that came with a certificate of authenticity. He would then have the paintings copied and sell the fakes, accompanied by the real certificates, to his Japanese clients; he then sold the originals at auction in the US. The whole thing unravelled with an almost Pink Panther-esque inevitability when twin paintings of an otherwise wholly forgettable Gauguin of some flowers in a vase were put up for sale simultaneously in two different auctions. (It is worth noting that, despite his conviction for fraud and his sentence of forty-one months, Sakhai denies wrongdoing.)

It was against this background that Andre later became involved in the art market himself and, by the time he and Inigo were introduced, in the summer of 2012, Andre was a seasoned collector. Despite his rambunctious persona, he was relatively discreet in his business dealings; he and Inigo were involved in many of the same artists' markets and yet Inigo had never heard of Andre. This stood in stark contrast to the young collectors – the usual inherited wealth wastrels and trust fund babies – Inigo was used to, whose tendency to indiscretion was bad for business.

When Andre first came into Modern Collections, Inigo was impressed that he was so knowledgeable about the artists he was showing. He was all the more impressed when Andre put several of the works on hold. (Putting something on hold means signifying your desire or intention to buy a work, but, like so much in the art world, no documents are signed or binding agreements entered into and such understandings are often reneged on for only the slightest of reasons, if any.) Several weeks later, Inigo had heard nothing further from Andre. He mentioned him to a specialist at an auction house, asking if he was worth following up with. The specialist's eyes widened and his answer was an emphatic yes. Inigo called Andre, who was holidaying in Ibiza, later that day. Andre bought all the works.

Andre is boyishly handsome. He dresses casually, almost always in dark-coloured clothes. He has a full head of rowdy black hair and an uncultivated beard wrapped around a mischievous face giving him the look of someone who enjoys practical jokes. In my whole life I don't think I have ever come across someone who seems so perpetually at ease; he always has the physical bearing and relaxed mien of someone who has been recently massaged. My lasting impression of Andre (and I only met him on a handful of occasions) is of him shrugging – not out of exasperation, but with an almost Zen-like acceptance of everything he encounters.

In a short space of time, Andre became much more than a client to Inigo. In Andre I think Inigo found someone who brought him back to the easy freedom of his high school years. Around him, Inigo's seriousness seemed to dissipate, their behaviour sometimes descending even into horseplay. They shared a love of backgammon – playing late into the night, betting bigger and bigger – and of electronic dance music, often going clubbing together in Ibiza. More than anything, though, theirs was a commercial bromance – Inigo was one of the most impressive young dealers in the world and Andre was an ambitious collector with a spotless reputation and a lot of money. In a time of frantic speculation and Wild West profiteering in the art market, their working relationship was perfectly poised to take full advantage.

Contemporary art has long been associated with big money and high price tags. Beginning in the 1990s collectors like Charles Saatchi (whose voracious collecting/speculating, sometimes referred to as 'speculecting', allowed him personally almost to define an entire art movement in the YBAs) confirmed a link in the public imagination between young artists' work and potential huge profitability. But, in the early 2010s, when Inigo and Andre started working together, the profits had seldom been bigger – or quicker. And the artists making the work had never been younger.

I have often wondered whether the financial crisis of 2008 had a role to play in the hothouse conditions of the art world over the ensuing years. After all those bankers and fund managers got caught (but not punished for) screwing the global economy, their activities were suddenly in the public gaze, their every moves watched, regulations enforced. They had no option but to play nicely. But it's not so easy to switch off your instincts (especially those which are so intimately involved with your brain's reward system), and those base, winner-takes-all impulses were not easily quashed. It is my belief that some of these financiers found an outlet in the art market.

A little while after I started working at Modern Collections I encountered a trader who worked at Goldman Sachs. We met at a winter wedding in the countryside and sat out the dancing part of the evening, preferring to smoke and drink by the fire-pit. He was a collector, I was a dealer, and we circled our way carefully towards the inevitable business of any conversation between two such people who have not previously met: buyer or seller?

At length, he told me that his initial interest in the contemporary art market was in the possibility of indulging his purest capitalistic instincts. Those things which he was not allowed to do on the trading floor at Goldman – act on inside information, artificially inflate prices, choose whom to sell to – were commonplace, even acceptable, in the buying and selling of artworks. There is no dedicated regulatory body overseeing the art market; prices are seldom openly displayed; ownership of works is often shrouded in legal mystery; deals are frequently sealed on little more than a handshake; and the storage of works in bonded warehouses and freeports can allow speculectors to avoid enormous sums in tax. He could therefore fully maximise the profit he knew was out there for the taking. 'The best thing about the art market,' he told me, 'is that it's completely unregulated. However,' he continued, 'the worst thing about the art market is that it's unregulated.'

When I started working at Modern Collections, the market was in the grip of what became known as flipping mania. Young, mostly male, almost exclusively abstract painters' works were changing hands on the secondary market for hundreds of thousands of dollars. Fresh out of art school, these young artists would show with galleries in London's East End or New York's Lower East Side and their paintings would sell for anywhere from $2000 to $15,000. (It was sometimes difficult to establish accurate primary market prices for these artists' works because galleries wouldn't give out prices; the easiest way to spot a non-serious gallery is that it has prices next to its artworks. This is in fact state law in New York, but go into

Gagosian or David Zwirner or Matthew Marks and you won't see a price tag in sight.) I have no doubt that a select few of the people who bought these paintings did so because they liked the works, but many bought them with only profit in mind. They knew that demand for works like these was so high that they could buy them and sell them again – either privately or at auction – frequently for ten times what they'd paid originally. The profit would be all theirs; the original gallery and the artist would see none of that massive return.

Along with Andre – as well as a whole other host of international players variously known as Houdini (James Lindon), Little Bruce Willis (Shay Rosen) and Hagrid (Carl Kostyál) – Inigo was making a killing. But Inigo couldn't just call up these galleries and buy the works himself; he'd had a rep since the day that *Art Newspaper* headline ran. Instead, he used a network of young, wealthy, drifting art hangers-on (one of whom used to come to the gallery wearing a single purple suede glove, whatever the weather) to buy the works for him. Either they or their parents had a sufficiently unsullied reputation that the galleries would sell to them and they would flip the painting to Inigo for a modest profit – say, double what they'd paid. These runners had a short shelf-life; as soon as what they'd done got back to the gallery their cards would be marked and their ability to buy curtailed, if not terminated. (So much of the art world is just rich kids who manage to break even on their travel expenses by facilitating a deal here and there.) The art world may be global, but its gossip network is as efficient as that of a small English village.

During the first couple of years that I worked at Modern Collections, I saw a wild array of awful art: interior-design-ready art, over-the-sofa art, Instagram-dull art and emperor-in-the-buff, you've-got-to-be-kidding-me art. It seemed as if the art world had become a swampy, endless horizon of artistic déja vu. My eyes felt like they'd been strip-malled. These were not artworks that asked questions (except perhaps for 'How much am I worth?'), and nor did they attempt to answer any. They were just assets, bearer bonds to be exchanged for money with the richest fool. This was the transubstantiation of art and greed into money and status.

Perhaps you think I'm exaggerating. Perhaps you think I'm a curmudgeonly traditionalist with an axe to grind, or that I'm grumpy because I didn't, like so many others, make out like a bandit selling these things. But hold your judgement. Let me tell you more.

Lucien Smith made his 'rain paintings' with a fire extinguisher, replacing the flame retardant with paint and mechanically spraying it all over the canvas. When one of these paintings sold in 2014, when Smith was twenty-five, for $372,000 (against an estimate of $66k–99k) the price tag seemed to redefine the phrase 'money shot'. Smith quickly got signed up by Per Skarsdedt, an Upper East Side secondary market dealer known for his impeccable shows of artists like Warhol and Bacon. Smith's 2014 show at the gallery, *Tigris*, was an exhibition of paintings apparently inspired by Hokusai, the Japanese woodcut artist of the Edo period; somehow they looked like military camouflage. In a review, the *Village Voice* described the exhibition as both 'undistinguished' and 'a shrewd career move'. In 2022, Smith's average price at auction was $22k.

Adam McEwan made his gum paintings by chewing bubble-gum and sticking it to blank canvases. (Rumour had it he got studio assistants to do the actual chewing.) They looked forgotten, like something decaying in front of your eyes, but people were climbing over each other to buy them. Indeed, once I did a viewing of a large gum painting (the asking price was around

$300k) and just as my client was leaning in for a closer look, a large red wad of gum fell off the canvas and on to the floor with a soft thud. The client was immediately put off, of course, but I had to fix the work before returning it to the owner. I called a conservator who said he had experience working with these paintings. When he arrived, I expected him to have some special adhesive. Instead, he spat in a cup and used his saliva to stick the gum back on the canvas.

And there were so many more besides: Dan Colen used M&Ms to make paintings; David Ostrowski's paintings had the aura of having been near someone who might once have held a can of blue paint; Christian Rosa, the quintessential emperor of new apparel, made 'automatic' paintings; Anselm Reyle filled his coloured Perspex boxes with what looked like tin foil. There were so many and the whole thing just felt so sad.

There will *always* be artists like these – art like that – but never before had so many buyers been so frenzied over such a small cadre of young abstract painters. Over a period of just a few years their nascent careers were all but annihilated by the money thrown at their art (money that they mostly didn't see) so that they simply didn't have the time and the space to develop artistically before the inevitable auction dump and the subsequent collapse in prices. Some of these artists doubled down and, ignoring the hype as best they could, went on to forge careers; others had breakdowns and dropped out of the art world all together.

The market has always had a say in the writing of art history but that voice has for the most part been *sotto voce* – a light pencil underlining on the page of artistic posterity. In the early 2010s, however, that plummy, moneyed voice became a deafening howl, drowning invention and originality in money in order to serve its bottomless hunger. And where there is the opportunity to make so much money in so little time and with so little effort, it will happen again and again.

For a young dealer on the make, those years were a gold rush. But, despite appearances, Inigo wasn't just trading young art for big margins. He was also starting to become involved in the trading of more 'blue chip' artworks.

In regular financial markets, a blue chip stock is one that performs steadily, regularly increasing in value, able to withstand fluctuations in the economic climate while still providing a return. Companies like Glaxo Smith Klein and Alphabet are widely considered sturdy in this way; their reputations have usually been built over decades, their status decided by tens of thousands of investors and fund managers. In the art market, the term blue chip is used to mean dead artists, artists whose oeuvres had been sanctified by a process of slow but inexorable price rises and the steady disappearance of works into museum collections. As the appetite for art buying increased in the 1990s and early 2000s the work of some living artists started to be viewed as blue chip, too. These markets were helped by blockbuster, world-travelling exhibitions which worked effectively as sales and marketing tools for dealers increasing an artist's audience and desirability; there's nothing more impressive than doing a viewing in the Tate or the Museum of Modern Art in New York (MoMA).

Damien Hirst sits squarely within this category (the early work, up to about 2003), as does Gerhard Richter, Yayoi Kusama, Jeff Koons, Christopher Wool, Bridget Riley – even Banksy. These artists have deep collector bases and global representation by the very best galleries. Their works are held in internationally renowned museums; they sell for millions of dollars.

Painters and sculptors are more likely to find themselves in this category than photographers and artists who work with photography as their principal medium, who sit uneasily in the contemporary art market for one main reason: their work is infinitely reproducible. If you're going to pay seven figures for an artwork, the logic goes, you want to be the only person with that image hanging on your wall. There is also the tricky subject of craft, but that's for another time; we're talking money here, not aesthetics.

There are, of course, a few photographers whose work has transcended this, some of whom – like Thomas Struth, Candida Höfer and Thomas Demand – are grouped together under the banner of the Düsseldorf School, defined by having studied under husband and wife team Bernd and Hilla Becher at the Kunstakademie Düsseldorf. The Bechers, while justly famous as the teachers of this group, were also celebrated photographers in their own right. Over decades, starting in the late 1950s, they travelled around Germany with an 8 x 10 view camera documenting industrial buildings such as cooling towers, grain silos and blast furnaces, making their pictures only on cloudy days in order to avoid shadow. The images they produced have a mathematical simplicity to them; they seem to be without comment, statements of pure and direct fact. The couple exhibited their works by type, in gridded groups of six, nine or fifteen. Together the photographs seem to form anonymous mausoleums, monuments to the benighted ambition of industry.

Many of the Bechers' former students went on to international success, but the undisputed king of the Düsseldorfers (at least in market terms) is Andreas Gursky. His photographs are as enormous as their prices and can feel like a tidal wave of image collapsing over you – sublime in both senses of the word. Gursky's pictures depict the complexity and bewildering abundance of contemporary life: the Chicago stock exchange at full tilt; a ninety-nine-cent store whose bright, tightly stacked shelves seem ready to disintegrate; a serpentine race-track devoid of cars but smudged with thick black tyre rubber like last night's mascara. They can reduce the vastness of our world almost to abstraction while enumerating details so precisely that they tip the viewer into the realm of the uncanny. Gursky is represented by White Cube.

Gursky's work had always sold for big money – their sheer scale and ambition necessitated a hefty asking price – and in the late 2010s his auction market was building steadily. In November 2011, only a month after the opening of Modern Collections, Inigo was in New York for the contemporary art auctions, the last of the annual season. All three major auction houses – Christie's, Sotheby's and Phillips – hold their auctions during the same week in the same city, competing for the same phalanx of plutocrats as they wander the globe. (Keen observers may notice that I didn't include Bonhams in that list; N.B. I said *major* auction houses.)

On the evening of Friday 11 November, in a crowded sale-room at Christie's in Rockefeller Plaza, Inigo raised his paddle to bid on Andreas Gursky's 1999 photograph *Rhein II*. The photo is one of Gursky's most iconic, showing the Rhein river in almost flag-like simplicity, digitally devoid of buildings and people. But Inigo wasn't trying to buy the photograph for himself; he was bidding on behalf of a client. This is not an uncommon practice and, while its principal aim is to protect the identity of the actual buyer, it can also help boost the profile of the dealer doing the bidding. A buyer might agree to an upper limit with their dealer, allowing them to read the room and act autonomously. More frequently, however, the two parties will be on the phone conferring in hushed tones; some dealers even cover their mouths with their hands lest their super-secret bidding strategy be rumbled by lip-reading spies. The atmosphere can be tense, the power dynamics in the room shifting constantly – at a sale at Christie's London I was present when a dealer, bidding with his phone glued to his ear, was sarcastically told by the young auctioneer to take his time. The dealer removed the phone from his ear briefly and growled, 'I will take my fucking time. I'll have a cup of tea if I want to.' He eventually saw off the competition to win the lot.

As the clamour of the room built around Inigo, a focussed calm came over his face and he raised his paddle again and again. The auctioneer climbed through the millions like they were just words he was rehearsing. The gavel came down. Inigo had committed to buying the artwork for $4.3 million, the most ever paid for a photograph at auction. In the saleroom, seated directly in front of him, was Larry Gagosian, by almost any measure the most powerful dealer of contemporary art in the world. Gagosian turned around in his seat, pointed his pen at Inigo and asked, 'Do you have a company?'

'No,' Inigo replied, 'I have a gallery.'

This brusque exchange between the new kid on the block and the silverback alpha was deceptively simple. On one level, it was Gagosian trying to figure out if the young man sitting behind him was someone he should invite for a drink and make a client, or was he the new competition? On another level, though, it asked something deeper about how art is sold: do you need a gallery at all anymore? In this instance, Larry G was trying to suss Inigo out: was he a private dealer or, less impressively, an art advisor? There can be a bravado among people who have started galleries, a feeling of being on the front line, that everyone else in the art world are merely civilians strutting around in camouflage. In my mind's eye when I heard that story – when Inigo told Gagosian that he had a gallery – the older man gave a barely perceptible nod of respect. In reality, however, he probably made a mental note to crush him.

But the thing that I began to realise when I went to work for Inigo the following year was that his business wasn't an art gallery. Sure, it *looked* like one, but it didn't operate like one. The traditional model of an art gallery is that exhibitions are staged and collectors come and buy: almost by definition, everything is available for sale. But at Modern Collections – and at many similar galleries the world over – things were different.

For example, in the staging of a big exhibition – the Gilbert & George *Bad Thoughts* show, say – some works would be on hopeful loan, the hope being that the owner, reticent to sell at first, would realise that she could live without the artwork and would respond positively to an offer during the course of the show. Others might be on a firm loan from an institution. But often anything that was for sale would sell before the show even opened. In the four years I worked for Inigo, I suspect I could count on the fingers of one hand the number of works that sold during or because of placement in an exhibition.

So what was Inigo doing? How do galleries like his operate? Obviously there was the downstairs viewing room, the sanctum sanctorum of financial discretion, but more often than not Inigo's clients didn't live in – or often even visit – London. A common misconception about London is that it's full of art collectors. It isn't. Not in a serious way, not in a New York or an LA way, and certainly not in a Brussels way (for rich Belgians, art collecting is like a blood sport). I remember Inigo once telling me about a lunch he had with the sales director of a new London outpost of a New York mega gallery. The director asked Inigo who the big London collectors were. Inigo laughed and explained that there weren't any. London was a place you waited for people to pass through – the Venus flytrap of the art market.

Some collectors, for whatever reason, still prefer to buy from a gallery that has a programme of exhibitions; perhaps it makes the process feel less transactional, more like they are indulging in a creative act of personal taste as opposed to moving money around. But the truth of it is that most sales happened via text or email. Art works would appear on Inigo's screen and be forwarded to a client's screen. Then a negotiation might be entered into on the phone or, if the deal was sufficiently large, in person; it wasn't unusual for Inigo to fly to the US at a moment's notice. All his clients took planes like the rest of the world takes the bus and Inigo had no problem keeping up.

Where the artwork actually was seldom mattered (unless you were calculating shipping and import taxes) and, for many buyers, whether they saw the work before buying it mattered even less. When a deal was reached, a conservator would be despatched to inspect and draw up a document that describes the material state of an artwork called a condition report. Then, as often as not, the work would simply move from one bonded warehouse to another, sometimes merely to a different area within the same warehouse.

While all this was extremely good for business, the fact that exhibitions (or, apparently, seeing the art in the flesh at all) were essentially superfluous to the business model meant that I had very little to do. By the autumn of 2013, I was deeply frustrated. Inigo was often away travelling for work, but even when he was in London, he was frequently aloof and distracted. I badly wanted more work; my role felt more and more like a sinecure, a golden hair shirt which I was increasingly keen to take off. I started to scrabble around for something that I might do which would be both useful and absorbing.

I did eventually manage to talk to Inigo about my concerns and we agreed that my role could be expanded to try to find artworks for sale. Inigo proposed a generous commission structure and gave me a shopping list of things he would be keen to buy if I could find them.

At that time, many bigger galleries were also busy snapping up artists' estates, trying to out-manoeuvre and out-schmooze each other to represent dead artists, competing for jurisdiction over their markets. There are several advantages to this: the prestige attached to a career that you haven't had to work for; the knowledge that you control what remains of supply and can work to manipulate demand; the ability to work with museums and art historians to shape or reshape a narrative to suit your commercial strategy; the authority to authenticate or to cast aspersion over artworks. There are downsides, too, of course: the widows, widowers and children of artists tend to be protective and controlling, with their own particular vision for the estate.

Inigo told me he'd become aware, via a Vienna-based British curator who also worked as an advisor to a wildly wealthy Belgian collector, that the American artist Scott Burton was due to have a retrospective in a Belgian museum. Works by Burton were also apparently going to be included in the inaugural show at the new Whitney Museum in New York. While his estate had been left to MoMA to manage, there were no dealers actively placing works. With the rumoured institutional interest, Inigo smelled opportunity.

I was due to go to New York in November to see a Mike Kelley work we'd been trying to buy for a while and Inigo asked me to do some Scott Burton research while I was there. And then, a few days before I was due to leave, Inigo called me late one evening.

'Remind me again when you go to New York,' he said as soon as I picked up.

'Next Monday morning,' I replied.

'How would you feel if we upgraded you on your flight?' he asked. 'I need you to carry something over for me and they give you more room in business class.'

'Always happy to be upgraded,' I smarmed. 'What do you need me to carry?'

'A client from New York brought me a Freud drawing to sell a few months ago. I offered it to my guy but the deal died on the vine. When I called the owner to ask where to send it back to and to ask for all the import declarations so we could ship it back to her, she told me she'd hand carried it on a friend's jet. No import papers means no shipper will touch it and I can't exactly send it via FedEx. So I need you just to slip it under your arm and whisk it through customs. Dress the part and do your whole posh English thing. You'll be fine.'

'I mean, isn't this slightly illegal?'

'Oh, definitely it's not *kosher*, but, look, if anyone asks just say it's a drawing by your grandmother or something. I'll have it wrapped super simply in brown cardboard. I'm sure no one will stop you. Have a good trip!'

On the Sunday before I flew I went for a long bicycle ride in the countryside to the south of London. After a few hours' riding, I turned a corner on a narrow lane to be met by the sight of an oncoming tractor very close at hand. I braked hard and my tyres lost their grip on the wet road. I lost control, fell and skidded along the road on my left side, tearing the skin from my hip to below my knee.

By the time I got back to London that night it was late and I was in agony. Unable to find an open pharmacy, I had fashioned a makeshift dressing from paper towels and packing tape.

That night I barely slept and I dreamed of raw steak. In the morning I screamed with pain and frustration as I pulled on my jeans. Thinking about it now – remembering the way my clothes stuck to the grazes and the gooey pain that resulted when I moved and the fabric tugged at the wound – I have no idea why I didn't cancel my trip. What I do know is that it never occurred to me.

At Heathrow I stumbled towards security with the Freud under my arm. I had no idea what would happen if I were caught, but the drawing was almost certainly worth a quarter of a million pounds and at that moment my principal worry was that I would stumble and put my elbow through it.

I caught a glimpse of my doughy, sweaty face reflected in the glass frontage of a sunglasses shop. I looked like I was detoxing and I was certain I would be stopped by the first se-curity guard I came across. Just then, someone asked to see my boarding pass. I gripped the package hard as I handed over my phone for inspection. 'Come this way, sir,' the man said calmly. He walked away with my phone, away from the long lines for security and turned a corner into a darker, cooler part of the terminal. Surely I was only minutes away from being put in one of those small, fluorescent-white rooms I'd seen in films. I mentally worded my confession, leafed through an imaginary Rolodex of one-phone-call people. But I needn't have worried. The man was merely directing me to the fast track line I was unaware I was entitled to use. With a deferential nod he handed me back my phone and moments later I had slithered through security.

It was before 9 a.m. on a Monday morning, but what I really wanted next was a drink. I knew, though, that I couldn't do this flight without first doing something about my leg. In the large airport pharmacy I asked for gauze, antiseptic and surgical tape. As I was paying, I saw that the gauze came in two-metre strips. Explaining my predicament, I asked the woman at the checkout if the pharmacy had a pair of scissors I could borrow.

'Oh, I'm afraid that'll be tricky,' came her reply. 'Since we're airside, I can't let you use our scissors. You could run off with them and hijack a plane and then where would we be?' She laughed nervously.

'I promise you, I can't run anywhere in this state. Surely there must be some way,' I pleaded. 'I need to do something about my leg.'

'Well, we can't lend them to you, but you might be able to use them under supervision in our consultation room. Let me talk to my manager.'

I hovered around trying to appear casual while at the same time trying to stand in such a way that my trousers wouldn't stick to my leg. After a few minutes I saw the woman coming towards me accompanied by an armed policeman.

The guy was enormous. Perhaps it was his expanse of black uniform, but there was just so fucking *much* of him, a T-bone steak in a stab-proof vest. I held the Freud tightly as they approached. 'I spoke to my manager,' the woman started out. 'He said if you're going to borrow the scissors, you'll have to be supervised by a police officer.' I looked up at the man's face. His eyes were elsewhere, doubtless scanning the horizon for threats. He gave no indication that he knew he was being discussed.

Officer T-bone and I were shown into a small room at the back of the shop. It smelled strongly of mildew and antiseptic. He sat down heavily in a plastic schoolroom chair and placed a pair of red-handled, blunt-ended scissors on the table between us. 'Away you go,' he said with all the flair of a tired father at a fairground.

I placed the Freud on the table and arranged the bandages and tape next to it. As I kicked off my shoes, I glanced at T-bone. He was staring straight back at me. Even sitting down he seemed to tower over me as I stood. When I began to undress I felt sure that the man would stop looking at me; we were in England, after all, a country marinaded in a juicy mixture of corporeal self-loathing and inherited embarrassment. I took off my trousers and draped them over the back of the other chair, but still he stared. When I turned around to reach for the gauze, I saw his hand on the Freud, his fingers lightly drumming on its cardboard enclosure. His eyes met mine and went down to the table before looking back at me.

For the next ten minutes I was locked in an intermittent ocular tussle as T-bone watched me, practically naked from the waist down, struggling to dress the wounds on my leg. His hand still rested squarely – almost possessively – on the middle of the Freud's cardboard sleeve. As I came to the end of my task and pulled on my trousers, I winced again, but this time not from the pain. Seeing that I would soon be ready to leave, T-bone had begun levering his massive bulk out of his chair and in the process pushed himself up on the Freud. From inside the cardboard came a single, seismic crack, like the sound of gin pouring over ice. Seeing my look of horror he followed my eyes again to the parcel on the table between us. 'What's in this thing anyway?' he asked me with a sneer.

'It's a watercolour by my grandmother,' I said meeting his gaze. The lie flowed out of me so easily, so unthinkingly. I reached my hand to claim my precious cargo, but still his meaty hand rested on it.

In those final few moments I had no idea what would happen. I wasn't conscious of holding my breath, but when T-bone finally removed his hand and opened the door, I realised my lungs were about to burst. The consultation room had been almost silent and the rushing noise of the airport hit me like a wave. I gulped in the duty-free air, the cheap perfume and the pubby mix of spilled lager and grilled bacon. It smelled like freedom.

When I arrived in New York I took a cab to an address on the Upper East Side and left the Freud, as instructed, with the doorman. He looked unfazed when I told him who it was for and I wondered how many precious artworks had been briefly in his care. As I would learn only long after I had returned safely to London, the cracking sound had been the wooden frame splitting at a corner, something that would be relatively easy to repair: the cost of doing business.

Over the next day or so it quickly became apparent why I'd found it so difficult to secure meetings: I had come the week of Thanksgiving and people were leaving town like rats fleeing a ship. In the MoMA archives I was almost alone on the Tuesday and completely alone on the Wednesday. As I riffled through Burton's papers – the letters he exchanged with manufacturers and the minutes of meetings he had with Max Protetch, his dealer – I realised that however much I could learn about Burton from his archive, I had yet to see any of his work in the flesh.

I spoke to the archivist on duty, a weary-looking man in late middle age with grey, tufty sideburns and a shop-soiled face. When I mentioned Burton, however, his eyes seemed to brighten like lights coming closer through a fog.

'Oh, I met Scott a few times in the eighties,' he told me. 'Such a nice, kind man. Such a shame he died so young.' (Burton had died from an AIDS-related illness in 1989.)

'Do you know if MoMA has any of his work on show at the moment?' I asked.

'No, I don't think so. He's a little out of fashion these days. But the best way to see Scott's work was always out there, you know. *In the wild.*' These last few words he said with a hushed excitement.

'Sorry,' I said, 'what do you mean?'

'Man, the best Burtons are all out there on the street, in Manhattan. Brooklyn even, if you wanna take the Q train all the way to Sheepshead Bay.' He jotted down some cross streets and handed me the paper. 'My favourite is the piece *inside* this building,' he said, pointing to a Sixth Avenue address. 'But it'll probably be closed for the holiday.'

The next day was Thanksgiving and I set out early. The streets were practically deserted under the sharp blue sky as I walked uptown from my hotel. Midtown Manhattan was an eerie movie set as I hunted for the Burton works the archivist had pointed out. At 51st Street, I turned west and found what I was looking for. In front of me was a wide expanse of concrete – a corporate gulley of struggling plants and litter and shadowy air. And then I saw what I'd been looking for. Scattered around the concourse were snatches of carved green granite, immovable tables and stools that looked like chess pieces in mid-play.

I sat at one and finished the coffee I'd been nursing for the last few blocks and thought about everything I'd learned about Burton. Early in his career he'd been a dancer and choreographer and I could see that in these works. I had previously been puzzled by Burton's art furniture, but now I was amongst it, I came to see it as a physical and enduring manifestation of dance. As I sat there on that cold, empty morning, I imagined all the office workers and couriers and weary tourists who had briefly sat at those tables; the lunches eaten and the cigarettes smoked; the tears shed and the hands held. All this was Burton's doing: the discreet, Oz-like choreography of anonymous dancers, locating and directing them in space and providing momentary respite from the frantic pace of daily life.

Back in London the following week Burton was all I could think about. I talked to Inigo and he seemed to share my enthusiasm. He showed me a list of Burton works that he'd been offered and together we selected a few to buy. I was enthused. My doubts about my job were fast receding at the prospect of this project. Over the next weeks I began a correspondence with Burton's former assistant, tentatively exploring the state of Burton's market and beginning to understand how the estate was handled.

A few months later, the Burtons arrived and Inigo and I looked at them together. They were beautiful things and I was keen to find more and to start putting together an exhibition. Inigo, however, had other ideas: he wanted to include the works in a group show with Sergej Jensen and Danh Vō, two artists whose creative concerns were about as far from Burton's as it was possible to be. Debate was useless; Inigo had works by Jensen and Vō that he wanted to market. We never again discussed the idea of working with the Burton estate and nor, to my knowledge, were any of the works ever sold. I had loved the idea of reviving Burton's career, but whether it had been mere infatuation or a strategy to contextualise more saleable work, it wasn't to be.

This further frustration came at a time of behind-the-scenes upheaval at the gallery. Inigo and Jopling's relationship had been going downhill in much the same way that Hemingway describes the onset of bankruptcy: 'Gradually, then suddenly.' I can remember at the time Inigo telling me about a meeting he'd had with Jopling in which Jopling had told him that the money Inigo was making was 'too much money for a young man'. Inigo left Jopling's enormous central London townhouse that evening reeling and the next day he showed his contract with Jopling to a lawyer. The lawyer was not optimistic, telling Inigo that Jopling effectively owned him.

In the coming months their already fraught association became acrimonious as Inigo attempted to extricate himself from his professional bond with Jopling. Inigo began to talk to other potential backers who might be willing to support him financially in a new venture. He also knew that, despite his lawyer's doomsaying, were he simply to refuse to sell art then it would hurt Jopling more than him.

Enter stage left Robert Newland. Rob had trained at McKinsey & Company, the global management consultancy firm, before going to work at Christie's, whence Jopling poached him to come and work at White Cube as a business strategist. He was brought in as mediator between Inigo and Jopling in an attempt to find an equitable solution to the discord.

Rob is compact and lithe, with thinning, close-cropped strawberry blond hair, a full deck of freckles and outsize glasses that give him the look of a laboratory technician. On the occasions when I encountered him, he had a twitchy manner when others were speaking, but when called upon to explain something, he would take on an instructive, almost paternalistic air, like someone used to corralling small children. He dressed casually and without flair in tee-shirts and jeans and seemed always to be acquiring new hobbies; he could be equally and entirely enthused by bouldering or triathlons mere months apart.

They made an odd couple: Inigo was urbane and charismatic whereas Rob was pedestrian and awkward. But I believe that they saw in the other something that they each individually lacked. Inigo's consummate salesmanship and flair was offset and complemented by Rob's levelheadedness and financial whizz-kiddery. Soon the two of them became firm friends, spending hours holed up in Inigo's Mount Street office or locked in hushed conversation at one of the many Mayfair bars and restaurants at which Inigo was a beloved big tipper. Inigo became almost entirely inaccessible in those months to any of us working at the gallery, and it is only after the event that we found out what was actually going on.

They developed a nickname for Jopling ('Bear') and even for the new White Cube gallery in Bermondsey ('The Abattoir'). Inigo's idiolect also underwent a change around this time and he began to speak in a janky financial-ese, employing terminology like 'finding the exit on the position' and 'the net-net result'. When discussing deals he would now speak of 'CAGR' (compound annual growth rate), which he pronounced with a low, big cat growl like one of Tom Wolfe's Masters of the Universe.

There was always something conspiratorial – something sniggeringly tête-à-tête – about their friendship and it didn't take long before Rob was effectively acting as a double agent in the negotiations between Inigo and Jopling. And then, not long after the legal wrangling was over, Rob quietly defected to work with Inigo full-time. While I'm not aware that he ever had a job title per se, from what I saw I think it would not be unfair to characterise him as having been Inigo's consigliere. He opened up a world of financial trickery that Inigo had only begun to know existed. As Rob pulled back the curtain, the possibilities must have seemed boundless.

The split that was eventually agreed to resulted in changing the name of the gallery from Modern Collections to Inigo Philbrick Gallery, as well as a change of livery from frothy white to a murky grey. By the end of 2014, Inigo had moved out of the space at 89 Mount Street and was renovating a new gallery on Davies Street, smack opposite his new favourite restaurant, Cipriani. The new space was in keeping with his increasingly private business model: it had no street frontage, just a brass doorbell and a door that opened on to a long, parquet-floored corridor – it didn't even have windows.

Inigo and Rob worked in two offices in the building above. One was stuffed with original Jean Prouvé furniture, Bang & Olufsen speakers and a built-in champagne fridge. The room also housed Inigo's collection of portable masterpieces – a tiny Basquiat, a miniature Warhol and a bonsai Calder, amongst others – coquettishly balanced on a mantelpiece. The other office, two floors up, was more sparsely furnished and boasted no artworks, merely a much scribbled-upon whiteboard and a conference table.

But before Rob went to work with Inigo in Davies Street – while he was still technically a White Cube employee – they both attended quarterly meetings with Jopling. These meetings were partly to discuss the artworks that were still owned jointly; they were also intended as an attempt to maintain cordial relations between Inigo and Jopling.

At one such meeting, Inigo was showing Jopling images of some Lee Lozano drawing he had bought from Graeme Steele (a former White Cube director who later moved to Hauser & Wirth in LA). When Jopling challenged Inigo for having purchased them, Inigo was confused. Jopling, Inigo told me later, seemed not to know who Lozano was. Inigo later told me that as he continued to be quizzed about the works, he became increasingly aggravated until he could hold his tongue no longer.

'You know, Jay,' he said, 'the whole point of this structure is that I'm here to invest money on our behalf and to make good returns. Thus far I think we both have to agree that my returns at worst have been satisfactory – if not exemplary – and if you're going to give me a hard time about particular artworks, or how many of a given artist we have, then, you know, I make the same money trading really aggressively as if I were to go out and buy a Mark Rothko that I really believe in. We'd have one work on the stock list, I don't even have to come to these fucking meetings and I'll sit on the beach wait for the Rothko to appreciate and then send you your share.'

As Inigo told me this story from his desert island refuge, I must admit that it stretched even my credulity. First of all, the idea that Jopling was unaware of Lee Lozano – an important artist whose work is in many major international museums – is a little ludicrous; Jopling is, according to everyone else I've ever spoken to, spectacularly knowledgeable. Given that Jopling has been one of the world's preeminent contemporary art dealers for over thirty years, it's difficult to give Inigo's portrayal of himself as a more confident and sophisticated dealer than Jopling much credence when viewed dispassionately. But one of the things that made it possible for Inigo to carry on his fraud for so long was the fact that he somehow managed to feel – to me and many others – wholly believable at all times. Indeed, for a couple of years before he fled, Inigo would repeatedly tell me that White Cube Bermondsey was losing so much money that it would soon drag the whole gallery into bankruptcy. I believed him totally. In fact, Jopling has recently expanded his operations, opening spaces in Paris, Miami and New York.

According to Inigo, Jopling quickly apologised and the situation de-escalated. The meeting came to a close and the three men had a drink together, after which Jopling told Inigo that he had business to discuss with Rob and Inigo left. Inigo and Rob had anticipated this and had previously arranged to reconvene for dinner later that evening.

Inigo went back to his office and tied up some loose ends. An hour passed, more. Finally Rob called, apologising for taking so long and saying that he would explain in person. When they met up, Rob told Inigo that Jopling had spent the past hour and a half discussing Inigo's throwaway comment about going and sitting on a beach. Jopling, Rob recounted to Inigo, was apparently concerned (as it turned out, justifiably) that one day Inigo would indeed end up sitting on a beach with his money. Inigo later told me that, after that meeting, his meetings with Jopling would always be denoted by the initials 'B.B.' in Jopling's calendar – Beach Boy.

When I was first working at Modern Collections, Inigo told me on several occasions that the company was more profitable than the whole of the White Cube operation. Even by his loose standards of truthfulness this felt like another bold claim, but it was undoubtedly true that Inigo was making a lot of money, both for himself and for Jopling. That evening in Jopling's office, however, the balance of their relationship changed. Inigo was still only toying with the market's dark arts at this stage, breaking ethical boundaries rather than legal ones, and doing so far beneath his employer's radar. But Rob's tutelage would soon equip him with an armoury of financial know-how, and Inigo was about to break free of any conceivable oversight. The really wild times were just around the corner and it would only be a matter of time before Inigo really did end up on a faraway beach with Jopling's money.

6

I was born and grew up in London and have spent the vast majority of my life here. Until I was eighteen and I began commuting by bicycle to my first job, I knew the city only in the abstract, as a tube map – a multi-coloured network that I imagined threading its way through the grey below. In those days, I would surface like a mole and scurry to my destination before submerging again into the bowels of the city, scarcely aware of even my most immediate surroundings. On my bicycle, however, I began to fill in the gaps, to feel the city's topography, and to sense its texture and its tremors. But joyous and convenient as cycling was, I soon realised that I was still only a spectator. If I were really to witness London – to be a part *of* the city rather than apart *from* it – I would have to walk it.

A little while after I started working at Modern Collections I started walking into Mayfair from my flat in south-east London, a distance of around five miles. At the time, I was obsessed with the writer Iain Sinclair and his London peregrinations, his notion that a city will reveal itself through a process of exploration on foot. Though it meant waking up and leaving home far earlier than usual, I would do this once a week at least, varying my route a little at a time until eventually I found a path I walked so many times that it felt as though I was somehow leaving my mark on the city. Most people when

I told them about my walks saw them as an affectation (which, of course, they were). My friend Ben Hunter asked if he could join me.

Ben and I had known each other since we met at the birthday party of a mutual friend in January 2008. We didn't become good friends until 2012, however, when we discovered that we were practically neighbours both at home and at work. Ben lived with friends in a rowdy house on a genteel street and worked in a St James's gallery shared by two dealers: one selling Old Master paintings, the other nineteenth-century sculpture. It might have been only a few streets away from Modern Collections, but it was a world away and I was keen to know more about it.

That first morning we met at the bottom of Ben's road and set off, saying little at first. Ben had a canvas tote bag over one shoulder and a suit jacket draped over his arm. He wore tortoiseshell glasses and sported a neat, full beard over his square jaw. It was the first time I had ever seen Ben in work mode; he had the preppy look of an earnest young art historian who was used to being listened to.

As we crossed the river at Vauxhall Bridge, Ben pointed to a side street that wasn't on my usual route. 'Fancy a bit of breakfast?' he asked. 'I know a great place just down there.'

When we arrived at the Regency Café there was a queue snaking out the door. Media types in skinny jeans and sloganeered tee-shirts mixed with steel-toed builders and fashion-forward Asian tourists. 'Trust me,' Ben said as I looked askance at the queue, 'it'll be worth it.'

There is no one art world. Instead, there are many, interlinked yet distinct worlds, and as we ate Ben told me what it was like to work in his. The men and women who worked in Old Masters tended to be longer in the tooth and more old-fashioned; the men wore tailored suits and red socks, the women chintzy dresses and velveteen Alice bands. They approached their work first and foremost as scholars, although often allied with a deft and ruthless commercial instinct. Their attitude to the objects they worked with could have a to-the-manor-born unconcern and in St James's it was not unusual to witness some red-faced old buffer staggering post-prandially down the street with a Cranach or a Bosch tucked under his arm, wrapped in yesterday's *Telegraph*. I recall feeling a jolt of horror when I witnessed one such dealer on an art fair booth touch up a Renaissance gold ground with a child's watercolour box. These precious artworks had survived for centuries, the logic seemed to go; a bit of grease or a light knock won't hurt. In the contemporary art world I'd come to know, you had to don latex gloves before touching anything; paintings travelled in climate-controlled trucks; and artworks were handled as gently as a newborn baby. All this surgical protocol felt designed with one thing in mind: to remind you of the financial value of the objects being handled.

Ben and I continued our weekly walks into the winter and the following spring, quickly developing a comfortable rapport. I've thought often about those walks over the ensuing years and wondered why they were so conducive to easy conversation. Neither one of us are morning people – in fact, quite the opposite is true – but there was something steadying about the forward progress of our walking conversations, the shared goal of a destination by an identical route, perhaps even something of the psychoanalyst's couch – the avoidance of eye contact, the regularity of the walks. Either way, with his stories, that first day and over the many weeks to come, Ben reignited in me the idea that art and art dealing could be fun. We discovered that we had a mutual love of Modern British artists, especially Frank Auerbach and Barbara Hepworth. We confided our belief that art could be something that can enhance daily life rather than merely embellish it and accrue value. Eventually, perhaps inevitably, our weekly conversations turned to what a gallery of our own might be like.

While we both enjoyed many aspects of working in the secondary market, we had the urge to work directly with artists, too. Our vision was of a gallery with an additional viewing room, a quasi-domestic setting in which emerging contemporary, modern and ancient artworks, as well as furniture and design, could coexist and enhance each other. The mixing of old and new was by no means an original idea (we were in thrall to dealers like Axel Vervoordt and Daniel Katz and to museums like Kettle's Yard in Cambridge), but at the time it wasn't being done by dealers of our generation, let alone in the context of emerging artists.

For months we obsessively honed our mutual pipe dream, but for months a dream was all it was until, in early 2014, I mentioned the idea to my mother. She was living at the time on the top two floors of a townhouse in Marylebone; the other floors were occupied by offices. The building was due to be sold and none of the leases were being renewed. We could have the first floor for the fixed term of a year. Ben and I agreed that it was too good an opportunity to pass up; now all we needed were some artists.

I first came to know the artist Christopher Page in November 2012, when a mutual friend called Simon Scheuer curated a small exhibition of his work at a gallery on New Bond Street. I had been to see the show at Simon's urging and liked it and I returned a few weeks later to hear a talk by the artist.

Though Chris spoke fluidly and eloquently about his work, much of what he said – I remember a lengthy, impressive digression into the French art historian Hubert Damisch's theory of cloud – went over my head. During the Q&A at the end of his talk I asked Chris a question about some aspect of his work which he answered with a quiet finality, in the manner of someone keen to wrap things up. When the talk ended the crowd stood around drinking warm white wine and not wanting to be the first to leave. Just as I was about to make for the exit, I felt a hand on my elbow and turned to see Chris. 'I wanted to apologise,' he said in his soft, narrow voice. 'I didn't answer you very well just now. The truth is I'm not feeling well. But I enjoyed your question. Can I think about it and maybe write to you?'

I was taken aback, unaccustomed to such earnestness. 'Of course,' I replied, jotting down my email address on a piece of paper. 'I'll look forward to it.' A few days later I received a lengthy email not just answering my question but expanding on it and posing a few in reply. Chris made reference to Walter Benjamin and Jacques Lacan, names I hadn't heard since Goldsmiths. The email ended with an invitation to come over for a chat at his studio. I readily accepted.

Despite this happening mere months after I had started to work at Modern Collections, it immediately felt more exciting, more engaging, than my day job. And there was a thrill of the illicit, too, an encroachment into a world I didn't have the credentials for: the almost sacred ritual of the studio visit wasn't something that I'd performed before, and certainly wasn't part of my brief from Inigo. Part confessional, part seduction, these encounters are generally reserved for curators, gallerists and, just sometimes, collectors. Studio visits offer that addictive sensation that you are seeing things before others. It was my first taste of the art world's primary currency: access.

The feelings I had had working at Modern Collections – feelings not just of commercial inadequacy, but also of professional redundancy – were brought painfully to the fore. What right did I have to go and talk to a real artist? What would I say to this clever, earnest young painter? In Chris's invitation, however, I sensed again the fizzy excitement of those early, all-night conversations with Inigo. It was the feeling I'd been hoping for, chasing, in returning to work with him; in reality, I'd hardly seen him in the months since I started, let alone talked to him. But while Inigo was flying around the world doing big deals, I was yet again searching for some kind of purpose in the city in which I'd lived my entire life. I had thought that returning to the art world, returning to work with Inigo, would bring me some sense of a future. There was something comforting – something approaching the familial, even – to that phrase 'art world'. It promised to be everything, an all-encompassing proposition. My father had always loomed large in my life, a difficult figure I was desperately unable to please, a shadow I was trying to shake off. But they say that imitation is the sincerest form of flattery, and I suppose I hoped that by inserting myself into a small part of his world I might garner the recognition and respect I had so long desired from him. I had grown up on a rich diet of art world legend and myth, surrounded by beautiful things and their stories, but in reality all I had found (once again) was commerce dressed up as culture.

Maida Vale in north-west London is a stretched-out, boundless kind of place; an area characterised by leafy, open avenues and long side streets. There are blocks of red-brick mansions trimmed with white, lacy stucco that lends them a prim domesticity, like a Victorian governess. It is not a neighbourhood that

I particularly like and certainly not somewhere I would have expected a young artist to have his studio.

Chris had sent me an address on Elgin Avenue, which runs right the way through it, and when I arrived I was confused to find myself at a shuttered nineteenth-century school building covered in scaffolding. I called Chris. 'Oh good, you're here,' he said, picking up. 'Sorry, I should have mentioned. Yes, it's all a bit confusing. Hang on just a minute, I'll come and find you.' Several minutes went by before I heard a clanking from around the corner. I followed the sounds and found Chris waiting by an open door. 'Come on in,' he said, patting my shoulder, 'you must be freezing.'

Chris was wearing an old overcoat as well as what looked to be several pairs of tracksuit bottoms at once. He wore his shoulder-length hair neatly off his face and I couldn't help noticing that his skin had an unhealthy indoor pallor, like a plant kept too long in the dark. He smoked constantly.

We walked down one dark and echoey corridor after another. Distant voices came from somewhere up ahead and music seeped out from behind closed doors. The place smelled of mould and stale cigarettes. The walls were strewn with children's drawings and noticeboards and sign-up lists. Eventually we reached a set of double doors inset with frosted security glass and Chris turned to me briefly with a here-we-are smile before pushing open both doors with a flourish.

The room was triple height and divided down the middle by a makeshift plasterboard wall. I noticed that the floor was parquet and I wondered what Mayfair gallery it would be installed in once the place was gutted. 'This was the school gym,' Chris told me with evident pride. 'My friend's studio is on the other side of the wall there. There are a few of us living here as building guardians until it gets redeveloped. It's not ideal, especially in the winter, but the rent is so cheap and I don't know where else I could get all this space. Anyway, what can I get you to drink? I have whisky.'

'Whisky's great,' I replied even though I'd brought beer; it was cold and I thought the whisky might make me feel warmer.

As Chris looked for the whisky and blew the dust out of two tumblers and then went off down the dark warren of corridors in search of ice and water from some faraway communal kitchen, I looked at the paintings displayed – for my benefit, I suspected – around his 'studio'. Quickly and surreptitiously, I took photographs while Chris was out of the room and it is those images I am looking at as I write. (To pretend I can exactly recall what I observed that evening would be absurd given how much we drank.)

The painting which I liked best, and which for years afterwards I wanted to buy for myself but had neither the space or the money for, was a tall, broad canvas called *Party in Seville*. It seemed to show a sliding door, but rendered as if in an architectural simulation. A warm rhomboid of summer light burst across it with a brightness which seemed to emit from the painting, as if somehow it contained its own light source.

Close at hand, hung side by side on the plasterboard partition, were two smaller paintings. As I approached them, I was puzzled to see that they weren't framed. Indeed, the paint-spattered 'painting' in the middle of what I thought was a frame was in fact a *trompe l'oeil* done directly on to the plasterboard itself. They were paintings of painting itself, abstractions of abstraction, but painted with a porcelain, Magritte-like finesse. I smiled as the paintings caught me in the act of looking.

Chris came back into the room with a pint glass full of ice and poured us both a drink. That night and two or three others over the following year, I would visit Chris and we would talk and drink and smoke late into the night. He seemed to me to be the whole package: a bright young artist who could talk convincingly about his work (not as common as you'd think); his work was complex enough to satisfy any intellectual needs collectors' bona fides might be looking to furnish, but so well executed (even less common) and visually arresting, too. He had studied at Central St Martin's in London and then under Peter Halley at Yale School of Art; he had shown with a few other galleries and already had the beginnings of a collector base, both here and in America. He was professional, too, and evidently ambitious. I didn't yet know whether he had what it would take to really make it big, but what I saw was more than enough to make a good start. (I didn't even consider taking Chris to Inigo: he wasn't interested in primary artists. Inigo only got interested once someone else had done the work of building their prices to £100k a canvas. He was a secondary market dealer to his core.)

And so when it came to finding artists to show in the gallery – the gallery we had decided we would call Hunter/Whitfield (we were so pleased with that /) – Chris was at the top of my list. In April 2014 I took Ben to Maida Vale to meet him and to see his work. We sat around and drank a few beers. Ben looked at the paintings – and I mean he really looked at them. Ben likes to get up close and personal with artworks; glasses off, nose practically touching the surface, hands caressing sculptures. It was something I found shocking when I first saw it, but it makes sense to me now. For Ben, I later came to understand, works of art don't exist in some precious, other realm, but are a necessary and intrinsic part of his life. That makes them no less special, no less worthy of respect; rather, his attitude to art objects is one of intimacy.

After a while, Ben gave me the previously agreed nod to tell me he was on board. I was supposed to do the ask; I had already told Chris that Ben and I were planning to open a gallery and I think I must have at least intimated to him that we would like to show his work – it's not the sort of thing I'm good at keeping to myself. But then I froze. I couldn't say the words; I had that chest-tightening feeling before asking someone out. For a while we just carried on chatting benignly. Ben caught my eye a couple of times. Still I said nothing. And then I heard: 'We'd like you to be the opening show in our new gallery.' Ben was never one for beating around the bush. I felt surging relief as he said it and then backslapping joy when Chris accepted. I looked over at Ben. We were on our way.

The intervening year went by incredibly quickly. In reality, it was a frantic grind of secretive planning (we didn't tell our respective employers until the last possible moment) and hard work. We had no idea how to write a business plan, let alone implement one. Our attempts to forecast numbers with no idea of prices, clientele or overheads were more fiction than anything else. We each had savings of about £5000; that would have to be enough to get us up and running. If we didn't manage to sell a good few of Chris's paintings in the first few months, those few months would be all we had.

I finally told Inigo about Hunter/Whitfield a few weeks after I got back from an art fair we'd done in Mexico City. I've always disliked art fairs – they have the feel of a large and glamorous wedding where all the guests loathe the bride and groom – and this one had been an unmitigated disaster. The gallery had only been accepted into the modern section of the fair rather than the contemporary section, meaning we were restricted to post-war art through to the end of the twentieth century. We'd scrabbled to consign a bad Warhol and a slapdash Picasso among some other forgettable minorpieces. At the last minute, we'd built a makeshift walk-in cupboard on the stand and hung a gold painting by the Italian market star Rudolf Stingel, which by the rules of the fair should not have been there. Few of us like it when the rules for everyone are applied to us and Inigo was a young man used to getting his own way. Circumventing the fair's regulations, however, wasn't mere high-jinks: by anyone's yardstick, flying five people and a bunch of artworks from London to Mexico is expensive. Stingel was in a market in which Inigo felt comfortable and his best chance of breaking even on the fair. By the end of the first day, word had spread about the hidden gold painting in the modern section. As the fair went on, the visitors to the cupboard grew in number until on the last day, when I arrived late to the fair, a small queue had already formed. It was the only reason people came to our booth.

Inigo had been travelling since the fair and looked exhausted as I sat down with him in his office, but I couldn't risk him finding out before I told him my news. When it came to it, I wondered if he'd known all along. He was eating a sandwich and turned to look at his laptop as I started speaking. 'So,' I started out. I could feel my pulse throbbing in my forehead. Inigo raised an eyebrow without turning back towards me. 'I'm going to open a gallery at the end of May. It'll be primary market so no conflict of interest and only open Thursday to Saturday to begin with so I can still work Monday to Wednesday here.' His reaction was almost non-existent. As I waited for him to say something, a piece of egg fell from the sandwich on to his laptop. I stared at it, fixated, even after he started speaking.

'Yeah, that's fine,' he said laconically. 'I'm really pretty easy about you and whoever else doing whatever on the side, so long as this place runs smoothly. So, yeah, I don't really care, so long as you get it all done, you know?'

'I will, of course. Absolutely. And we're going to have an opening dinner in the space. We'd love it if you would come.'

'Of course, man. I wouldn't miss it.' He smiled briefly in that moment, a warm, genuine smile that I can still recall to this day. I wondered if he were perhaps a little proud that I was making a go of it without him, finally relinquishing my childish hold on his coattails. Our relationship had suffered in the time I'd worked for him mainly through my expectation that our friendship could remain the same and that neither of us had changed; perhaps he was simply relieved that I was on my way out. Inigo's motive for hiring me was never entirely clear to me. It wasn't that I was underqualified. I was entirely *un*qualified.

Inigo was a transactional person and working for him always made me wonder if I weren't merely a pawn in some elaborate game. His gallery really didn't need an exhibitions manager. For a long time I took it for a mix of friendly benevolence and a well-founded belief that I would have done anything he asked of me. Years later, combing through the many documents he sent me, I came across a long email correspondence between Inigo and a lawyer who was helping him renew his visa. The solicitor had requested to see my pay slips, as well as those of another long-standing employee. While I have no more concrete evidence that this was the only reason that Inigo kept me around and on his pay-roll, it was the odd nature of our friendship that made me persistently question its legitimacy. But proof was needed, it seems, that Inigo had been employing UK citizens.

The next few months were taken up with renovating the space in Marylebone, signing up and pandering to artists, buttering up and inviting potential clients to the dinner and myriad other tasks big and small. Within a week of our planned gallery opening, Inigo's new space on Davies Street was due to open, too, and I had to oversee the installation of a show pairing Mike Kelley 'Memory Ware' works and Sterling Ruby spray paintings. (In pretentious jest, I called the show *Spray, Memory*; I had just read Vladimir Nabokov's memoir, *Speak, Memory*.) Working two jobs, seven days a week I began to grind and clench my teeth so hard at night that I had occasionally to massage my jaw muscles in the morning – and once had to resort to opening my mouth with a ruler – simply in order to yawn.

Chris had moved from Maida Vale to a smaller studio in south-east London not far from where I was living. Either Ben or I would drop in each week to see Chris's progress. If there is one thing, one memory, that I could save from those days it would be those visits. Discussions the three of us had could sometimes be identified in Chris's work weeks later. I felt – I still feel – a very deep pride that our shared project had been an impetus for the beautiful paintings Chris was making. To be, even in the vaguest, slightest, most distant way responsible for assisting in the creation of that body of work is something I will always cherish.

In mid-May the space was ready. The drab, seaweed-y carpet had gone and the floorboards below polished; the dusty strip lighting replaced with square LED panels that hung on a wiring system Ben devised and which spread a clean, bright, even light over the whole place. We had transformed a room into a gallery. Our office-cum-viewing-room-cum-sitting room next door was decorated with antiquities and furnished with a round G Plan table.

The gallery dinner is sacrosanct, part of the contemporary art world's catechism. Generally held either the evening before or in the hours after a show's opening, it is typically a boozy affair to celebrate the artist in the company of the people who really matter: wealthy collectors. Sure, you need to pad the room out a little: all that money and ego can act like opposing magnetic forces. So you invite some art writers, a curator or two, other artists and maybe some civilians, too, if you've got room. What you don't do is invite other dealers.

The gallery dinner is, in truth, a symptom of an infrequently acknowledged reality about the contemporary art world: it is in large part a service industry designed around the needs and desires of very rich people. Collectors – and this in my experience is truer of those people who buy emerging contemporary than more seasoned (wealthier) buyers who are likely bored with the whole damn scene, and possibly of anything else the world has to offer – enjoy the glamorous circus which surrounds and accompanies their purchases. It can be a question of identity, too, I suspect: how much nicer to think of yourself as an art collector or patron of the arts rather than an oil trader or a hedge funder. It's a quick way of trading in hard cash for cultural capital and social acceptance (in a certain sphere), of moving from being defined by your wealth to being defined by your taste.

Over the past few decades the art market has boomed, often in the face of dire global financial downturns. There are many reasons for this, many reasons that people feel comfortable investing in expensive artworks when financial markets, even housing markets, are down. Like fine jewellery, artworks are a portable way to park money and can be easily stored in tax havens like Switzerland to avoid the prying eyes of, say, divorce lawyers or tax inspectors. Add to that ethically grey trading practices and the potentially massive returns that can be made for doing next to nothing. But, to my mind, it's the mad global hamster wheel of dinners and parties and studio visits and fairs and auctions – not forgetting the intoxicating, intangible and priceless X factor that is *access* to all the above – that has kept the market as buoyant as an oligarch's yacht. If you're one of these guys, following the art caravan around the world gives your life sumptuous and predictable structure. Frieze New York and the attendant auctions are your reason for being in New York in May; Art Basel is your reason for being in Switzerland in June; you sail your yacht to the Aegean in July because there's a new foundation opening on Hydra; October rolls round and it's time to be in London and then Paris for Frieze London and then Foire Internationale d'Art (FIAC); and then finally, just when you thought you couldn't take any more, it's time to gird your loins for one last hurrah and get some winter sun at Art Basel Miami, after which you'll definitely deserve your ten days on St Barts.

All this is to say that when we gave our dinner – a joyous, chaotic affair catered by my chef brother-in-law – it wasn't really something we wanted to do, and not something that we imagined would bear financial fruit. People were congratulatory to Ben and me and adulatory to Chris. They ate and drank; I gave a brief speech; and Inigo, who arrived late in a fugue of cologne, his shirt unbuttoned in a way that signalled that summer was coming, was a source of fascination for all. He was seated next to a wily aristocrat-ish former dealer who at the end of dinner said to Ben and me, 'Who on earth was that American I was next to at dinner? Total shark. I rather liked him.' I relayed this to Inigo the next day, to which he replied, 'Ha! Takes one to know one.' I briefly wondered whether he was proud of me.

*

The next evening was the not-so-private private view. We had no idea what to expect, no idea how many people would come. The conditions of our lease meant that we had to hire a doorman to stand on the front steps and keep a limit on the numbers coming in. We considered it an absurdity but we were wrong. A trickle of family and friends arrived when the doors opened at 6 p.m. Gradually the room filled up with voices, with the golden clamour of admiration. I was walking the perimeter of the room, ensuring people weren't getting too close to the paintings. I looked out of the window on to the street. Below was a writhing mass of people, a line around the corner. We were already at capacity in the gallery.

I tried persuading people who'd been in the gallery for a while to move on, but eventually we gave in and told the guy on the door to let it rip. The room filled up until the noise and the crowds were almost unbearable. To this day I am amazed that none of the paintings were damaged.

That night went by so quickly, all too quickly. It was a dangerous, happy feeling like the moment in a dream when you think you're falling but realise instead that you are flying. I have a video of it all buried somewhere in the digital detritus of that period, shakily shot by my father on his phone. He was already unsteady then and had brought with him a kind of walking stick that unfurls to become a makeshift chair, the sort of thing older people take to picnics. From his low-slung perch, he panned his phone slowly around him. Because of the angle, the footage is mostly of people's torsos, sometimes a double chin, but there's a point where the camera slowed to show me in conversation with someone I don't recognise. I turned towards my father and smiled for the camera, and what I saw in his face, I think for the first and only time, was pride. The video trembles and then ends. I looked on as he began smilingly to cry.

I could tell you how that felt; the words came to me that instant and I've had them in me ever since. But I need it to remain mine and mine alone. Because although the gallery is now gone and the house it was in is long sold, that's where he remains, my father, an immovable and beaming star as the chaos spins around him.

We ran the gallery for a year at that space and put on some shows that I'm still genuinely proud of. Emerging galleries like ours often seek to find their artists at art school degree shows and competition for the best artists is stiff, gallerists elbowing each other out of the way to sign up the new hot thing. Through Chris, however, we met two artists: Jeffrey Stuker and Thomas Hutton. Jeffrey, who makes exquisitely rendered, conceptually taut computer-generated films and imagery, had been one of Chris's teachers at Yale and Thomas was a friend and fellow Yale alumnus.

I first met Thomas in Venice in early 2015 when we were both there for the Biennale, Venice's biannual festival of contemporary art, international grandstanding and competitive Negroni drinking. It was the first time I'd been to the Biennale and right away I wished I hadn't come. Private jets were nose to tail at the airport and the Venetian lagoon was choked with sinister mega yachts. That evening a colleague went to party on a boat belonging to a family of Israeli former-arms-dealers-turned-arts-philanthropists who have enthusiastically been washing their bloody reputation in the sweat of young artists' hard work for decades now. At the dinner, my friend sat down next to a woman with the priceless skin of taut, plasticised youth, whose opening conversational gambit, in a pinched voice of indeterminate origin, was to ask, 'Tell me, did you fly here commercial?' My friend had been on the same budget flight as me that morning. We had made it into the easyJet set.

Thomas and I met for lunch the following day. Over a bowl of pasta he showed me image after image on the cracked screen of his phone. As well as sculptures and drawings, he made what he called 'architectural interventions' into the spaces in which he showed. What he proposed worried me, however: he wanted to 'entomb' half of the room's walls in a very fine grey cement. He would accompany this intervention with his drawings, miniature pointillist ink drawings of exquisite beauty, also 'entombed' in frames of Thomas's own design. Despite my initial fears, *Stone Anchor* (as the show was called) was for me the most satisfying of all the exhibitions our gallery did, by which I mean that all the ideas in the show meshed cleanly and harmoniously together, as in a well-oiled lock. It gives me pleasure to think about it, even years later.

In October 2015 we showed an artist called Rebecca Ackroyd. She had just finished three years at London's prestigious Royal Academy and her show with us, *Taken Care*, was her first as a graduate. Wax mouths and hands and ears pushed their way between the bars of what looked to be chopped-up dish racks stuffed with cast wax plates; dismembered souls constrained by a cage of polite domesticity, cleanliness masquerading as moral purity. Amongst these were five towering headless figurative sculptures made with medical plaster of Paris over chicken-wire frames, some of which had necks that reached like chimneys to the ceiling and whose concave bellies were filled with coal.

Certainly that first year was hard work but it never exactly felt like a job. At that level it's not a job, it's love for the artists you're showing; for the world that's giving you a chance; a love of working for yourself; and a love of a friendship that had come to mean more than all of it. And yes, it was a love of doing deals – although those were few and far between early on. Working with, and then later for, Inigo, I had come to see deals as the be all and end all of working in the art world. But working directly with artists (rather than simply with artworks), I had come to see relationships as paramount. This is not to say deals weren't important (indeed, we worried constantly about where the next deal was going to come from), but my fondest memories of those days are of conversations that went on disjointedly for weeks; fraught conversations about the gallery's direction and future; rich, challenging conversations with artists; and conversations with collectors which were by turn frustrating and elating. It was much of what I had hoped for when I worked in publishing, a sense of cultural midwifery, of helping works of art come into being and then showing them to the world.

In the late summer of 2016 I had stopped working for Inigo and the gallery had moved to a space in Clerkenwell, an area of east central London. The space was a marshy-smelling room with an undulating floor and diagonal walls; not ideal, but we could afford it – just. Finding good clients was always far harder than finding good artists, and we thought we were being terribly clever: equidistant between the upmarket galleries of Mayfair and St James's and the conceited edginess of the East End galleries and project spaces, we were sure that we would be able to ensnare collectors crossing town from one hub to the other. Sadly, we were wrong; no one came.

By the time we left Marylebone for Clerkenwell we had a few proper collectors on our books, mainly buyers of Chris's paintings. I went on holiday with them, I arranged studio visits for them, I sat through rich, torturous dinners with them and, sometimes, long nights at infernal nightclubs staring out past the velvet rope of the VIP area like a member of a harem. I was as much these guys' hired friend and London concierge as I was their art dealer. Was it significant that they were mostly older, gay men? Perhaps. But, as I said before: service industry.

When the new gallery opened in time for Frieze London 2016, I was hopeful that our opening show would attract the sort of attention that we'd been lacking. Thus far, given our secondary market backgrounds, we had been viewed with suspicion by some of our peers: too commercial, too business-minded. And so, instead of opening our new space with a show of saleable paintings, we approached an artist called Adam Gordon (another Yale pal of Chris's).

A body builder, Adam arrived from New York laden with pre-prepared lean meals and immediately asked us to find him a gym he could use during his stay. Over the following fortnight he slept in the gallery, slowly and almost imperceptibly changing it. He installed a glass divider – essentially a second shopfront – near the front of the gallery space. The entirety of the press release, written by Adam, reads as follows:

> *The gallery space has been bisected by a glass partition. There is a simulation of natural light. The gallery remains almost entirely empty aside from a curtain. Visitors are kindly asked to refrain from touching the glass.*

To this day I am not wholly sure what this show was 'about'. I assume all Adam's work is, roughly speaking, about control: self-control and the control of others, as well as the structured and engineered loss of control. (A previous show of his, in New York, consisted of a woman he hired from Craigslist to travel to the vicinity of the gallery twice a week. No one but the woman knew when or if she would be there.) Whatever

Adam's intention for his show with us, *Secession 2000*, I loved the idea of opening a new gallery, lovingly renovating the space and then denying people access to it.

There was of course no opening – Adam forbade it and there wouldn't have been any room anyway – but over the course of Frieze week we welcomed a few bemused visitors to the gallery. We also missed out on a few. Our Middle Eastern billionaire was coming across town in his chauffeur-driven Bentley but soon turned around when he got stuck in traffic; and our bicoastal American millionaire, who had been going to come and see (with a view to buying) a new Chris Page painting we had installed in our upstairs viewing room, rang to say that he'd just bought a $1 million painting from an international mega gallery and that was his spending done for the year.

Several things were at issue here, although we didn't fully understand them until much later. Firstly, it was clear that we needed to be in central London: art fairs have made collectors lazy. They represent a one-stop shop where art of all ages and stripes can commercially coexist in a kind of giant, moveable, upmarket Walmart. They are a truly terrible way to look at art: imagine eating 500 slices of pizza and then trying to tell the difference, trying to discern quality, let alone remembering what the first slice was like. You can't. Fairs exemplify the new-found shopability of art: they've made art *convenient*, like a department store or online shopping. So many collectors have become habituated to this way of seeing and buying art that when they come to a city like London, where the auction houses are all within easy walking distance from the best hotels and restaurants and a phalanx of high-end galleries, that the idea of travelling two miles by car (these are not, by and large, public transport people) to a gallery like ours, let alone one really out in the sticks, becomes somehow too onerous. The big galleries – whose business models increasingly mimic the art fair model of catering to all budgets (relatively speaking) and all tastes – are slowly suffocating the lower end of the market. Not only do these galleries have the resources to do umpteen fairs a year and to be in the smartest parts of town, but some of them are also picking up artists straight out of art school. Slowly but surely, in the way algae chokes the oxygen out of a pond, the enormous concentration of power in the upper echelons of the art market is suffocating opportunity at the most fertile level, the place where artists and money are not necessarily directly equated, and where careers have time and space to develop: the emerging gallery.

For a gallery like ours, the choice was stark: figure out a way to be in central London or stay where we were, accept that collectors would seldom come to our shows, and do several art fairs a year. Neither option is cheap. On the one hand, all fairs are a gamble: you've no idea who will turn up and there are often ludicrous barriers to entry such as holier-than-thou requests to bring some unsaleable installation or performance before you're permitted entry with artworks that might actually make your gallery some money. It's a widely accepted rite of passage that lends your fledgling gallery's cultural capital to the fair at your financial expense. We decided that to begin with we wouldn't do fairs, but would try to establish a solid gallery programme in London. And when the opportunity of a space in St James's came up, in a building owned by Christie's and where all the dealers pay domestic council tax rather than Westminster's punitive business rates, we leapt at it.

7

Hugo de Ferranti has a ten-acre voice, a booming blend of English officer-class indifference and Riviera poolside weariness. His year-round bronzed skin tells not only of his distant Italian heritage, but also of his active weekend rural life. He is neither tall nor short, neither stout nor slim; his close-cropped hair is grey and his eyes are the colour of Arctic waters in a nature documentary. In a crowded room he has the ability at once to give you his full attention and to scan passers-by for people he knows and thinks you would enjoy or benefit from meeting. This is made all the more remarkable for the fact that he is that most ironic of things: a partially sighted art dealer.

This combination of attributes results in a man who is as widely loved as he is known. When I first met him, Hugo was sitting down at a gallery booth at a London art fair, and from my position behind him I could read the enlarged type of his phone as he dictated a text message into the microphone. Suddenly the screen changed and I could see the words 'HRH . . . ' on his phone. With ineffable smoothness, Hugo waited a beat, sat himself up in his chair, and answered the call. 'Highness, how *aaarrhre* you?'

By the time I got to know him, Hugo was working for a St James's gallery called Hazlitt Holland-Hibbert. St James's is the area of London most closely associated with London's aristocratic past, with its proximity to the royal palaces and its men-only 'gentlemen's clubs' . (Hugo is a member of White's, the most back-slappingly traditional of the lot, where he enjoys flouting the rules by wearing all-black custom Nikes instead of the requisite dress shoes, claiming not to have noticed what he was putting on his feet that morning.) The windows of Jermyn Street gleam with brass and leather and silk – the shiny new trappings of old money – and you should not be surprised to encounter red-faced men in tweeds blustering along the street carrying shotguns newly serviced from Beretta. The twelfth of August may indeed be glorious, but not for the grouse.

Hazlitt, Gooden and Fox, where Hugo had worked for many years, and of which Hazlitt Holland-Hibbert is the modern and contemporary diffusion line, is as venerable as they come. Established in the mid-eighteenth century, they were official art dealers to the Queen and specialise in the sort of pictures you hang in a house whose outdoor space is referred to as 'the grounds' rather than 'the garden'. In 2002, with the late-to-the-party recognition that modern and contemporary art were on the rise and had become the focus of the market (and that it should perhaps be shown differently to its centuries-older antecedents), James Holland-Hibbert, a man of almost two-dimensional gauntness but three-dimensional poshness, opened up shop in the neighbouring building. Hugo has been a fixture ever since.

And the gallery does not fuck around. While they do not technically work as artist representatives, the list of names they have shown and worked directly with is a formidable rundown of the artists now collected under the auction house umbrella label of Modern British (or 'Mod Brit', if you want to sound in the know). Auerbach, Freud, Bacon, Riley and Hepworth are just a few of the seven-figure heavy hitters James and Hugo can help you lay your hands on. They seldom do exhibitions – certainly no more than two a year – and their parqueted rooms exude a cultured serenity which does half the work for them. There is an apartment on the top floor with *two* sitting rooms.

While Modern British art is the gallery's stock in trade, Hugo is a more adventurous soul and will happily do a deal wherever there is a deal to be done. (He told me he once sold a small Robert Motherwell painting in the back of a New York taxi.) At the point I first encountered him – waiting nervously for him to finish that mysterious royal phone call – I was still working for Inigo, but behind the scenes I was already setting up the gallery and Hugo felt like the kind of man I ought to know. He soon came into Inigo's gallery and the two of them hit it off like Scotch and water. For the next couple of years, the pair did innumerable deals, lunching together most weeks at Scott's on Mount Street, eating the kinds of fish which are now nearing extinction, looking for all the world like father and son in a Ralph Lauren advert.

Together Inigo and Hugo did some pretty big deals with some pretty big players, including but by no means limited to: Hugo's HRH to whom he would sell things as they rode horses in the desert; Olyvia Kwok, the granddaughter of a Red Army Chinese general, in whose Knightsbridge home a phalanx of Netherland dwarf rabbits ran free; the film producer and co-founder of Working Title Pictures, Eric Fellner, best man at Hugo's first wedding, who had a penchant for the French artist Louise Bourgeois. Hugo introduced Inigo to the niche of English society which is not itself a rich seam of collectors, but whose (often foreign, largely oligarchic) business associates are. Charm the upper classes and they'll give you the key to the castle.

As with many of Inigo's relationships, however, things

soured precipitously. Inigo's ability to form intense friendships with mostly male, mostly older art dealers was matched only by his willingness to let them fizzle and implode under the weight of exasperation and wilful neglect. It was a mystery to me then, and I wonder now whether this attitude was a conscious one, or rather whether it was part of any kind of plan. There aren't many of the kinds of people that Inigo was routinely pumping and dumping, certainly not enough for this pattern to last a whole career. His deceitfulness was bewilderingly self-destructive.

In this case it all went wrong when a Monet deal went south and Inigo did his disappearing act: phone calls cancelled on the second ring; texts and emails roundly ignored; attempts to find him at the gallery (where he seldom was anyway) rebuffed by members of staff instructed to tell anyone who asked that he was 'travelling'. Hugo would come to the gallery – sometimes two or three times a day – beseeching my colleagues and me somehow to rouse Inigo, his tone alternating between fury and exasperation. Eventually, however, he could push no more and in early 2016 their friendship ended in a bitter and mutually assured froideur.

Any implosion belches out detritus in its wake and in the messy ending of Inigo's relationship with Hugo, I saw opportunity. While Hugo had performed the role of ferryman for Inigo into London high society, Inigo in turn had opened Hugo's eyes to the heady world of contemporary art – and when I say contemporary, I mean art where the paint's still wet and the money to be made is liquid. By this point, of course, Hunter/Whitfield was underway and, while I was by no means the art world wunderkind that Inigo was, I felt that I might step into the breach as an understudy Virgil.

*

When I first got to know Hugo, the gallery was still in Clerken-well. Those were tricky days. The gallery was making money, but barely; we were perpetually on the cusp of being financially secure, but never quite getting over the line. We were getting by with the occasional secondary market deal, while sometimes whole exhibitions of the primary artists we were working with would go completely unsold.

Fruitless days were spent on the phone trying to persuade collectors and dealers to visit us. I knew that someone like Hugo could make a real difference – with his blessing and access to his contacts we might just make it. I was under no illusion that, were it not for my association with Inigo, Hugo would likely not have given me a second's thought. Inigo had had the endorsement of some pretty powerful art world players when he started Modern Collections. I needed some help of my own and Hugo looked like my best hope.

For several months, I had no more luck persuading Hugo to visit us than I had had with any other major client; he is not a man who likes to stray far from Chelsea or the West End. When, however, news reached him that one of the artists we represented was starting to be talked about in the kind of hushed tones which in the art world mean money is to be made, Hugo came cantering across town in a black cab.

When he arrived that day in May 2016 at the gallery on Great Sutton Street, I was equal parts nervous and excited. It felt like something of a triumph to get him to come, this man who would think nothing of selling a Freud before breakfast and a Riley before lunch. If he was impressed, it could mean an entrée into his world of buyers and power players.

As he got out of his taxi he was mid phone call and I heard him saying, 'Oh, but you really must see it. It's really one of the best I've ever seen . . . The price? Oh, come on, let's not discuss such vulgarities now. Come and see it first . . . This afternoon? What are you doing for lunch? Great. See you at the gallery. One o'clock. OK, bye.' By this time he was already in the gallery, his face mere millimetres from the surfaces of the delicate paintings hung on its walls. I watched him, fearful that flecks of saliva might mar the surface of the paint. His taxi was waiting outside, grumbling blackly.

'Orlaaaando,' he purred, 'how good to see you again. I love your gallery. How long have you been here? And these paint-ings, they're faaabulous. Tell me about the artist.'

I'd been rehearsing my spiel all morning – at breakfast with my girlfriend; in my head (and out loud) on my cycle ride into work; and in the office until the moment Hugo arrived – and then, just as I started, Hugo began speaking again, but not to me.

'Hi, yuh, my client is coming to see the Hockney at lunch today,' he said into the AirPods which seldom leave his ears. 'He likes the picture, but I think he's seeing another with someone else . . . No, I don't know who. It's all very infuriating.' Hugo was wandering around the gallery, he was inspecting each paint-ing in turn, pressing his face to within whispering distance of its surface, occasionally turning round to me to point at the paint-ing and make a face that emoted an almost lusty pleasure, all the while continuing his conversation with the seller of the Hockney.

The exhibition wasn't large – only five paintings – and Hugo made his way around the space slowly becoming visibly more excited by the artworks on view. Their bright colours and deft brushwork, he later told me, seemed to him to shimmer like desert heat. Eventually, as Hugo had almost come full circle and was approaching the door, his phone call was over.

'Which ones are available?' he asked me.

'All sold,' I said. (Whether it had been true or not, and in this instance it was, it's what I would have told him.) He was suitably impressed and disappointed; the show had only been open twenty-four hours. He'd missed the heat and he knew it; heat is everything in this game.

We'd anticipated this and I'd spent much of the previous day trying to extract a painting which had been consigned to an exhibition in nearby Shoreditch. The owner of the gallery was furious that I was taking the painting back. He was on his way to Tokyo but had somehow managed to harness enough of the first class cabin's Wi-Fi to harangue me from 38,000 feet. Thankfully the phone line soon went dead.

'IT'S MY FUCKING PICTURE I FORBID YOU TO TAKE IT!!!' came a message not long after, but by that time I'd wrapped the picture and was in a cab travelling across town ready to hang it in our viewing room in preparation for Hugo's visit.

I always felt that art should be something one lived *with* and that as such we should, in the gallery, always have somewhere that I could present works in something approximating a domestic setting. The office was decorated like a living room, with a sofa and chairs at one end and a long dining table at the other where we could give dinners. Alongside artworks by gallery artists, I occasionally displayed other pieces I was selling on the secondary market, as well as antiquities and ceramics that we bought at auction. When Hugo saw the painting I had to offer him, it was hung on a light grey wall, above a mid-century Scandinavian sideboard supporting a Roman bowl.

'Mmmhh, wow, yeah,' he growled as he moved closer to the painting and swapped his phone from the hand he usually held it in while speaking into the hand he used to take photos. He began to snap away indiscriminately.

'Anyone else seen it?' he asked, not wanting to find out later down the line that a friend – or worse yet, a frenemy – had rejected it. I explained the situation with the Shoreditch gallery.

'Mmmhh,' he replied, figuring – probably correctly – that not many market movers had been to see the show. 'And how much are you asking for this?'

'How much would you say such a masterpiece is worth, Hugo?' I had a feeling Hugo would enjoy a little bit of old school obsequiousness. I was right.

'Mmmhh, well, it's a beautiful thing. Fifteen?' Either Hugo knew someone who'd bought one of these paintings and already had a rough idea of pricing or it was a lucky guess; either way it saved us both some embarrassing haggling. I couldn't let Hugo buy it for more than other people had paid for similar works lest he find out and feel short changed, and I couldn't let him have it for less in case other buyers got wind of it and thought that Hugo was getting the special treatment. (For a world that claims to live and breathe secrecy, it's remarkable how often precisely the people you don't want knowing your business seem to have intimate knowledge of it, as if they go through your bins each morning.) 'We're actually asking sixteen,' I said, 'but I can let you have it for fifteen. As it's you, Hugo,' I added, just in case I hadn't ladled out enough slime by now. Every primary market artwork sold to an individual (a 'private') has a 10 per cent discount priced in; more if it's sold to a museum or a foundation. If you bought something from a gallery and you didn't get at least 10 per cent off, quite frankly you got mugged.

Hugo was silent, staring at me intently through his lopsided spectacles – one side has the look of a bulbous monocle, the other a regular lens. He looked at the picture again and then back at me. I began to think I'd said something wrong. Was he expecting a bigger discount? A harder sell?

'Sold,' he said, and shook my hand as he removed his glasses. He snapped one last photo of his new purchase.

Moments later, Hugo was back on the phone ('What do you meeean the shippers haven't arrived yet? My client's coming in for lunch. Today!') and heading downstairs to his still-waiting taxi. The whole visit had taken no more than ten minutes. It turned out to be one of the most fruitful ten minutes of my career. Over the next few months I would receive frequent phone calls from Hugo asking me if I knew such and such person; invariably I didn't and invariably Hugo would send them or bring them into the gallery and invariably they would buy something and invariably Hugo would invoice us for an introductory commission. Typically 10 per cent of the sale price, it was money well spent. While this may seem like financially prudent bonhomie – the incremental debut of a new protégé – it was also a clever hedge on Hugo's part.

Unlike financial markets where, on the level of the individual, no one really knows what anyone else owns (unless, of course, like Elon Musk, they take to Twitter to repeatedly tell you), in the art market, *who* owns what is of paramount importance. By persuading and cajoling his friends and clients to buy works by this particular artist, Hugo was not only helping to build a market for the artist, but he was making sure that the *right* people owned the paintings – people who would come to him if they wanted to sell on; people who had other *right* paintings in their homes, and the *right* dinner guests, too. The art world is a realm of secrets, covetously held and judiciously used. Hugo, like any great dealer, is a semi-permeable receptacle of these secrets, as wise as the hills and as cunning as a snake with an abacus. As Inigo was wont to say, 'When you know, you know.'

*

In August much of the art world engages in a mutually agreed hiatus. Galleries and dealers close shop and scurry off on holiday wherever their clients are sunning their monied hides. (Hugo, however, likes to go and enjoy a couple of weeks' silence in a Greek monastery.) The summer can also be a good time if you're a buyer; the very rich get nervous if they feel their money isn't doing things for them, not necessarily making them richer, just moving. It's a question of fluidity rather than liquidity and, if you time it right, August can be a great time to persuade otherwise recalcitrant sellers to agree to lower prices just to keep their river of money flowing with frothy, white-water rapidity.

I hadn't heard from Hugo for a few weeks and felt almost bereft when the three or four calls a day winnowed to none. Then, in early September, he called and asked me to lunch. We had already done a considerable amount of primary market business together in the relatively short time since he'd first come to the gallery and it had been, I felt, energising for him to have a new gallery to tell people about, a new artist to champion – not to say a youngish new dealer to do business with. It was around this time that we abandoned the dank Clerkenwell space in favour of the tiny gallery in St James's, all the better for Hugo to bring his clients to. Things were looking up.

Over lunch at Hugo's favourite St James's restaurant, Boulestin, where (at least in my company) he always ate the same thing – an off-menu pasta dish with quinoa and broccoli, known to the staff as 'Mr De Ferranti's Pasta', followed by two oat milk macchiatos and a Madeleine – he asked me if I still had clients from my days working with Inigo: big clients for big deals. I didn't. The truth was that at that stage Hugo *was* my big client; indeed, not far off being my only client.

'Oh, yes, quite a few,' I said, stuffing my mouth with bread to prevent another lie emerging from it.

'I bought a few things over the summer. Bought 'em well. Thought perhaps you might have someone for one or two of them.' (This is another odd bit of art dealer patois: 'Do you have someone for a [insert artist's name]?') On this tantalising note, our lunch was suddenly curtailed when Hugo spotted Viscount Linley, son of Princess Margaret – a grinning marionette of a man with clicky heels on his shoes and gaping lapels on his jacket. Hugo quickly went to join him at his table, leaving me with the bread basket and the bill.

For a while after that I heard very little from Hugo. In vain I called and texted to follow up. But we had a gallery move to orchestrate and soon my focus was elsewhere. And so I was surprised to receive an excited call from him early the following January, as the art world rumbled sleepily into action after its post-Miami Basel rest, to offer me a Christopher Wool work on paper.

'Have you got someone for it, do you think?' Hugo asked me after he'd sent me an image.

'Oh, I think I have just the client, yes.'

'Great. Just one thing: your client's not Inigo, is it?'

'No, Hugo, it's not Inigo,' I lied.

There is a rootlessness to the very wealthy in the twenty-first century, a floating ease in both place and time that is mirrored, or perhaps emboldened, by a certain kind of space. Oases devoid of responsibility or obligation allow one an escape from reality that is almost womb-like in its comfort. In the Connaught Bar, if you can bag a table (it was named 'Best Bar in the World' by a panel of 500 so-called experts in 2020, the year in which, as I recall it, everyone had to stay home in order to get a load on), you will be surrounded by an international array of players united by one thing only: money.

As you walk in you will be greeted by a server in a school-uniform grey dress, black-patent-leather-belted primly at the waist. You'll note the way piped music seeps into the room like an odourless gas, and the way the lighting, which manages somehow to maintain a crime scene lustre whatever the weather outside, pools between the tables and chairs and glances off the glass table tops and brass fittings and the painted silver panelling. Think air travel in the 1960s with a touch of netherworld glamour. You've seen it in a movie. Have you got a reservation? We're rather full tonight.

The guests are ensconced in cashmere and softly shrugging leather; crisp, dark denim in stark juxtaposition to the falsetto glint of diamonds and the low-energy glow of rose gold. Their torpor is somehow moribund, borne of the ennui that will always affect those for whom any kind of satisfaction is gratuitously imminent. The room shimmers non-dom status – the financial equivalent of diplomatic immunity – and they talk of elsewhere, always elsewhere, as if the present moment were fraught with some kind of difficulty.

None of this matters to Inigo, who saunters in a full twenty minutes after we are meant to meet, though ten after I've arrived – in this game, with these guys, you adapt to habitual tardiness – and mouthily whispers 'Sorry, playboy, just a minute more' as he continues his phone conversation with whatever hapless intermediary is doing his bidding this time. 'Just tell him to calm down. We're all going to make a lot of money on this one. My guy's got the condition report now – finally.' Shift the blame, stall, whatever works. 'Shouldn't be long now, then we can all get paid. Hey, listen, I have a call on the other line, I need to take this.'

He puts his phone face down on the table between us and then thinks better of it and turns it over. Notifications roll in like the wheel on a Vegas slot machine. His hair is wild and his tan sandy and beaming. I feel the contrast to my winter London pallor. As always, he is expensively fragrant. He's been in Australia for Christmas and is riding the jet lag wave, so he tells me, ready to rage all through my night, his day. At the Connaught Bar, the rough comes with a side helping of smooth.

'I'm starved,' he says, sitting down heavily next to me and pouring himself a glass of sparkling water. 'The food on Qantas is just fucking dire. Everything tastes like kangaroo shit. Let's get some snacks.'

A waitress comes over as if by magic and greets us with a 'Good evening, Mr Philbrick'.

Without looking up, Inigo reads from the menu: 'We'd have the truffle croque madam [£45] but hold the fries, the crispy sushi salmon sashimi, the shrimp satay and the Ibérico ham [three plates for £42] and a bottle of the Dom Perignon – the '08 [£295]. And another bottle of water – in fact, just keep the water coming. That should do us for now.' He flashes a smile at the waitress, who flashes one back. Inigo unbuttons his jacket and leans back with a sigh, glances with an eye-roll at the messages flooding in on his phone and says simply, as if it were a statement of unequivocal fact: 'Funny world, my friend. Funny fucking world.'

'How do you mean?' I ask. I agree, how could I not, but I'm not sure if we're on the same page as to why.

'Us, dude. This!' He casts an eye over the room and raises his arm as if he's conjured it all and could whisk it away in an instant. 'Madness.' Just as I am about to agree, his phone starts to ring and the champagne arrives and he's gone, back into deal mode.

'I spoke to him just now, he's panicking but I told him we have the condition report so we should be able to invoice soon.

Huge invoice. It'll block out the sun in his inbox.' This kind of big money banter continues for a while and I zone out slightly. It's intended to dazzle, I guess, make you think about the destination, not the journey, the turbulence. I sip my champagne which, despite my knowing that it's a) vintage and should taste amazing and b) incredibly expensive and should taste amazing, merely tastes how all champagne tastes to me: coppery and cold and fizzy with the lingering aftertaste of sweet vomit. I wash it all away with the ham, the nutty fat coating the inside of my mouth as I ponder how to pitch Inigo on the Christopher Wool I'm not meant to show him, let alone sell to him, and which feels like it's making my phone warm – actually *hot* – in my pocket.

I've had the Wool – known about it, that is – for a week. I've checked Hugo's facts as best I can; it was sold at auction for *a lot* less than Hugo's asking, but a respectably long time ago, in 2014 (anything more than a couple of years is acceptable), and the Wool market has moved a lot since then, probably because Inigo's been involved. He's the kind of guy who moves markets. I've no idea whether it has changed hands privately since then (Hugo says not), but if anyone has this kind of information it's Inigo, so ideally I'll show him the picture on my phone and gauge his reaction. His poker face is pretty good, but I've known him longer than most and the flow of champagne shows no sign of letting up. I like my chances.

Four hundred pounds' worth of snacks and fizz are dealt with in under half an hour, although Inigo has been on the phone or texting or on Instagram exchanging memes with a client or a would-be client more or less the whole time, so I haven't been able to find a moment to show him the Wool. Inigo pays the bill and gives crisp twenty-pound notes to everyone we've been in contact with since we arrived and then we bundle ourselves back into our coats and, already warmed by the champagne and the bonhomie, step out into the velveteen frostiness of a London January evening.

The cold bites at our faces grinning with booze, but we haven't far to walk; Inigo seldom leaves Mayfair, unless, that is, he's leaving via an airport. We walk into Cipriani – the Italian restaurant he jokingly-but-not-so-jokingly calls 'the canteen' because it's opposite his gallery and he eats there almost every day – where he is greeted like a son returned from war. Inigo hugs the maitre d' and hands his coat, a soft blue thing with an astrakhan collar that engulfs his neck like a headlock, to the Russian coat check girl and she flutters her lashes so hard they seem to blur. I give over the jacket I have worn to cycle into town, still slightly damp from my efforts, and receive in return a pitying grimace. I agree: the reflective patches aren't very Mayfair.

The room is decked out like the interior of a ship, though less the cruise-y kind that pensioners die on and more the kind that Billy Zane wears white tie on. Polished teak and brass portholes that look on to nothing and blue and white nautical linens and sturdy, short-stemmed ship's wineglasses: this is not a room for the mere Haves, this is a room for the Have Yachts.

'The food here is just like your Italian grandmother would make,' he tells me as we sit down, 'if your Italian grandmother were a really bad cook and charged you a lot of money.' I couldn't care less: there is a dessert trolley.

Inigo takes the menu in hand and looks it over imperiously. Two Gin Gimlets have arrived and I already feel my buzz. He orders for me, something he enjoys doing for everyone he dines with – or more accurately, buys dinner for (Inigo is always buying). I feel suddenly like a housewife from the 1950s and the burnished edge of my boozy confidence is dulled ever so slightly. Is this the point? Is it a tactic on his part? Generosity as a form of power?

I can feel the distinct lack of messages coming into my phone in my pocket as Inigo's continues to vibrate and glow next to his cocktail. I know only that on mine there is a collection of pixels that could make or break my gallery. Pasta dishes arrive one after another and ruby discs of beef carpaccio and *vitello tonnato* the colour of American tan tights all jostle for position on our round table. Inigo texts with one hand and holds his fork in the other. I'm thankful, briefly, for Inigo's distraction as I try to soak up the alcohol sloshing around in my system, as I try to neutralise the insulin spike in my blood.

Eventually I feel better. Inigo has put down his phone to talk to the maitre d', a lurching Italian man in a white dinner jacket who's come over to make a joke about something Inigo had texted him while we'd been in the restaurant. When he's eventually sauntered away, I seize the moment.

'You still in the Wool market?' I blurt, failing to channel my inner Gordon Gecko.

'Always,' he replies.

I think I can detect a glimmer of surprise at my question, but Inigo puts a forkful of rigatoni into his mouth and waits for me to continue. Your move, playboy.

I take my phone out of my pocket and delete an alert telling me I have a text from my mother. Then I quickly put the phone on airplane mode, a trick Inigo had taught me by proxy: you don't want your clients seeing a stray text pop up when they're looking at a picture on your phone. I find the image and drop the phone on the table with what I hope seems like nonchalance, as if selling Christopher Wool paintings is something I now do all the time at dinners in yacht-themed restaurants. The phone skitters over the starched tablecloth and knocks over a glass of water. Wryly amused, Inigo wipes the corners of his mouth with his napkin and then uses it to dab the water from the phone's screen.

He looks at the image for no more than five seconds, zooming in on one corner with a quizzical expression. The Wool, *Untitled (D305)* from 2006, exudes a frantic delicacy, the handiwork of a haphazard genius. The printed surface of the paper has the punky aesthetic of a 'zine comprised entirely of torn-up Rorschach tests. Anger and confusion are enmeshed in a sombre monotone web splotched with great greasy splats of pigment. This is if you view it in person. On my iPhone's damp screen, however, the Wool looks far from impressive – but that is hardly important to Inigo at this moment; the collection of backlit pixels don't actually represent the Wool qua artwork, they represent its fungible monetary value. What we're looking at is a sales document, a trade to be executed, not an aesthetic experience. This is business, not art.

'Nice. You direct [directly in touch with the owner]?'

'Yes. Client is in LA.' Double lie: I'm only in touch with Hugo who is either in west London or the West Country. The painting is apparently in Switzerland, though I've no idea where the owner lives or who she is (or even if the client is a she), but LA sounds impressive and Inigo knows I've been there recently seeing an altogether different client – a man to whom we together tried and failed to sell a painting on the eve of the 2016 presidential election, figuring that an ebullient mood the morning after would make the sale a shoo-in.

'What you asking?'

'Six.' Inigo basically only ever trades in US dollars, so there was no need to burden this snappy financial repartee and the hundreds of thousands aren't even worth mentioning. What do you think this is? Retail? My net to Hugo was $450,000. Still room to play.

'Hm. I could do 450.'

'500?'

'Okay, done,' he tells me, passing me back my phone and motioning to a loitering waiter. The whole thing is over in less than half a minute. 'My friend here would like to see the dessert trolley, please.' And then, turning to me, 'They have the most insane ice cream, too. It's like the stuff you had when you were a kid but for about ten pounds a scoop. I guess the price somehow justifies eating kids' food. There's chocolate sauce and they bring you sprinkles. What a fucking world.'

The ice cream comes, great frothing heaps of it that look like torn-off clouds, and we pour over the hot chocolate sauce from a silver jug with its handle wrapped in a napkin tied in a bow. The ice cream collapses with a fatty sigh and we dig in. 'Oh, one thing,' says Inigo just as I shovel in a large spoonful. 'This deal doesn't involve Hugo, does it?'

Through my mouthful of ice cream, I lie.

8

In the introduction to his bestselling though little-read book *A Brief History of Time*, Stephen Hawking tells the story of an astronomy lecture given by a well-known scientist, possibly the philosopher Bertrand Russell. In the lecture, Russell describes how the Earth orbits the sun and the sun, along with billions of other stars, orbits the centre of our galaxy. Towards the end of this lecture, so the story goes, a little old lady at the back of the lecture hall stands up to lambast Russell. 'This is all nonsense!' she cries out. 'We all know that the world is really a disc resting on the back of a giant celestial turtle.' Amused but patient, Russell addresses the old lady. 'Ah, madam, but if that is indeed the case, upon what does the turtle rest?' 'No, no, professor,' she spits back, 'you can't fool me. It's turtles *all* the way down.'

I can't remember which of us read this story first or where (certainly neither of us ever actually read Hawking's book) but that little old lady's retort of 'turtles all the way down' became something of an in-joke at the beginning of Inigo's and my careers. Hawking uses the story to illustrate the theory of infinite regress – an infinite series of interdependent entities which rely on or are produced by their predecessor in the series; we used it as byword for a deal with too many players involved.

Let me explain. For the Wool deal, Hugo may or may not have been directly in touch with the owner, but for the sake of this example let's assume that he was and that the price they had agreed was somewhere in the region of $375k–425k net to the owner. Hugo then comes to me and tells me I need to net him $450k, which would be great for him if his net to the owner is towards the lower end of the aforementioned scale but still pretty good if it's towards the upper and everything goes smoothly: $25k is not a bad rate for a few phone calls. I then go to Inigo and we agree the deal at $500k. So Hugo is making between $25k and $75k; I stand to make $50k; and Inigo presumably thinks there's enough room for him above the half million mark to make at least 10 per cent, that is, another $50k. And just like that, somewhere between $125k and $175k is created out of thin air, a few phone calls and an expensive dinner. When you make money in this way – almost alchemically, miraculously, unsure of really how it came about – it can have one of two effects: it can make you feel immensely clever, or it can make you feel like a fraud. It made me feel like a fraud.

This is all very well and good – everyone needs to put caviar on the table – and if deals like these were a rarity then everything would be A-OK. But while this is a private deal between anonymised individuals and their supplicant intermediaries, the price achieved sets a benchmark for all involved and, since the circle of people who operate at this level is pretty small, word gets around fairly easily. Expectations are raised and a market quietly moves until similar prices are reached at auction because everyone who buys and sells at the big auctions knows what's being achieved privately and then the growth is locked in. And all this, not because there is any inherent value in the artwork, but because there were so many turtles in the chain.

The day after Inigo and I sealed the deal I woke up with a musty head that was cut through by a sense of elation. This was the single biggest deal I had ever pulled off and it came at just the right moment. I was struggling to get collectors to come to the gallery and sales had been sluggish. A deal like this – to all intents and purposes a virtual deal, albeit one with a real payout – was perfect.

I sent Inigo a text thanking him for dinner and, fully expecting him to write and tell me he'd changed his mind, asked him which of his companies I should invoice for the Wool. To my surprise, he replied immediately in a direct and businesslike tone. 'Send it to Jess [Inigo's assistant] addressed to Inigo Philbrick Ltd. Thanks.' More than a little incredulous, I played it cool, waiting a full half hour before sending the invoice, having checked and rechecked that our bank details were correct. I sent it off, cc'ing Inigo. Ten seconds later came his reply: 'Someone's keen.'

And for a while that was that. The payment terms on the invoice were thirty days and I was sure Inigo would use the whole thirty. All I had to do in the interim was keep Hugo calm. We arranged for a condition report to be carried out in the Geneva warehouse where it was being stored. I never knew the name of the conservator who carried out the report; it came on headed notepaper and the signature could have been Charlie Chaplin's for all I knew. The (scanned) piece of paper – its cursory examination represented by the most threadbare, clinical language – was merely a stepping stone on the road to fifty big ones. Inigo accepted it without comment.

Payment was due on 12 February and on 11 February, a Saturday, I was giving a dinner for my thirtieth birthday at a restaurant near my flat. Inigo came and sat next to my father. My father liked Inigo but was wary of his roguishness; he liked to tell me he was sure Inigo would end up in prison. That night, however, each time I looked in their direction, they were red-faced and laughing, Inigo frequently refilling my father's glass. At the end of the evening, Inigo sidled up to me with a sheepish look. Surely he wasn't about to cancel the deal on me, not today. But before I could ask him anything he asked, 'What are you doing next week? Come to New York. We'll have a rager.'

'Sounds good,' I said. 'Let's talk on Monday. And any news on the Wool payment?' I was too drunk to sound casual. Panic sounded in my voice like a faraway foghorn.

'Monday!' he replied, and stepped into the protective darkness of a waiting Mercedes.

By late Monday afternoon I hadn't heard anything from Inigo. I was refreshing my bank balance every hour and Hugo was calling me with the same frequency, his tone alternating between annoyance and sympathy. 'We've all had late payers. Part of the game. But do you know why? What's your guy saying? *When* will he pay? Just tell me that. My client's already going crazy.'

'I spoke to him this morning,' I told him. 'He's been travelling. Assured me he'll pay this week. I'm going to New York this week, I think. I'll try to see him there.'

Inigo hadn't returned any of my phone calls on Monday but in the evening I received an email from British Airways informing me that Inigo had booked me on to a flight to New York the following morning. I called him again. He picked up on the first ring.

'What's up, player?'

'I got an email from BA. You booked me on a flight to New York?'

'Yessir. See you over there.'

In the First World War the British navy employed a form of ship painting called dazzle camouflage. Warships were painted in bold, chaotic black and white stripes and zigzags that made the ships look like modernist zebras afloat on the high seas. The patterns were intended to make it difficult to determine a ship's speed and direction of travel. The intention was not to conceal but to confuse – to make it impossible for the enemy to work out what was really going on.

This was sometimes what it could feel like to be in Inigo's orbit. Blinding displays of generosity at the moment you least expect it. At the time, I remember feeling a thrill at the prospect of the trip. A chance to relive the good old days. See some exhibitions, go bowling, even. Now I can see that I played a role for Inigo, not by any means at his behest, but entirely at my own instigation. I was a source of nostalgic reliability for Inigo, an on-tap wellspring of mutual history. It was a history which I thought mattered equally to us in the present as we had shared it in the past. But I was wrong: much as he enjoyed the occasional weekend regression with me, Inigo only looked forward.

Over the next few days we drank some beers; we went bowling. A serenity always came over Inigo whenever we went bowling. I always felt that for him it must have been a lingering remnant of his teenage years in suburban Connecticut, at odds with the sophisticated man about Mayfair he had become. As we rolled downtown in a cab, Inigo's usual frenetic energy faded. He put his phone in his coat pocket and let the cold from the open taxi window blast the jet lag from his eyes. Arriving at the alley in Chelsea Piers, he slipped inside while I smoked a cigarette overlooking the Hudson river. Despite the late hour in London, Hugo had called me twice while we were in the car and I had had to cancel the call. I thought Inigo might have seen Hugo's name flash up on the screen, but it wasn't until the second call came, two minutes after the first, that Inigo gave me a sideways look of wry amusement. As I smoked, I composed a text message to Hugo. 'With client now. Will send update in the morning. O.'

As we bowled Inigo's face seemed to soften at the mouth. He moved like liquid, with a camply self-aware grace, his right leg kicking up and back as he flung the ball hard and true along the boards. He paused after each release and watched the ball not only as it hit the pins but for a long time afterwards, as if somehow expecting a different result. Watching him bowl I remembered that Inigo is American. For all his expensively down-at-heel suede Euro loafers, his tailored Milanese suits and shirts and his international man of business mannerisms, his roots were in the New England suburbs. He got stoned in strip mall parking lots and crashed his friend's father's Lexus drunk on stolen beer. And he bowled – bowled whole youthful days away – till his fingers were raw.

Inigo can at times be surprisingly masculine, comfortable discussing the relative attributes of home improvement stores Lowe's versus Home Depot and can talk knowledgeably about power tools; he can read a team's baseball stats in the newspaper and just from that describe their most recent game, play by play; he can shotgun a beer like a frat house bro. He may have been an auction room maestro by his late twenties but the bowling alley was always his true arena. He could really sling it.

Between turns, Inigo flirted with two women bowling next to us and soon enough we were doing shots with them and bowling in pairs. I remember little more about them save that one was tall and brunette and the other short and blonde. Their eyes had the wet sheen of gemstones underwater and both wore perfume in such quantities that it amounted to something like an anaesthetic. Inigo had taken an enormous, three-bedroom suite at the Plaza, and soon the four of us were crammed into a town car heading north on Sixth.

The suite came with a night butler, and Inigo had phoned ahead on our way uptown to order room service. Soon after we'd arrived back from bowling, the doorbell rang. I walked to another wing of the suite to open the door.

'Good evening, sir. I have your champagne.' The man in front of me wore a purple waistcoat fastened with gold buttons, which gave him a festive look, like an embarrassing uncle at a Christmas party. His name badge said Elvis.

'Well, you'd better come in, Elvis.'

As he was opening the champagne, Inigo and the brunette appeared. 'Fantastic, just fantastic,' Inigo said to Elvis. 'Keep it coming,' and he handed him a twenty-dollar bill from his pocket. Inigo always seemed to have secreted cash about his person.

'Your burgers will be here shortly and I'm around all night if there's anything else you need.'

'So you can bring us anything we want?' asked Inigo.

'Yes, sir. Is there anything you need?'

'I don't know. Guys, is there anything we want?'

'Could we get a PB&J?' the brunette asked. 'We don't really eat meat.' Nervous giggling emerged from the blonde as she chewed gum incessantly.

By the time Elvis came back things had escalated. The brunette was on the phone to the White House trying to get through to Donald Trump. 'I just really need to talk to *my* president. I'm staying at the Plaza, and I think he needs to know THERE ISN'T NEARLY ENOUGH GOLD HERE ANYMORE! This is a gold emergency. Defcon fuckin' gold, baby! We want Trump back at the Plaza. Screw his Mexican wall, Fifth Avenue needs the Donald!' The wine had eroded my anxiety and for a brief moment I forgot about the Wool and Hugo and the invoice and the anonymous seller and the money and the gallery. I wondered what moment in my life had lead to this, what crucial and irrevocable turn in the road had brought me to prank-calling a president from a hotel he used to own. Inigo was red-faced and weeping with laughter, holding a half-eaten burger in one hand as he struggled to chew.

There are moments when I wonder if this brief, wild interlude really happened, if it might have been a Xanax-induced simulation. But I still have a cupboard full of tchotchkes – soaps, an embroidered Plaza Hotel laundry bag, a loofah – purloined from the room. Even then it felt like all that couldn't last.

For the rest of the trip, Inigo would flit around town all day in the back of blacked-out cars seeing clients, doing his thing. I saw a few exhibitions in between fielding Hugo's increasingly irate phone calls. All three nights we were there I would quiz Inigo about the Wool payment as lightly as I could, aware that the suite I was staying in was his, my business class return flight on his dime. Each time he dodged my questions like a boxer, parrying with a seemingly inexhaustible array of reasons and excuses. I knew he was lying, but I chose to believe him anyway. It was the course of least resistance, the coward's way through.

I woke up on the last morning to find the suite empty, his bed unslept in. A note scribbled on a piece of hotel notepaper informed me that he had hopped on a jet to Arkansas, gone, so he would later tell me, to see a member of the Walton family about a Basquiat. It was, for me at least, just this kind of thing that made his excuses so infinitely plausible.

In the art world, what is termed 'discretion' – but which others might call deliberate obfuscation or outright lies – is as essential to the everyday existence of the market as money. If all the turtles all the way down knew about each other, how would any of them make a buck? A circumvented art dealer is a broke art dealer.

But, as much as we were all lying to each other, we were also all engaged in a collective act of self-delusion: deliberately choosing not to question whether these things are *worth* these enormous sums of money, that the market can value them in advance of history's verdict. The money that has been injected into the contemporary market can only ever be seen as speculative at its core. Because, unlike tradable concrete assets like timber or grain, trading artworks is always trading futures in the hopes that fashion will dictate their continuing rise in value; necessity, that keystone of economic forces, does not apply. This makes the art market wildly unstable: vast sums of money change hands, often sealed by little more than a handshake, for assets that have no intrinsic value and whose quality has been decided by an international phalanx of tastemakers whose quixotic desires serve only their own ends. Woe betide the art market when the apocalypse arrives.

Certainly value – the value of the Wool – was the only thing that mattered to me as my plane landed back in England. As soon as I turned on my phone I saw deluge of messages, voicemails and missed calls. Almost all of them from Hugo. I checked with the bank: nothing in.

I sent Inigo a message straight away. 'Still no Wool funds, bro. Can you ask bank what's going on? O.' And then, as an afterthought, trying to seem relaxed: 'How are the Waltons? Say hi to John-Boy from me. X.'

Despite what I knew about Inigo's modus operandi – the infuriated clients, the late payments and the long, obdurate silences – I felt certain that Inigo wouldn't treat *me* like that. Surely this must all be some misunderstanding; over a decade of friendship would stop Inigo from screwing me around. And so, in the face of mounting evidence to the contrary, I convinced myself that Inigo was telling me the truth. I decided that, if it came to it, I would pay Hugo the deposit. I was betting it all on my friendship with a man who habitually lied to my face.

I went home and fell asleep fully clothed. What with the Xanax I was by then semi-reliant on, the booze and the jet lag, my body had no idea what time it was. Some hours later I woke up to my phone ringing in another room but I got to it just as the caller hung up. Missed call from Inigo. I rang back straight away but got his voicemail. Moments later, a text: 'Spoke to bank. They apologise, say they sent money but it bounced. Can you double check bank details and resend invoice and will pay first thing in the morning? I.'

This seemed plausible. It had never happened to me, sure, but then it wasn't like I was accustomed to receiving or sending regular international payments of half a million dollars. For all I knew, this was part of Inigo's daily grind, massive wads of cash bouncing around between accounts, sometimes too big or too ungainly to fit in.

I resent the invoice having checked the bank details. They were correct on the original, so I assumed it was human error somewhere in Switzerland. Secure in the knowledge that it was now under control – that things were most definitely happening – I went back to sleep.

The next day I did something foolish. I had slept in such a way as to make me feel like I'd been washed clean by mountain streams and I awoke with renewed hope. After a lengthy bath I donned my crispest shirt and my bluest jeans and made my way into town to see Hugo.

I found him sitting outside Franco's, a restaurant on the corner of Jermyn and St James's streets whose extreme loucheness is matched only by its exorbitant pricing. Hugo was on the phone, his AirPods firmly in place. I ordered an espresso and sat back, basking in the cool February sun and the warmth of the heat lamps above my head. Cigar smoke wafted from a nearby table.

'Everything's going to be just fine,' I told Hugo once he was off the phone. 'There was a problem at the bank and the money bounced back. They're resending it today so we should have you paid out by teatime.'

'You're sure? I don't know how much longer I can keep my client from pulling out. She's really spooked.'

'Hugo, you can tell her that if there are any further delays, we'll give her a 10 per cent deposit to secure the deal.'

'Oh, that's great. OK, fine. I'm due to talk to her in a few hours. I'm sure that will calm any frayed nerves.' Hugo ordered another bottle of sparkling water and then turned to me: 'So, what are we going to sell next? Have you got anyone for a large Henry Moore? It's in California, beside a tennis court, but I don't see why that should be an issue, do you?'

The next morning, before I'd had time to check the gallery bank account, I received a message from Inigo: 'Stuck Arkansas with shitty wi-fi. Payment scheduled yesterday but missed the international deadline so won't leave my account until today. Should credit yours after the weekend. My bank manager will call to explain. Sorry. I.' Inigo and his implacable I.

Inigo was rapidly becoming seen as one of the best secondary market dealers, not only of his generation, but in the world. He was, so he would tell me, regularly dealing with some of the biggest players in contemporary art, from household name galleries like Gagosian and Hauser & Wirth to the kind of rarefied secret money that is the stuff of most art dealers' dreams. He was ahead of trends, asking tomorrow's prices for today's paintings – and achieving them. His collectors kept coming back not simply because he seemed to have the most amazing access and to be able to help them acquire artworks that would improve the value of their collections and provoke the envy of their friends, but because when they came to sell – and they almost always did, through Inigo – their initial eye-watering outlay would be rewarded with a robust return. Inigo, everyone agreed, was the real deal.

Inigo's message sealed it for me. If I was going to save the deal, I would have to send a deposit. I remembered that Hugo had told me that he would be out riding in the morning, so I knew I had a few hours' grace until I would have to explain to him what was going on. If he were going to cancel the deal, I figured, why wouldn't he have done it already? It was Friday. If the money was with us on Monday, the $50k deposit was a quick sticking plaster on a minor wound, saving both the deal and my relationship with Hugo. I decided to pay the deposit. I wrote to Inigo: 'I have to pay client a 10% deposit to keep her from pulling out. Can you guarantee money on its way?' He replied just '💯'.

I sent Hugo a message telling him that he'd have the 10 per cent in his account by close of business, with the rest to follow on Monday. He replied only 'Thanks'. I transferred the funds and tried not to let my eyes linger on the remaining balance of the account. There was just about enough to last the business two months if I took no salary.

I never heard anything from Inigo's bank manager. All attempts to contact Inigo over the weekend were unanswered.

On the Monday I was going away on a trip I'd been talking about with my oldest friend, Jamie, since we were thirteen. If we still knew each other by the time we both turned thirty – in that then impossibly distant year, 2017 – we told ourselves that we would learn how to ride motorbikes and then go ride them in Vietnam. An early mid-life crisis for the both of us.

Jamie and I met at the airport early. I love airports. Once through bag-checking and the indignity of removing items of outerwear while others look on, I always feel a sense of calm come over me. A good airport offers that rare thing: the guilt-free indulgence of late capitalist mores in combination with day drinking.

I fully expected the deal would close while I was in the air and so, when Jamie and I opened a bottle of wine at around 9.30 a.m., I turned off my phone for the first time in months. Forty-five minutes before the flight we both took a half bar of Xanax, washing it down with the last of the second bottle. As we meandered to the gate we saw something of a commotion as passengers spoke to the flight attendant and then, over the public announcement system, came the news that the flight was delayed. As we would soon come to learn, the plane had hit a flock of birds coming in to land the night before and the engines needed to be inspected. The delay lasted nine hours and we were all bussed to the Radisson Heathrow, where Jamie and I promptly emptied our respective minibars and made for the pool. We then both passed out by the pool only to be shaken awake hours later by an airline representative, receiving a sardonic round of applause when we finally made it back on to the bus to the terminal.

Over the next two weeks, as Jamie and I rode through the verdant landscape of Vietnam, the money did not appear in my account. Throughout long days of riding, I could feel my phone vibrating in my pocket as Hugo called me again and again. I had no idea where in the world Inigo was, but my messages received no responses and my phone calls were rejected. I tried to come to terms with the very real prospect that if Inigo reneged, I would have no recourse. In the art world, deals like this are seldom legally binding but instead are sealed by what is risibly known as a gentleman's agreement. Everyone simply trusts that there is enough money to be made that everyone will work hard to push the thing through. When it works, it saves on contracts and lawyers' fees; when it doesn't . . . well, I was about to find out.

By the time Jamie and I reached Hội An – halfway down the Vietnamese peninsula – on 4 March, I had become jittery through lack of sleep. I no longer felt able to ride safely. In a last-ditch attempt to rouse Inigo and to conclude the deal one way or another, I sent him an emotional and desperate message: 'Come on, man, can you please just let me know what's going on? This has been going on for so long now and it's incredibly frustrating – not to mention hurtful as my closest friend – when you just ignore me. If there's an issue, can you just give me a call and tell me so we can figure out how to move forward?'

Several hours later came his reply: 'Frankly O, not ignoring you – it is auction week and this is one of a few open ended transactions which am juggling to complete on top of the normal deals that go into the running of my business.' The message continued in the same tone: 'Who has time to massage the nerves over and over again – what you get paid for is managing your client. Funds have been organized yesterday and the payment was sent towards end of day for credit Monday. You will have them Monday afternoon and then onto the client. If that isn't good enough for her she can keep the 50k and take a hike. See you soon.'

I flew home two days later on Monday 6 March. When Tuesday came and still there was no money, I took the tube across town to Bond Street and walked the short distance to Inigo's gallery on Davies Street. I rang the buzzer and pushed the door hard when I was let in, not caring that it hit the wall behind it as I walked through.

Several members of Inigo's staff were there – people I knew and liked. They seemed surprised to see me but were friendly in the face of my brusqueness. 'Where's Inigo?' I demanded.

'Upstairs in the office,' his assistant replied. I turned on my heel and made for the stairs, staring up at the CCTV, which I felt sure Inigo would be watching from the comfort of his Jean Prouvé desk two floors above me. At the stairs, my way was barred by Rob Newland, Inigo's consigliere.

'You can't come up,' Rob told me. 'Inigo's in a meeting.'

'I can wait.'

'You know he's not going to see you, Orlando. You need to calm down.'

'My gallery will have to close if he doesn't honour this deal, Rob. I don't understand why he's doing this.'

'Let me talk to him – is this still the Wool deal?'

'Yes. The invoice is a fucking month overdue. I've put up a deposit. I'm going to lose it all.' I slumped on the stairs at Rob's feet. 'Just please get him to pay it. I've got until Friday before my client pulls out with our deposit.'

'I'll do my best,' Rob said.

I shuttered the gallery for the next couple of days and tried to figure out ways of raising the money to keep the business running. I filled in reams of loan application forms for the bank only to find at the end that the business had not been trading long enough to qualify. By Friday afternoon, I was on the phone to Hugo for the fourth or fifth time that day. As we spoke, I was refreshing the bank's website again and again, madly expecting a different result. Suddenly, the screen seemed to have changed.

I looked closely, trying to figure out what was different. I hit refresh again. The money was in.

'Hugo, I'll have to call you back.' A cold hard 5 followed by five gaping os were right there in front of me, incontrovertible and galling. I refreshed the page: still there.

It was just before 3 p.m. I sent Hugo a screenshot of the balance, carefully blurring out the name of the depositor, with a message that read: 'Paying you now, Hugo. Please call your client.'

Inigo and I still hadn't spoken by the June of that year when I was going through the auction catalogues and I suddenly saw the Wool staring up at me from a page of the Phillips evening sale book. The sale was a few days away and the painting was on view at their Mayfair auction room.

When I got there it took me a little while to find it and I wandered around looking at the different lots, trying to imagine what convoluted deals had brought them to this point. I turned a corner and there it was, bathed in the early summer light streaming in from Berkeley Square, cheek by jowl with a Joe Bradley painting. I stood in front of it for a long while, reliving the mad journey that had resulted in its presence here. Standing in front of the Wool I registered it – the printed-upon Japanese paper and its over-layer of spray paint with its whirligig virtuosity – but nothing more. In that moment the painting was its price tag, as were all the works that surrounded it. I don't profess to know what art is, but it wasn't this – at least not any more. It might, however, be what it has become.

It wasn't long after all this that I began to think seriously about leaving the art world. I don't mean to imply that this ordeal was the main cause; at the time I don't think that would even have occurred to me. The success Inigo had achieved was phenomenal, a marker against which I could not help but hold myself. What the Wool deal made me realise, however, was that I didn't have what it took to make it in the same way as he had. And I didn't want to. Too often, I let my emotions get in the way. What I felt as betrayal and manipulation, Inigo saw merely as the cost of doing business, a weakness to exploit – a means to an end.

To this day Inigo and I have never properly discussed what actually happened in this deal. Whenever I tried to bring it up, I was met with deflection and obfuscation. It was made all the more confusing by how it ended, too. The auction estimate for the Wool was £150k–250k, far less than Inigo paid for it. It sold for £293,000, a loss of nearly £100,000.

From what I know now, however, this may well have been a symptom of the larger financial chaos that was gradually consuming Inigo's life, just one deal out of many where money was being moved from one pot to another with ever increasing strain. At the time I wondered whether the loss he made selling the Wool at Phillips might have been somehow intentional – a ruse to devalue some larger Wool work he was negotiating on, perhaps – but I suspect that was fantasy on my part. It was in all likelihood proof only of his fallibility, evidence that things were slipping out of his control. But, like everyone else around him, I saw what I wanted to see: a wunderkind, a shooting star, an artist of the deal.

9

There are a lot of gaps in my story. There are days I'd rather forget, some I can't; others have simply vanished like a magic trick. In February 2018 I began to lose control of my life. The abrupt ending of a new, intense romantic relationship – in retrospect, no more than a hopeless attempt to paper over the widening cracks in the rest of my life – as well as a worsening relationship with my dying father were enough to contend with. The final straw, however, was the sudden and precipitous terror I felt that what I had been doing on and off for over a decade was destroying me. What I had for years convinced myself what I should be doing – that which would make my father proud, would impress Inigo, would give me a sense of belonging and purpose – suddenly seemed the cause of my deep unhappiness, a life that had been revealed to be a lie.

I all but stopped going into the gallery. I was of no use there anyway. Instead, I spent long hours in the bath, mixing Xanax and tramadol with cheap whisky and beer. I woke one evening freezing in the bath. I had fallen asleep and the water had cooled around me. On the edge of the tub was a razor blade, so flat and grey I thought it might not be there at all. I reached for it, touched it, but couldn't do the next thing. I dropped it in the water and got out slowly and deliberately and crawled into bed wrapped in my wet towel and slept.

In the morning, I saw the razor blade still submerged in the bath water. I called the therapist I had recently begun to see, who asked my permission to call my emergency contact: my mother. We agreed I should go somewhere for a while, somewhere I wouldn't be able to hurt myself. All I had to do now was wait.

Later that day I felt ridiculous. I called my mother, tried to get her to call the whole thing off. She told me to pack a bag, told me what to pack. In the evening, I took a minicab across London to the hospital. I could see on the driver's GPS screen that the journey was nine miles. In my palm I had three squares of Xanax left. I knew that I wouldn't be allowed to bring them in with me. Every three miles, I took one of the squares, the method somehow as comforting as the impending oblivion the pills brought.

When we arrived at the hospital, I had to be helped from the back seat by the driver, a stony-faced man who lifted me under my arms with a stern tenderness. I felt my body as he must have, as a pathetic weight, something to be rid of. He deposited me in the hospital's reception area. Within an hour I had been shown to my room through a series of electronically locked doors to which I had no key. My door, however, did not lock. An emergency light made a distant whine above me.

The next few days were impossibly hard. Withdrawing from Xanax only increased my anxiety. I was still in the world, but no longer a part of it – a helpless spectator tended to by nurses and orderlies. Days passed and nothing seemed to change. At first I was allowed no visitors and I left my room only to smoke, always in the company of a short, plump young Filipino man whose job seemed to be to shadow patients on their cigarette breaks. A psychiatrist prescribed me Wellbutrin, which gave me vivid and violent nightmares. Despite the snow outside my window, I sweated profusely in my bed; one morning an orderly offered me an adult nappy. My situation felt glacial, terminal. I had nothing to give and wanted nothing in return.

On my fourth day there, I woke up famished. I'd hardly eaten since I'd arrived. In the canteen I piled my plate with eggs and bacon and tomatoes and toast. I sat down to eat in a corner near a gap in a partition behind which I saw half a dozen emaciated young women and girls. As they stared down at their plates a matronly woman stood over them, her reproachful glare watching their every movement. They were spectral, almost gone. One young woman – about twenty, I guessed, though it was difficult to tell – caught my eye and started to rock back and forth, to shake like someone fervently praying. Low screams came out of her as she inhaled. The matronly woman hurried over, her glare suddenly softened. She escorted her charge out through a side door.

I got up to sit at another table, scanning the room for a free seat as far away from that partition as possible. As I walked through the tables, I passed a grey-haired man I recognised from the smoking area, where he seemed to be a permanent fixture. 'You'll not sit there again in a hurry,' he said. I stopped at his table, unsure what I should say, unsure if he intended malice or kindness. He kicked a chair out and motioned for me to sit down. He introduced himself, using his full name.

'The painter?' I asked.

'That's me,' he said. The grisailled man in front of me was a very famous artist, practically a household name. 'This your first time here?' he asked me. I nodded. His question made me feel it wasn't his.

After breakfast we went out for a smoke. It was bitterly cold, but we must have spent an hour out there. He'd checked himself in, he told me, after a lonely Christmas binge of cocaine and Scotch had gone on for almost six weeks. His wife and children had left and his drug dealer had moved into his spare room. I told him about the gallery and my desire to quit. 'The art world's not what you think it is, trust me,' he warned. 'Get out while you still can.'

I spent much of the remainder of my time there in this man's company. Neither of us could face the mandated group therapy sessions and so instead we smoked and watched entire DVD boxsets of *Frasier*. On the day I left, I wrote down my phone number and told him to call me when he got out. We could see some art together, I suggested. I never heard from him, of course. We'd served our purpose for each other.

And then, barely two weeks after I'd left my flat, I was back. The pristine snow that had fallen while I'd been away now sat in grey, lumpy drifts everywhere. The flat was cold and empty. I think I'd expected to come home and feel different. That first night my mother came round and we ordered Chinese food and she watched me warily as I drank and ate little. She didn't want to leave, offering to stay on the sofa. As soon as she'd left, I wanted to call her, ask her to come back. I didn't want to be alone. I turned the radio on and went to bed.

Some days after I came home, I went to the opening of a show at the gallery. No one knew I had been unwell but I felt out of place among my friends and peers and left early. The gallery had been a place I felt not only at home, but took pleasure from. It was the only thing in my life I was proud of. Now all that had gone. No depression is unique but as an illness it is so isolating, so howlingly painful, that it is impossible to believe anyone has ever survived the same depths of feeling. I was untethered and alone.

In the coming weeks, I realised with a heavy certainty that I would have to quit the gallery. I was a deadweight and my heart hadn't been in it for months. It was a wrench, another wound among the many, but it was what I needed, even if to this day I think about the decision often, unsure what emotion it will bring. It may also have saved my life.

Inigo and I saw each other only very occasionally around this time. I heard grapevine whispers of his move to Miami, of the gallery he had set up there and the emboldened extravagance of his lifestyle. Once, he invited me to fly on a private jet to Ibiza with him and some friends to see the DJ Solomun play his last set of the season at Pacha. On another occasion, I joined him and his girlfriend and some of their friends for dinner at Min Jiang, a Chinese restaurant at the top of the Royal Garden Hotel in Kensington. The restaurant's windows offered panoramic views of London. Below us Kensington Gardens, one of the most expensive residential streets in the world, looked paltry and down at heel.

Inigo and I had never really had the kind of friendship where we knew the other's friends. He certainly showed little interest in meeting mine and I always had the feeling he was slightly embarrassed to introduce me to his jet-set pals. Probably with good reason: I loathed them on sight. I felt they had taken away my fascinating friend, inducted him into their moneyed clique.

As Inigo leapfrogged his way up the art world food chain, the people he surrounded himself with gradually but noticeably changed. At the beginning, he had mentors; next there were wonky auction house guys whose understanding of the market was all head and no heart; then there were the serious collector-collaborators, all with serious money, many of them esoterically Belgian; lastly there were the frivolous sons and daughters of the sinister rich, playing with their parents' cash after they'd figured out the really good parties weren't in the fashion world anymore. These people were bored-by-it-all rich, fuck-you-don't-talk-to-me rich. They spoke with barely varnished ignorance and displayed unconcealed contempt for people less wealthy than themselves – which was almost everyone. They spent their money like water precisely because it wasn't their money. And, Good Lord, were they dull.

That evening at Min Jiang, in the late summer of 2018, we were joined by a ragtag bunch of wealthy under-forties. There was a German aristocrat who looked as if she was made of icicles and a man who told a long story about his having punched a billionaire in a nightclub whom he had perceived as anti-Semitic. I don't remember anything else of the conversation that night but I do recall watching Inigo as he spoke to his guests. He laughed and gestured animatedly, looking for all the world just like one of them: a very rich young man for whom great wealth was as ordinary as air. I wondered if he was faking it, or if I had simply deluded myself about how well I knew him. Maybe there had always been multiple Inigos waiting to reveal themselves; certainly the Inigo at dinner that night was a pale imitation of the young man I had met twelve years previously. He had vanished into his bank balance.

But while life had been going badly for me, around this time things were also beginning to fall apart for Inigo. It would be easy to see his change in social circle as part and parcel of a trading-up, but to me it now seems like an act of desperation. Although I had taken his evasions and brinkmanship in the Wool deal personally, it was in fact part of a general pattern of behaviour that had now caught up with him. He had fallen foul of convention too many times in the London art world – as well as the worsening of his relationship with Jopling, Inigo was on the outs with a number of influential players on the London scene – and his finances were, as I now know, stretched to breaking point. He was going to greater and greater lengths to make things add up, doing things that were far beyond the realms of art dealing. Inigo had always worked at the edges of the acceptable in the art world – and those are some pretty distant boundaries – but until he was talking to me, years later, from the comfort of his desert island hideaway, I had no idea the lengths to which he had gone to stay afloat.

Much has been made of Inigo's crimes; they have been portrayed as the devious, cunning, manipulative actions of a cartoon villain. But there were things Inigo did that haven't been fully reported – deeds which havered on the line between unethical and plain old illegal. And some of these misdeeds seem to have led him into realms which are closer to conceptual art than art dealing: while trying to stay afloat, Inigo was unintentionally questioning notions of authenticity, authorship and value – even the very nature of art itself.

Inigo told me this story in May 2020, on the phone from Vanuatu. He started tentatively, as he did with many of the anecdotes he told me in those conversations, wanting to get his facts straight, his details in their proper order. But whether there was something in my voice which spurred him on as I murmured assent, or if he simply found his footing, his telling of what happened seemed suddenly to unspool from the reel of his memory, as if a great and powerful fish were pulling us both farther and deeper than we had ever meant to go.

In the dog days of summer 2018, in the shadowy cool of a locked garage in Mayfair, something glistened in the dusty half-light. Temporarily housed in this unprepossessing box was a treasure that simultaneously did and did not exist. For weeks now, the garage had been the scene of mysterious comings and goings by people who, instead of decamping to Mykonos and Ibiza with the rest of Mayfair's residents, were here, spending endless hours practising alchemy, attempting to resurrect the dead. The subject of this feverish industry was a vast expanse of gold, almost five metres square. Something that was 'destroyed' and yet still existed; something that was bought for chump change – $300,000 – and had already been sold for $1.75 million; something that the new owner had never seen.

The garage at the centre of this story is normally home to an ever-changing array of expensive classic sports cars: the street where it is located, Carlos Place, hugs one side of the Connaught hotel, sluicing out at its other end into Grosvenor Square. This summer, however, it was playing host to something potentially much more valuable: a painting by the Italian artist Rudolf Stingel. A great expanse of gold, it's one of the 'Plan B' series – think hushed AmEx tones rather than a shimmering Trumpian glare. The lower section displays a regular bas-relief pattern that appears to recede towards a vanishing point. The upper section, meanwhile, is a perfect golden sky, an uninterrupted plane of pristine purity. Or perhaps it once was. For a closer look reveals a cluster of dark stains in the centre spanning about one metre. Still closer, the attempts to remove the damage are evident, attempts that, according to a condition report from July 2016, resulted in 'a cloudy dark spot in the centre of the painting'. The damage was so considerable that the artist declared the painting 'destroyed', saying he didn't want any restoration work to be done on it. But a painting does not cease to exist just because an artist wants it to disappear. And nor can she or he decide what becomes of it once it has left their hands.

Works of art of this calibre – of this price point – are usually kept in climate-controlled warehouses, in freeports or countries with no income tax. So you might be wondering how this paint-ing, albeit damaged, came to be in a room designed to store cars.

In the summer of 2016, two years before the painting arrived in the Mayfair garage, Inigo received a phone call from a contact who said he thought he'd come across a good deal. This contact relayed to Inigo that he had a connection at an insurance company who would occasionally offer him written-off works of art that the company had 'bought in' as part of a settlement. One such artwork was the Stingel painting. For Inigo, who in that same year had told the Art Market Monitor podcast, Artelligence, that he was 'pretty centrally placed in the Stingel market [and that] on the secondary [market] side, it's pretty rare for paintings to transact without my having some sort of tangential involvement', this was a potentially brilliant opportunity.

The contact told Inigo that the damaged painting could be acquired for $300,000, around one tenth of its market value in pristine condition. So Inigo, who had a close working rela-tionship with Christian Schiedemann, the conservator with the most experience working on Stingel paintings, bought it right away and paid his contact a finder's fee of $150,000, which, as far as I can tell, is as far as his involvement went in Inigo's scheme. Inigo was confident that he could persuade Schiede-mann to work on the painting and thereby make good his investment.

Inigo still hadn't seen the painting for himself, but then again it's not unusual for dealers or collectors to buy high-value artworks sight unseen, facilitated by a global network of shippers, art techs, photographers and conservators. Viewings are often done on FaceTime or by trusted advisors. And in this instance, despite the poor condition of the painting, Inigo felt comfortable enough about his relationship with Schiedemann that, as he said to me, he could 'get him to do something that an insurance company couldn't'. It soon became apparent, however, that this wouldn't be the case.

Schiedemann had spoken to Stingel when the painting was first damaged. The artist considered the painting destroyed and had asked him not to work on it. Inigo told me that he had pleaded with Schiedemann, arguing that if the artwork in question were a Mark Rothko – Schiedemann is also a highly respected conservator of Rothko paintings – he would be willing to undertake the work. Schiedemann agreed, but said that with Rothko he wasn't able to ask the artist himself as he was dead, and so felt safe assuming that he would have wanted it restored. With the damaged Stingel, things were different. Stingel was alive and well and living in New York City.

Inigo had reached an impasse. He put the problem painting out of mind.

At this time, Inigo was running an art fund on behalf of the Israeli-Canadian billionaire Marc Steinberg, and pretty much had carte blanche over what the fund bought and sold. So, without mentioning the damage to Steinberg, Inigo sold the painting into the fund for $1.75 million, pocketing the difference. For a while, he thought nothing more of it; Inigo could be adept at ignoring his problems. He continued to make attempts to persuade Schiedemann to restore the painting, even visiting him in his studio to press his case in person, but the conservator stuck to his guns and so the painting remained in Inigo's storage, its fate uncertain.

Then, without warning or precedent, in the autumn of 2018, Steinberg informed Inigo that his business manager, who ran his family office, would be coming to do an audit of the artworks that the fund held. In addition to the damaged Stingel, catalogued as having been bought directly from the artist's studio, this visit presented a number of other problems. In the inventory there was, for instance, a Félix González-Torres piece, *Untitled (Welcome)*, which Inigo was meant to have bought for the fund but in the end hadn't. While the money had been transferred out of the fund the deal had fallen through and Inigo kept control of the money. With nothing to show Steinberg's business manager, Inigo improvised. The artwork comprises a stack of rubber welcome mats, so Inigo found a hardware shop in America that stocked the same mats that had been used to make the piece. Buying a hundred of them, he had them FedExed overnight to his gallery. As he unboxed them the next day the sweet, pear-drop smell of new rubber filled the gallery.

No amount of Diptyque room spray or frantic wafting of auction catalogues would fully banish the smell, but Steinberg's man walked around the gallery with a check list detachedly looking at and ticking off each artwork in turn, the way one might do a headcount of young children getting on to a bus. 'He had no idea what the fuck he was looking at,' Inigo told me. He kept the Stingel painting in its travel frame, behind opaque polythene, in a narrow storage space behind the gallery wall so that the man had to peer in. Inigo had propped another crate in the space which just obscured the stains on the upper part of the painting. Steinberg's man went away satisfied.

Emboldened, perhaps, Inigo started to think of ways he could avert future close calls. He told Steinberg that he had agreed to sell the painting to Andre Sakhai and simultaneously sent Steinberg 10 per cent of the money, promising the remainder within ninety days. Inigo of course hadn't sold the painting to Andre, but had in fact planned eventually to pay Steinberg out himself, taking back control of the damaged work. He sent the 10 per cent and thought about something else.

As time passed, however, Steinberg became increasingly agitated about payments to him. Inigo, fearing discovery of the painting's damage, decided instead to sell it for $2.5 million into a joint venture that he told me he ran and co-owned with Jay Jopling, though I only have Inigo's word for it. 'That gave me enough to cover the profit that I needed to pay Steinberg, take my profit, a good little deal,' he recounted from Vanuatu. By this point, the damaged Stingel had generated, via Inigo, almost $2.5 million in profit. Neither of the two parties whose funds had fuelled this profit had ever seen the painting in the flesh, nor were they aware that, not only was it damaged, it had also been disowned by its creator.

Moving the painting into the joint venture's ownership allowed Inigo to 'kick the can down the road a bit . . . At this point it's finally somewhere where I just don't mind leaving it. I just need to get it into a situation where it's in good enough condition that I can say I bought it in good faith.' Since no conservator would touch the painting, Inigo had to take matters into his own hands. He started to research Stingel's production methods and the materials he used to make the 'Plan B' series, eventually managing to track down the specific metallic enamel paint that the artist used for the gold layer. He spoke to people he knew in Stingel's studio, as well as conservators who had worked on the series in the past. The advice he got was encouraging: the new paint, if properly applied, would mask, 'at least in the short term', the areas where the water damage had oxidised the paint.

Although the damage was restricted to the upper portion of the painting, all of the areas of gold paint would need to be resprayed in order to produce consistent colour and coverage.

This meant that the exposed layers of white, primed canvas would have to be individually masked off. Using dental silicone – the gooey stuff a dentist puts in your mouth to take a mould, which turns remarkably hard remarkably quickly – with agonising precision, this process took three people three months working full time.

Were you to have walked past the garage in Mayfair that summer, there were two things you might have noticed. The first would have been a solvent-y smell of fumes that would likely have got you high had you sniffed them. The second was a noise like a recording of a far-off propellor plane, played loudly and close at hand. That was the sound of the fans blowing that smell through the windows at the top of the doors, out of the garage and into the deserted mews and your nostrils.

All the time the painting was in the garage, Inigo was, as he recounted to me, 'under massive pressure from Jay, who is aware that this is one of our bigger investments, and thinks that I've bought it from the Stingel studio for a collector . . . and thinks that it would be an amazing work to bring to an art fair because he shares my enthusiasm for the "Plan B" pictures. And I'm there waiting to see if it's even possible to fix this fucking thing because it's this time bomb that's either a goldmine or a blackhole.' According to Inigo, at this time Jopling was under the impression that the painting was stuck in New York, rather than in a garage less than a mile from White Cube.

Once the painting had been resprayed and the paint had dried (this took three weeks with the fans going) the process of removing the silicone began. 'This isn't like removing a strip of masking tape,' Inigo told me. 'This is going in with dental tools to hand pick these spots – I mean, microscopic spots – of silicone' off the painting. Working like archaeologists with the kind of tool that goes 'ping' against your teeth – the kind of probing tool Lawrence Olivier uses to torture Dustin Hoffman in *Marathon Man* – a crew of amateur restorers painstakingly removed the silicone from the painting. Inigo meanwhile was stalling Jopling, telling him one lie after another: the painting was stuck in customs; he had another client to offer the painting to; anything he could think of. Finally, after weeks of this and under almost tooth-cracking pressure, the painting was ready.

With relief in his voice, even years later and with thousands of miles between him and the painting, those events still had him in their grip, Inigo told me. 'I move it to my office, I call Jay, I say, "Hey, come see the painting." He comes to see the painting and I send in a conservator to make me a condition report and it comes back in pristine original condition. And so we've taken this artwork that was destined for the scrapheap and, having bought it for $450k, turned it into a painting which is now worth $2.5–3 million.'

From a commercial point of view, this was alchemy, or as close as you can come to it. But to you, this might seem like something else – at best sharp practice, at worst a fraud of a moral, if not a legal, kind. If you dig a little deeper, though, it raises some interesting questions about authenticity and ownership. The painting was damaged, but did the artist the right to declare it destroyed? He's a powerful figure in the art world, so it's understandable that the conservator wouldn't touch it. And should Inigo have hired a bunch of people without conservation degrees or letters after their names to restore the painting? If you buy a painting 'by' an artist, aren't you expecting it to have, at least in part, been painted by them – not some mysterious third parties wielding dental equipment and a spray can? But works are restored all the time, and if the end result is that another, highly reputable conservator gives the work a clean bill of health – and I've seen the condition report, it got an A+ – what are we to think? Isn't the whole letters-after-names thing just another example of gatekeeping?

Some fakes – those by the Dutch forger of Vermeer paintings, Han van Meegeren, for example – are now collected in their own right. As Inigo finished telling me about his Stingel restoration project, I wondered whether the painting might itself attain some level of celebrated notoriety one day. Surely it is no longer merely a Stingel, but now a Philbrick-Stingel, an unwitting painterly collaboration. Either way, that painting is still out there, still asking questions. That's something that will last. That feels to me like art.

10

Each day in the late morning, his back as straight and strong as the pencil he keeps tucked behind his ear, Piers Townshend rides one of his three over-sized cargo bicycles from his home in Stockwell, south London, to his studio in Vanguard Court, in the nearby neighbourhood Camberwell. Piers pedals with the contented rhythm of a man happy in his work, sometimes stopping to buy a loaf of bread or a tin of sardines or a block of cheese for his lunch. He is a man whose deep appreciation of the quotidian – of the gentle cadence and infrequent disturbances of his day-to-day existence – he has heightened to something approaching a philosophy. Once, he spotted me walking along this same stretch of road in the same direction as he was cycling and dismounted to walk me back a few hundred yards just to show me a small patch of violets that he had spotted growing at the base of an elephantine plane tree. He has never, to my knowledge, used an emoji.

The entrance to Vanguard Court is sandwiched between a former piano factory now converted into apartments and Southwark Register Office. As you make your way over uneven cobblestones, the modern world seems to drop away and a London of the 1950s unfurls before you like a film set. The noise from the busy main road behind you softens and then vanishes, the quiet only broken by the shrill dive-bombing of ring-necked parakeets as they criss-cross the sky above with their ai-kai-kai-kai call and their feathers the bright green of new leaves.

Originally the site of a manufacturer of omnibus chassis, Vanguard Court was, from the 1930s until the 1980s, the factory of a prominent manufacturer of lightweight suitcases. Today it is privately owned by a family, and the mews is now home to an array of artists, artisans and craftspeople. It is a sliver of yesteryear that I loved from the moment I first visited it.

Piers's studio is a room packed full like a midden. The painted wooden floor is pebbly with the rivets that once held machines. In a space in which you could just about fit a decent-sized car, there are countless tools, many esoteric and specific, some home-made or refashioned, others merely broken and redundant; three plan chests; a cast-iron nipping press; a plastic sink so large you could sleep in it with your legs outstretched; a suction table; and innumerable rolls and reams of different papers from the thickest felty blotters to the wispiest cigarette papers. Plant life forms a garland around the whole room, succulents and ferns and nasturtiums and geraniums clambering over each other wildly.

The walls, where there is space not taken up by tools and things-leaned, are adorned with a variety of artworks. There is a black and white photograph of the German artist Joseph Beuys and a coyote; a childhood drawing by Piers's son, now in his thirties; a small painting of an old woman by his late mother; and a small ironwood nineteenth-century Benin sculpture of a lioness with a cub in its jaw that sits atop a light box and seems to be protecting everything in the room – not only the precious things that take up temporary residence there but also Piers himself and the occasional acts of brinkmanship he must perform in order to save them.

Piers is tall – six foot one, at least – and has the strong, broad shoulders and wide, open chest of a man who has done manual labour and who, despite his years, is still very active. He has a full head of grey-white hair, which covers his ears. When you tell him something that pleases him – as I did when I told him that among the conservators at the National Archives he is known as the Indiana Jones of paper conservation – his head emerges from his neck like a giant tortoise waking up from a nap. His smile, when it really comes on, is better and brighter than any other I know.

How I first met Piers and how I came to work for him are two separate but linked events and he and I have different memories of them both. In 2017, we were preparing to move the gallery from the space in Clerkenwell to the new one in St James's. Even in the relatively short time we had been in business, we had amassed a great many artworks – some unsold by artists we represented or had shown and others I'd bought in order to sell on. The gallery's storage space at the back was small and chaotic and this was one of the many reasons for the move – and in the process of excavating it we opened a box of unframed drawings given to us by an artist we were representing. This man was by far the most difficult of the artists the gallery worked with over the years, as well as one of the most talented. I wore gloves to unwrap each one in turn. When I reached the bottom of the box and began to unwrap the last drawing, I saw something horribly wrong: the square of masking tape that was meant to hold the tissue paper enclosure together had instead become adhered to the artwork.

Carefully but stupidly, I tried to remove the tab of tape myself. Although the tape mercifully was stuck to the rear of the sheet, it came away with a thin layer of the paper beneath and the skinned patch (as I later learned to call such things) was clearly visible on the artwork side, registering as a dark shadow on the front and thereby ruining it.

This was a disaster. At the time we were stretched perilously thin; after a period of bad sales, we were paying rent on two galleries while we renovated one. In that same instant I could hear the artist's voice rebuking us – for my stupidity, for my carelessness. Regardless of the cost – the gallery would owe the artist 50 per cent of the piece's asking price – I knew that something like this could destroy an artist relationship that was already in a precarious state.

In a moment like this there was only one man to call: Simon Mitchell. For years one of the top technicians at White Cube, Simon had left to work with Inigo when he opened Modern Collections in 2011. Simon, who is originally from Yorkshire, came to London to pursue a career as an artist but, like so many who try to make a career showing their art in galleries, he ended up working behind the scenes to make ends meet. Despite his having spent over a decade living in London, his warm Northern burr is undiminished and when he picked up the phone to me that day I can remember the relief I felt. Within a few minutes, he had sent me an email introducing me to a paper conservator who happened to be out of town but who, in turn, gave me Piers's number.

When I called Piers, he took a while to pick up but answered eventually with a deep 'Hullo, hullo'. As I explained the problem he didn't say anything, but finally, when I'd ceased my hysterical wittering, he said, 'Well, you'd better bring it to see me.'

At the appointed time, I arrived at Vanguard Court and rang Piers's bell, to no response. I called him, with similar results. Ten minutes passed. Twenty. Just as I was preparing to leave, I heard a loud vehicle turn through the gates. The noise was fearsome, like a handful of gravel in a washing machine, and I watched as Piers, sitting bolt upright, rode in on a camouflage-green 1942 Harley-Davidson, Don Quixote-style on his furious mechanical donkey. I knew then and there that I wanted to be his friend.

Once I showed him the picture, he seemed tentatively confident that he could repair it and we left it with him. Over the next few weeks, I rather forgot about Piers and the damaged drawing and the angry artist as I struggled to wrap up one gallery and finish renovations on another, so that when he eventually did call me and launched straight into telling me what he'd done to the drawing, it took me a little while to place his voice.

'After I'd softened the edges of the skinned area with a cuttlefish bone to lessen the shadow,' he started by saying, and then, before I could interject, 'I tried first with the micro-cellulose powder. This didn't work well, though, because your paper contains optical brighteners and I couldn't match the colour. So I lined the sheet with an inter-layer of thin Japanese tissue and then with a similar paper to the original. Anyway, it's done now, you can come and collect it any time.' He paused and then added, 'Afternoons are best.'

I went back to collect the drawing a few days later and found Piers in the middle of a delicate operation with a pair of tweezers and some flakes of paint that had come away from a painting. 'Come in,' he said. 'I must just finish this, but the kettle is on. Do you like Lapsang? I'm afraid it's all we have.' And with that he replaced his magnifying goggles and bent over the painting with his tweezers in one hand and a fine paint-brush in the other. The 'we' made me expect an assistant who was temporarily out of the room, but no one came.

Though Piers suffers from arthritis and both his thumbs

are locked straight, I have seldom seen another person so dextrous or so gentle in their movements. Paper conservation, as I would come to learn, requires a deftness of hand that takes many patient years to acquire. Each of his movements is a masterclass in the physical expression of care.

It was late in the afternoon and the building around us was quiet, save for the birds outside and the kettle slowly heating up. I cleared a space on a chair underneath a billowing fern and watched Piers work, his mouth pursed into a silent whistle. I went about making the tea, feeling like an explorer as I gingerly reached through the fern and felt for the teapot. Piers finished what he was doing and turned to peer at me through his magnifying goggles. Quickly taking them off, he mopped his brow with a handkerchief that he produced from his pocket. Seeing that the tea was in the pot, he put his arm through the fern behind me and, without looking, produced two small bowls, one orange and one blue, both with gold rims, into which he poured the hot tea. Passing me one, he sat down and sighed, gazing out of the window. The branches of the trees in the nearby park, still in partial leaf, swayed against the setting sun like some Gothic tracery come mysteriously to life. The room filled with the smell of the smoky Lapsang and the ambient rumble of the modern world seemed impossibly distant. Neither of us said a word.

I have read that it was when working as secretary to James Joyce that Samuel Beckett began truly to understand the importance of silence in dialogue; Joyce, reportedly, could sit for hours in the company of another and say nothing at all. Beginning with that quiet interlude in the early autumn of 2017, I learned that sometimes having nothing to say – whether it be for one minute or ten – generally means that I should say nothing.

This was at first an alien concept; I'd spent years talking to sell art, to persuade and cajole, to flirt and demand and lie. I was well-practised in the much-derided language of 'artspeak' that has come to define so much of what is loathed and misunderstood about the contemporary art world.

Beginning on that first day when I went to pick up the drawing at Piers's studio, I have since spent countless hours in contented non-conversation with him. Six months or so after that first visit, when I was in the midst of the series of events that I would later come to recognise as 'my breakdown', I apparently sent Piers a couple of emails, though I have no recollection of these nor indeed do I have access to that email address any longer. Piers can't find them either. In them, he tells me, I asked, 'on behalf of a friend', for advice about how to get into conservation.

At that time I still loved art and wanted to stay in contact with it in the intimate way which had come to be the only remnant of being a dealer that I liked. My next question was to ask myself: well, what are you realistically qualified to do? Apart from working as a photographer's assistant and a stint in book publishing, I had been an art dealer my whole professional life. In one respect, I was enjoying the possibility that the moment held – I could live abroad, perhaps, or study again; in another, I was immobilised by fear that what I'd done in walking away from the gallery – from all that had been built, of which I became proud only when it was too late – would be a regret that would haunt me for the rest of my life.

And then there was the final, niggling worry: look at your hands, you moron, you're covered in tattoos, spidery blackness all over your skin like a trap. When you run your own business you can look how you like, but when you're asking someone to employ you, it's a very different matter, and I was convinced that this would be the final nail in the coffin of my undoing.

Back then, I still occasionally showed up at the gallery when there were things I needed to go through in order to perform the task of dividing up the flotsam of the previous four years. What I remember most keenly was a sense of heat at the back of my head and neck. Every so often, I would go for a walk, ostensibly to clear my head, but in truth these were farewell tours. On one of these, I went into Christie's and, as I walked through the viewing rooms, my ability to staunch the tears fell away. I pushed past a frightened security guard trying to find my way out and got lost in a building I had known since childhood. As my composure crumpled I could see the busy main lobby at the end of the corridor, replete with dealers and collectors.

There were three doors in the corridor. The first was locked. I tried another, opening the door in the expectation of resistance and instead flung it into the wall of the room. Inside the small beige room were two men in their late sixties and an old woman who looked as if she were dressed for mass. On the table between them were two boudoir-appropriate nineteenth-century bronzes – Alfred Gilberts, possibly – fey, gym-sculpted young men with a look of let's-get-this-over-with written across their placid faces.

Three sets of eyes stared at me in disbelief. Before I could say anything, the man closer to me simply stood up and in one fluid motion, staring straight past me, closed the door. As he did so, I heard him say, 'I do apologise, Lady —. I don't know what the world's coming to. I knew his father many moons ago. Tricky man.'

I was rescued by Alice, a friend who worked at Christie's, who must have been alerted to my presence. Alice and I had become friendly since I'd started working for Inigo and we occasionally had boozy dinners together to swap art world stories. She guided me down a series of unseen corridors and through doors that beeped when she opened them with her key card until we found ourselves in a storage area.

Porters and art handlers passed me with a curious look and when Alice left to make cups of tea, I found myself reaching for one of the many grey moving blankets scattered around. These rough felty expanses were a fixture of my childhood, since they were always present in the boot of my father's car, presumably in case he should spot some priceless sleeper in a Devon junk shop, which never happened. For a long time I associated their peculiar musty smell with our holidays.

When Alice returned, she found me bundled in one of these blankets breathing it in, lost in memory. As we talked and drank our tea, I watched as the art handlers in their claret red aprons moved artworks with the reverence of priests carrying icons. I could feel the panic draining out of me, for now. I resolved then that whatever I did next should involve this enviable unseen proximity. I may have been done with the art market, but my real relationship with art was only just beginning.

I rang Piers a few weeks after I got out of hospital in the spring of 2018 and asked if I might come round to see him. This time when I arrived, Piers had a client with him – a cheerful man who had the look of a bawdy glutton from a Gillray cartoon. He held a small portfolio of Indian miniatures which Piers, with the delicacy of someone handling the unhatched egg of a rare bird, was transferring one by one on to a light box. Thereon, the paintings themselves seemed to recede and disappear and a dense cartography of paper fibres came to the fore – islands and gullies and crevices and gentle accretions of material that looked to me like the satellite imagery of another planet, my first glimpse of a new world.

As we looked at each of these former rectangles on the light box, their edges nibbled by insects and time, I began to see that paper is less of a two-dimensional flatness and instead a portal masquerading as surface. Piers pointed to where the paper fibres – in this case probably some mashed-up kind of reed – had knitted together in an orderly matrix, and other spots where the tendrils overlapped each other like takeaway noodles dropped on a damp street. He showed me where some of these works had been repaired before, their scars cleverly concealed by delicate infilling and dirt which had been invisible before Piers lit them from beneath; and he showed me where certain insects had eaten away at the paint because its binder contains something sweet like xanthan gum. You can differentiate between various paper-eating insects by their bites, he told me; some are round and shallow while others are sharp and deep.

In time we looked at all of them and Piers stroked his chin as he tried to concoct an estimate. 'I'll have to see how I get on with one or two before I know,' he said to the man. 'Leave them with me and I'll have a play.' The man departed and Piers filed the artworks away in the white plan chest that towered over us both in the corner of the studio. I sat down and he made the tea this time while I wondered how to phrase what I had come to ask. In the end it just spilled out of me, the sort of sentence a nervous sixteen-year-old asks: 'Could I . . .' I faltered '. . . possibly come and do some work experience with you here?'

Piers definitely heard me. He was looking straight at me when I asked him and it's not a big room. But he didn't answer straight away. He didn't answer for what felt like five minutes. He made the tea and sat down. 'I suppose that might be possible,' he said. 'I've never had someone here.' His voice was deep and I could tell that this was an actual decision he was having to make about something he hadn't quite anticipated. 'I've had people over the years, of course, but that was before I was in this room. But yes, why don't you come for a week and we'll see.'

I can't sit here and tell you I thought conservation was my calling. As Piers has said to me on a number of occasions, 'Conservation is nobody's first choice, but it is often their last.'

Conservation is a profession that calls on a wide array of skills and knowledge pools. Art history is a happy bonus; chemistry is a must, as is a familiarity with pigments, solvents, adhesives and hand tools. For obvious reasons, you must not be colour blind and you must enjoy – or be able to tolerate – repetitive tasks and long hours in exchange for often imperceptible results and remuneration.

Piers's own route was circuitous, including stints as a bricklayer and taking a degree in the unusual joint honours of Zoology and Psychology, but he eventually found his way to the Paper Conservation Diploma at what was then Newcastle Polytechnic (now Northumbria University), and from there to the North West Museum and Art Gallery, operating out of a funereal Victorian villa with a large garden in Blackburn, and finally to the Tate Gallery in London. He spent the next thirty-three years there, the bulk of them as head of paper conservation.

When Piers joined, the British Museum had just transferred its enormous holdings of J. M. W. Turner works to the Tate and, for the next decade or so, Piers was almost exclusively engaged in the conservation of Turner's works on paper – some expansive, employing his usual swathy chromatic licence; others bare-boned like kindling – as well as his many sketchbooks. If you have seen a Turner on paper at the Tate, you have likely seen Piers and his team's handiwork.

During this time Piers supplemented his Tate salary – also, as he might put it, to vary his diet – by taking on extra-curricular work from dealers and collectors. Working in his attic or, when possible at weekends, in the conservation studios at the Tate, he took on a wide array of jobs, from the Leonardo drawing that had rust stains where the artist had pinned it to a board while working on it, to the naive marine scenes of Alfred Wallis. Then, around 2011, with retirement looming, Piers started renting the studio at Vanguard Court and he left the Tate for good in 2013. In a highly uncharacteristic move, the Tate's director, Sir Nicholas Serota, spoke – glowingly – at his leaving party.

When I came for my first day of work experience, in late May 2018, Piers didn't have a lot on. It was a warm day and he was wearing a tee-shirt whose neck looked as if it had been pulled at repeatedly by a small child. His customary boots had been replaced by leather flip-flops and his hair was on the feral side of leonine. 'I've got a few prints that we' – 'we' already! – 'need to put in the bath, but I'm running low on blotting paper so I thought I might pedal over to see old John Purcell. Paper merchant. He's just in Brixton and it's such a nice day . . . Did you cycle here?' he asked hopefully. I had.

There is an ageless quality to Piers when you see him ride a bicycle. The way he pedals denotes a certainty of purpose rather than any sense of hurry. Today the bell on his handlebar was slightly loose and announced his passing to the whole yard. Charlie the sheepdog ran in his wake.

We rode the short distance to Brixton and arrived at an unprepossessing single-storey building with peeling white paint on the brickwork. People in high-vis jackets greeted Piers in the yard as we locked up our bicycles. Inside, the warehouse was cool and dark. Seemingly endless shelves rose twenty feet towards the roof and reams of paper hung out like great white tongues. The floor was thick with a dust that deadened our footsteps. 'I'll go and look for our blotters,' Piers told me. 'Have a wander around. And don't forget to touch!'

As I walked up and down the aisles of the warehouse I saw paper from Germany and Korea, Italy and Japan; grey paper, the colour of a bad mood, and creams and whites and pinks like stamped-on petals. As instructed, I touched as many as I could reach; at one point I climbed on a lower shelf to reach a speckled green sheet and lost my footing, pulling the paper down with me. Its grainy flecks – known as inclusions – were woody, seemingly distinct from the sheet but inextricably part of it. When it fell to the floor, the sheet had the look of a bird's-eye view of a rainforest.

In touching these papers, I realised that the gesture felt oddly taboo. I was so used to handling anything within an art context with extreme caution, as if at any moment I might mar or break it. Coming into contact with these pieces of paper – lumpy, sandy, glassy, rough – started the process of making art something for me again, of pulling it back from a commercial realm to one where these objects existed within a more stable, more tactile reality.

Back at Vanguard Court, Piers spent a good ten minutes or so communing with his plan chest, opening one drawer after another, and taking out prints and drawings and watercolours for brief inspection. Eventually, he found what he was looking for and laid it down on the table between us. The reality was disappointing: a rat-brown sheet depicting a fox-hunting scene. It looked like the kind of thing you'd hang on the wall of a pub.

'What can you tell me about this?' he asked.

'Hm,' I said. 'Can I touch it?'

'You certainly should.'

'Shouldn't I put on gloves or something?'

'But then you wouldn't be able to *feel* anything. Go on now, just pick it up.'

The paper was stiff in my fingers, like a ginger snap, and felt as if the slightest bend would break it. Around the margins, the sheet was freckled with holes and brown flakes fell on to the white tabletop as I held it. 'Don't worry about those. We'll put them back later,' Piers said, gathering them up into an envelope from which he had deftly removed the sticky lip with a scalpel.

'It's a mezzotint,' I said hesitantly, 'and it's [reader, I assure you I didn't intend the pun] "foxed"?'

'Foxing' is a generic term for the marmalade-coloured spots that can appear on old paper for a variety of reasons, from mould to iron inclusions in the paper resulting from its being rolled out by metallic cylinders in the mill. On this mezzotint, the foxing likely resulted from ferrous particles left over from the printing process, which then rusted in humid conditions. The paper itself had acidified and embrittled as the cellulose was exposed to sunlight and air.

'First we need to do a surface clean,' Piers said as he donned an apron and came at me with a cheese grater. He looked more as if he were about to prepare a soufflé than restore a print. I stepped back. Piers took a rubber eraser from his pocket (Piers's pockets were a perpetual *Wunderkammer* of boyhood treasures: always a wood-handled Opinel penknife and a whittled-down pencil and his spectacles and a handkerchief; often a pebble or the stone from some fruit or other; and once, a whole Camembert that he claimed to have entirely forgotten about). He used the shredding side of the grater to grate a good amount of the eraser on to the print and then, using his hand flat and stiff, he gently rubbed the print with the eraser bits. The bits darkened, but not much. The print looked no different.

'This isn't doing much. Time to give it a bath.' Piers filled a small plastic tray – the sort of thing you find in darkrooms filled with chemicals – and boiled a kettle since there was no hot tap in the studio. When he had added enough from the kettle for the tray's water to be the temperature of what he deemed to be that of a baby's bath, Piers added a good glug of magnesium bicarbonate, which he said would help to deacidify the paper, halting or at least slowing its enbiscuitment.

Using a pump-action Japanese bonsai sprayer filled with deionised water, he lightly sprayed first the back and then the front of the artwork. I watched on in horror as the paper convulsed and curled up like a sea creature reacting to the tentative touch of a predator.

'Can you see,' Piers asked me, 'where those dark lily-pad patches are forming and the paper is soaking up the water more thirstily? That's where the paper's sizing – the stuff they put in paper to make it strong and a bit less absorbent – has been eaten away by mould spores. It's generally made from rosin, pine resin.' As he was speaking, my eyes were fixed on the print as it writhed uncomfortably and eventually lay flat. After thirty seconds or so, he tested the paper for 'floppiness'; it bent like a lettuce that had been too long in the fridge. Satisfied, Piers laid a sheet of Reemay – a polyester mesh material designed to be a supportive underlay for wet paper – on the surface of the bath. I watched as it seemed to hover on the surface tension of the water, then darkened intermittently and sank like a discarded sock.

And then I did something I never imagined I would do, let alone witness, something that felt a bit like a baptism for both me and it: on Piers's instruction, I deliberately submerged an artwork in water. Piers handed me the dampened print and I held it tightly between between my thumbs and forefingers. I carefully flung it out in front of me, allowing the air to float the paper gently down on to the surface. There, for the briefest of moments, it rested on the meniscus of the water and I stared at it neither sinking or swimming, simply poised between one thing and another.

Piers moved in quickly to push the whole sheet under the water. His actions were a little rushed but, as he explained, 'You want to submerge the whole sheet as fast as possible. If you don't, and there's stuff which is going to come out in the wash, you'll get a tide line on the page which can be murder to get rid of. It's what the wonks call a "wet-dry interface".' He sighed. 'I'm afraid it's been the subject of a few too many PhDs.'

Over the next twenty or so minutes, while Piers went back to rootling through his plan chest, I stood over the bathing print as it stewed in the cooling water, gradually turning it a fecal brown. When it was time to remove it, Piers instructed me to lift the Reemay sheet out first. 'Our print will be fragile now, so we need to give it some support. Hook your fingers under the Reemay and pull it up slowly. Wait just a mo' while I get you a bit of blotter.'

He laid a piece of blotting paper next to the tray and gave me the nod. 'Time to hoik him out.' Inanimate objects were often 'him' or 'her' to Piers, an affectation I found twee to begin with, but which I am unashamed to say I have now adopted by osmosis. It is, somehow, part of a wider Piers ethos: if one thing matters, everything matters.

Holding on to the Reemay only, I slowly pulled it out of the water and the print clung flat to it. As I did so, swirls of dark brown came out of the water, the whole lot the colour of weak tea. When it was at rest on the blotter, Piers leant it at an angle to avoid water pooling on its surface. 'This is the time when we need to be most careful,' he told me. As I was about to pour away the water in the tray, Piers stopped me and inspected it. 'Hmm,' he said, 'it's not quite brown enough. Sometimes when we wash something that's really brown, you can boil down the water afterwards, reduce it right down, to make what I call paper extract. You get a sticky, shiny goo. Here,' he said, rummaging in a drawer. He handed me an old 35 millimetre film canister. I peered inside and could just about make out a dark snot substance, like pitch. It smelled like the distillation of every old book in the world.

'What do you use it for?' I asked.

'It's useful for toning in paper when you're making repairs. Filling in gaps. It can help the new paper look old. But we'll get to all that tomorrow. It's home time now, I think. I'm cooking sausages tonight.'

The next day my father died. My brother rang me at just after nine in the morning. It was a sunny day and the strong light coming through the windows meant that I couldn't see the name on the screen of my phone. As soon as I heard his voice, I knew what must have happened.

Dad had been ill since the previous summer. An infection that started in his kidneys spread to his lungs and soon he was in a cottage hospital in Warwick, on a ward where countless grey men lay dying. Amid the smell of disinfectant and un-emptied bedpans there was a whiff of Soviet Russia about the place. I felt glad that my father was unconscious. I wished I were, too.

Soon, though, he was moved by ambulance to a hospital in Coventry, a space-age place with long white corridors and gummy linoleum floors. There was a Marks & Spencer in the lobby and a helipad on the roof. On my first visit he was barely conscious in intensive care, pumped full of fluids and squishy like a waterbed, delirious, grinning and pink. His eyes were a forceful denim blue. I can't remember having noticed that before.

The next time I came he was on a normal ward and more aware of his surroundings. I fed him red jelly with a plastic spoon and his mouth made a smacking noise as his tongue pushed it to the back of his throat. He couldn't speak much and I didn't know what to say, so I read to him an article from the *Antiques Trade Gazette* about a Ming vase that was coming up for auction at a saleroom in Yorkshire. I'm not sure he was aware, let alone interested.

By the time he was ready to be discharged, his already weak muscles had atrophied to almost nothing. His Tony Soprano bulk had disappeared, and with it his ability to embrace me, to hold me close like he used to and slap me on the back in that way that said 'This a hug is between men', at the same time calling an end to it before things got out of hand and emotions were demonstrated.

His house was ill-equipped for his recuperation and so he was moved into a home in a town three miles away, a place with swampy air and rubber-coated mattresses. The walls were the colour of prosthetic skin and a man two rooms down the hallway shrieked unacknowledged, night and day, like a car alarm. When I asked an orderly about it, she said, 'Yeah, he does that. He's losing his mind.' After six weeks, on a cold Sunday morning in October, Dad came home in a minicab whose rear seats could be removed and a ramp produced so that his wheelchair could be strapped in place. He looked stiff, almost stately as he arrived. Held under his arms by the driver and me, and gripping a walking frame, he insisted on walking the short distance from the car to the house. His collar gaped at his neck and halfway up the path my stepmother had to pull up his trousers to prevent them from falling down.

In the kitchen, as my stepmother paid the driver, I grappled my father into a chair and gave him a cup of coffee. He looked at the tattoos on my hands. 'You're becoming so lower class,' he said. After that we didn't speak for months.

In the New Year, with his improvement static, all four of my father's children gathered at his house to discuss the situation with him and his wife. There was no one thing wrong with him, no specific malady to point to and treat. We asked his wife what she wanted to do. She said she was fed up, she just wanted to go back to France, to live out her days in the seaside town of Saint-Jean-de-Luz. After a life in which he had left two wives – two families – my father was suddenly faced with the prospect that this one might leave him.

That was the last time I saw him alive. He woke up one morning at the end of May and listened to the eight o'clock news. Then he fell asleep again and never woke up. When I arrived at his house at lunchtime with my brother and sister, my stepmother was there with my other sister, who lives nearby. The door to the room where he'd died was closed and I could hear his bedside radio still on. We sat on the small, shady terrace outside the kitchen not saying much, eating Bombay mix and drinking warm white wine. There were crows on the lawn pecking out moss for their nests and a huge copper beech in a neighbouring garden shuddered in the wind.

My stepmother asked me if I wanted to see the body. 'The body' – so quickly no longer my father. The Austrian novelist Thomas Bernhard called it 'this terrible *was*', and now I knew exactly what he meant. The curtains were drawn but the sun had found its way through somehow and a beam slanted down just above his face. I saw dust motes hovering in the light above his mouth, ajar, and for a brief moment I thought I saw them moving in sync with his breath. There's been a terrible mistake, I felt like shouting, calling to the others to come quick. But the skin on his face told a different story, slumped down heavily over his bones like uncooked pastry. His eyes were open, gawping and drying out, his hair smoothed back from his forehead. Above the fireplace and on every available surface in the room, pots and bowls and small sculptures in bronze and porcelain and wood sat shiva, gazing at him mournfully, their lifeless, tearless eyes downcast at the passing of their careful keeper.

My siblings had encouraged me to embrace him, to touch him for one last time. I tried talking to him at first, tried to say goodbye, but nothing came. I touched his face, which I was surprised to find wasn't cold, as corpses always are in novels, but rather tepid and slightly clammy, like clay. My father simply wasn't there anymore and he never would be again.

At the time, and for a long while after, I felt nothing. And so, the day after my father died, I went back to work with Piers. He made no mention of what had happened, didn't ask me how I was – which was a relief because I wouldn't have known how to respond. We drank the burnt coffee that Piers makes in a Bialetti Moka on a laboratory hotplate and stared out of the window for a while. Piers had never known his father, a pilot who died four months before he was born, in May 1948, when he was flying JFK's sister, Kathleen Cavendish, to the south of France.

Death, or its aftermath, is often a shared experience, but not this one. I wonder now if I put him in an awkward position:

a young man he hardly knew, whose dead father hadn't yet been measured for his coffin, just kept turning up, asking to be given something, anything, to do. That day he directed me to a lithograph of a garden with topiaried yew trees and closely cropped lawns and a dark blue evening sky.

'Do you see those little dark flecks all over the surface?' he asked me, passing me his magnifying goggles. Small shiny marks like chubby black hyphens peppered the whole of the print. 'They're, well, um . . . They're fly vomit. Po-faced people will call it frass but let's not beat about the bush.

'We need to get rid of them before we give him a bath. If we don't, they'll stain the paper when we get them wet.' Briefly raising his goggles and giving me the look of a man about to go on an adventure, Piers pulled a scalpel from his red, crushed velvet tool roll, then lowered his goggles again and bent over the lithograph with his scalpel in hand. The blade was tiny and with a gentle curve like the bottom half of an S.

Some of the tiny black marks popped off cleanly, others pulled away minute patches of pigment, exposing the paper beneath. 'We can touch those in later,' Piers said without looking up. 'The important thing when you're doing this kind of work is not to dig too deep. Think of it like picking at a scab – be careful not to make it bleed. Anyway, I'm stealing all your fun. Here, you have a go.'

I perched on the stool – a stool Piers had fashioned from the engine block of a London taxi he used to drive – and picked up the scalpel.

With Piers watching me closely, I zeroed in on my first victim. It came away, but left behind a blinking white patch of the paper underneath. My heart sank. 'Not to worry,' said Piers, 'but try, if you can, not to use the point of the scalpel. Use the bit just where the flat edge at the end starts to curve around.

That way you're less likely to dig yourself a hole or – Heaven forfend – shoot through the paper.' I repositioned the knife in my hand and tried again. This time the frass leapt away at the lightest touch. 'That's the ticket,' he said. I didn't look up, but I could hear his smile.

After that Piers busied himself again looking for something or other among the rubble of paints, pencils, knives, brushes and implements for poking, scraping, slicing and lifting that fill the drawers and cover many of the surfaces in the studio. His is a process that demands rumination – 'chin stroking', he calls it – and no decision is ever rushed or taken lightly. Whether Piers developed this unconsciously as a conservator or because of it no longer matters; it is precisely how one should be for this kind of work. Knives must always be sharp, measurements taken at least twice, and decisions weighed until something as near as possible to absolute certainty is arrived at. It is a manner of being that is antithetical to the modern world. It is a methodology inspired in equal parts by chastening fear and long experience. Its endeavour is the preservation of beauty.

For the rest of that day my mind was empty and quiet. Piers picked things up and put them down, found something he wasn't looking for and moved it somewhere else. It was the most peaceful I had felt in years.

That evening, I had a drink with Inigo. It had been a warm late spring day and we sat outside a restaurant on a busy square near my therapist's office. Plane trees were bursting into life against the reddening sky and black cabs scurried past us like beetles. As usual, Inigo had been travelling, flitting between Europe and the US, even Russia, he told me with what seemed like deliberate mystery. The last time I'd seen him had been the previous December and I was happy to be in his company again. It was easy, even comforting, to slip into the roles we played for each other; the Orlando I was that evening was a young man whose father hadn't died. We drank a bottle of wine and ordered another. Inigo and my father had liked each other and for a while it felt good to talk about him as if he were still at home among his things, listening to his music, reading in his chair, those things that weren't his any more.

Inigo didn't know I'd left the gallery, but expressed no surprise. Perhaps he knew all along I wasn't cut out for it. I told him that I was planning to become a conservator. His eyes brightened. 'Ah, good. I could do with someone to write me some favourable condition reports,' he said.

We held a small funeral at a crematorium in the Oxfordshire town of Banbury, a town that always smells of burning coffee because of the Jacobs Douwe Egberts factory there. The crematorium itself suggested a motorway service station, more car park tarmac and ailing saplings than anything else. In a hall which felt as if it might play host to line-dancing nights, an officiant none of us knew spoke about our father as if they'd been old friends. I watched two fat wood pigeons perform their aggressive mating ritual on the grass outside the window as my nine-year-old nephew, his glasses steamed up with tears, read a passage from *The Selfish Giant* by Oscar Wilde. As we left, Siegfried's Funeral March from Wagner's *Götterdämmerung* played on the speakers.

Piers was in Greece for much of the summer and, having noted his return date in my diary, I got in touch with him after what I felt was an appropriate time. He was back in his studio already, watering his beloved jungle. 'Here,' was his one-word reply to my lengthy message. I cycled over.

As the days started to cool, Piers and I fell into a rhythm.

Around eleven each morning, Piers would let me know he'd arrived in the studio and I would pedal the short distance from my flat. Mornings were definitely a time for limbering up, inspecting artworks which had been left to dry overnight or which were recovering from some chemical treatment or other on one of the two gauze screens where these things rest mid-process. The afternoons were when things got serious. The afternoons were when the tools came out. It has, on occasion, occurred to me that some conservators got into conservation *because* of the tools. I would be lying if I told you this was not part of my motivation.

The most common things people bring us are not of great value; works of art on paper are, generally speaking, less expensive than, for example, works on canvas – what are known in the trade as 'easel paintings' in order to distinguish them from wall paintings, which are obviously a whole different ball game. This is, both for the market and the conservator, where the (relatively) big bucks lie and, as such, Piers spent a lot of time trying to discourage me from getting into paper conservation, often forwarding me job advertisements and pointing out the limbo-low salaries on offer which stood in stark contrast to the lofty qualifications and experience required to apply. It is a central irony of the art world that the care of the objects so highly valued by their owners are entrusted to people they are willing to pay so badly.

But I was in a privileged position, not just because of my upbringing, education and relative financial security, but because I knew that money not only didn't make me happy, but that its nature can be corrosive, that it can cause an insidious craquelure to appear over the surface of everything it touches. Paper is an everyday thing, owned by everyone. An early Picasso drawing worth hundreds of thousands of dollars can be as important to its owner as the scribbled drawing of a child who has died. I wanted somehow not only to be in touch with art that mattered to the culture, but art that mattered to people. In working with paper, I realised this was possible.

It is not unlike a parent bringing their sickly child to the doctor. With ailing artwork in tow, they arrive, nervous, cowed. 'Please can you help?' they ask as they hand over their precious parcel. They look around the studio, at the clutter that somehow maintains a balletic dance between manageable chaos and hoarding-in-need-of-intervention; at Piers and his Beethovian hair; at me with my just-out-of-jail tattoos and generally feck-less air; and they wonder: can this be the place?

Most often the reason for our clients' visits result from one of three things: light, water or framing. The picture arrives and is stared at. It is removed from its frame and, once the whole thing is disassembled, Piers will hem and haw, turning the artwork over in his hands as he turns over options in his mind, occasionally asking me starter-for-ten questions to see if I'm paying attention. And then, The Book comes out, a great green ledger with a stapled-in pink ribbon that was once tied around some chocolates acting as place holder. Into The Book, owner, dimensions, medium and a brief treatment plan are noted, as well as an estimated cost for the works to be carried out. Out come the tools, and the pipette filled with water for testing pigments to see if they will run; reds and yellows are always the likely candidates, followed by bold blues. The process from first poke to last press can take anything from a week to months and can range in results from barely noticeable to almost magical. Even Piers, with his forty years of experience, is sometimes surprised by the outcome.

For me, the joy of it all is that the same problems affect all works of art on paper and, if you're Piers, whose industry-wide reputation is not only one of sensei-level expertise but also one of enveloping kindness, you get all manner of things and people turning up at your door. Frequently – at least once a month – other paper conservators who have a problem they do not know how to solve will call or email Piers for advice, which he will dole out without hesitation or charge or the creation of mental debt.

In the years I have been working alongside Piers we have treated some of the most exquisite artworks I have ever seen, as well as some truly reprehensible efforts. A Rembrandt, which was on paper so thin I felt the need to hold my breath while I was near it, exemplified the other reason I like artworks on paper: you get to see the artist's process. The small sheet bore the sketched faces of four people, quickly rendered, but with the shining acuity of the Dutch master, each eye seeming like it might blink at any moment, each mouth curled into a wry and knowing smile. The almost certain knowledge that the sitter was present while the drawing was made (not by any means always the case for easel paintings) engenders an immediacy, a closeness that is almost electric.

There were others, too: the Paul Thek sketchbook in which all thirty-eight pages were covered with densely worked pencil drawings, frustration and sadness and lust discernible in every furrowed line; the unfinished Lucian Freud preparatory drawing of his father where the missing mouth is perfectly stood in for by a sheet-wide crease; and the Aubrey Beardsley drawing that had been torn up by the artist and rescued from the wastepaper basket by his sister and diligently put back together by Piers, 120 years later, like a flimsy jigsaw puzzle. Sometimes we learn more about an artist from what they don't want to show than what they do.

And then there are the clients. There is the fabulously wealthy British art dealer who collects American slave auction posters from before abolition and who, rumour has it, once brought a young Black artist to show her his golliwog collection; there is the bottom-feeding dealer who always grumbles over his bill and then proceeds to pay not only in cash, but in *coins*, counting out each pound like an art world Scrooge.

Piers once told me a story about a dealer he was working for – a dealer who claimed that Piers's restorations had put his son through private school – who came to stand over Piers as he worked. As the man pushed Piers to work faster, Piers told him that he'd been up since three in the morning sweating blood for him. 'Couldn't you sweat just a little more?' the man replied. Dealers who come to us always seem to want things better: flatter, brighter, the staining even further banished, tears and creases more invisible still. Their satisfaction is never guaranteed and we are often tempted to remind them that we're conservators, not magicians.

Private clients can be demanding, too, but it's the first timers I always enjoy the most. When they come to collect the drawing they thought ruined, or the family photograph album damaged in a flood – things they thought without hope, beyond repair – their faces seem to radiate a mixture of shock, wonder and joy. Whether you own no more art than some posters and postcards, this is the reaction it should provoke in you. I feel sure this is a big part of the reason Piers keeps working.

One morning in June 2021, Piers and I cycled over Vauxhall Bridge, through the gathering swelter of a London summer's day, to Tate Britain. For reasons of workload, when the Tate brings in pictures on loan which need conservation attention the work is given to external conservators on a trusted list.

Piers, as you might imagine, is on that list. We had been asked by one of the registrars to come and work on a Paula Rego painting – possibly her most famous piece, *The Maids* – and we arrived laden with tools and adhesives. As we signed in and walked through the riverine corridors beneath the Duveen Hall (the Tate was built on the site of a former prison, which itself was built on a drained marsh), Piers was greeted like a long-lost friend by everyone from security guards to curators.

I had to work hard to keep my cool. As a dealer, privileged access to an exhibition install like this would have been nearly impossible even to imagine; here I was, though, on the other side of the looking glass, casually wandering through the show where paintings were being removed from their crates, their owners' information displayed for all to see on the paperwork that lay around. Rego's over-life-size paintings with their stern, squat women and grimacing, obedient men and allegorical, self-knowing animals – all those big still eyes stared down at me, singling me out as the imposter I felt.

As we reached the place where *The Maids* was to hang, the painting was still in its crate. We hung around – since an exhibition install of any size requires a lot of hanging around, as if it were a vital part of the process – while the Tate technicians gathered their tools and checklists and ladders; *The Maids* is over two metres tall.

The painting, which was for many years owned by Charles Saatchi, dates from 1987. It depicts the real life story of the Papin sisters, Parisian maids who, in 1933, randomly and without obvious reason murdered the mother and daughter of the household in which they worked. The image is fraught with psychological menace, from the reaching, finger-like tree branches in the background to the fearsome wild boar in the foreground. The maids, who stand so close to each other that they seem almost to overlap, loom over their employers. The mother is placid and unassuming, captured in the moment before her death; the daughter's arms are raised in horrified alarm at the violent grip of her impending doom.

It is an odd quirk of the art market that easel paintings, no matter their size or maker, generally achieve higher prices than works of art on paper. Since at the point when *The Maids* was painted, Rego liked to work on the floor, paper was the obvious choice, but at some later date the picture was stuck down on canvas by the now-defunct north London mega framer John Jones. Now that the painting was into its fourth decade it was starting to show signs of ageing. In several places, the paper was coming away from the canvas and we had been tasked with sticking it down again.

The Tate art handlers moved with careful alacrity around the crate, silently passing each other tools as if communicating by telepathy, occasionally uttering a whispered 'One, two . . .' as they lifted something in unison. With the painting finally out of its crate, it was laid to rest on five wooden boxes, one at each corner and another supporting the cross beam. Soon the Tate technicians dispersed and Piers and I were left alone with the vast expanse of the painting, its great size in contrast with the frailty of its surface. It made me feel unwieldy and clumsy as if for no reason at all I might suddenly fall on to it.

As we got to work, gently levering small spatulas under the edges of the paper to check the adhesion, I heard the tinny babble of transmitted conversation from a neighbouring gallery. Piers and I craned our necks around the corner and saw a cull of curators gathered around a tripod with an iPad in its grip. On the screen, disembodied in the way that the pandemic had made us all too accustomed, was the face of Paula Rego. For years I'd admired her work – after all, I'd begun my career in the art world by selling it – but this, I realised, was the first time I'd ever seen her, ever associated a person with the art works I'd traded and looked at. In her face I could see the faces of many of the young women who populate her paintings, much older now. Unlike her paintings, she seemed weary; her presence on the iPad and the way the curators directed her gaze and moved the tripod around like a digital wheelchair made her seem impossibly fragile and remote.

Back at the painting, we injected adhesive between the paper and the canvas and used pieces of mount card held in place with small clamps to ensure the glue would do its work. The job took all day and most of the next and while we waited for the glue to dry both Piers I spent a fair amount of time wandering through the galleries, enjoying the paintings, some of them on the wall, others leaning casually on blocks. There were no wall texts yet, no indication of date or owner.

We packed up our things at the end of a day and a conservator friend of Piers's sidled over to say goodbye. She looked down at *The Maids* and sighed. 'Such a famous painting,' she remarked. 'It's always on the road, always flying around the world like a celebrity. But it's not good for it, all these small repairs, all these hands lifting it up and down.' As she walked away slowly, I realised the implication of what she was saying. The more the work travels, the better known it is, the more engorged its price tag. But all the flights, the turbulence, the humidity and changes of temperature and minor knocks and bumps eventually take their toll on these finite objects and, as with almost everything, money takes its pound of flesh. Eventually everything becomes a dollar sign – it's just the way art is judged now.

As an apprentice conservator, though, I felt that getting to work on art like this was a deeply special moment. I thought about the first principle of conservation, its core tenet: revers-ibility. Everything a conservator does to an object should be capable of being easily undone. Coming full circle from having sold works by Paula Rego to helping preserve one, I wondered whether somehow this principle might be applied to me, too, that I might be able to start over again and do better this time around. Up close I could see that many of these paintings had been attended to over the years, their scars visible only because I was looking. All these artworks had been given second chances; might an art dealer get a second chance, too?

11

Years ago, long before all this, Inigo told me a story about a client of his who once took out his iPad at dinner to show Inigo an image of a painting he had recently acquired. As Inigo pulled his chair around, the better to see the screen, the guy typed in his passcode. The screen opened on to the website of a dominatrix. Inigo's client closed it very quickly. Inigo pretended not to have noticed and the client rallied, pulling up the image of his new painting and handing the tablet over for Inigo's perusal. The rest of the evening passed convivially and perhaps the guy really did think Inigo had been looking elsewhere at the embarrassing moment.

But Inigo wouldn't miss something like that, and nor would he miss an opportunity to turn it to his advantage. Over the course of Inigo's continuing relationship with this collector, he told me, there were times when the man would dither about a purchase or sale. Whenever the prevarication became a problem and Inigo's easy charm had failed to produce his desired end result, and since Inigo knew the man to enjoy being told what to do, he would do just that, calling him and clearly and forcefully instructing him – *commanding* him – to buy or sell.

And it worked. For years, Inigo was incredibly good at getting people to do what he wanted, and surely that's what power is at its most pure? He had what it took to be one of the great dealers of his generation. His obsessive knowledge of the market and art history and his ruthless business instincts were matched only by a seemingly bottomless hunger for more. But a part of Inigo's power – the mystique of youthful success which swirled around him – was to a certain degree built on a foundation of half-truths and outright lies. This, combined with his hubris and his ravenous greed for more and bigger deals, would prove fatal. Eventually, after years of shoring-up and temporary fixes, this foundation absorbed one tremor too many and began to crumble.

What Inigo did was incredibly, wildly complicated and I am not sure I fully understand it. Indeed, there were times during the conversations he and I had about what he'd done when I wasn't sure he totally understood it either. I couldn't help feeling that it must have been a relief no longer to have to retain the baffling volume of lies he had spun for so long. I was no longer working for Inigo when the majority of these deals went down, and although I have a massive amount of information from him at my disposal, there is lot missing. The process of working out what may have happened has been rather like working on a jigsaw big enough to cover a football pitch, during which you belatedly realise half the pieces are missing. So I hope you will forgive me when in the following pages I am honest with you in my ignorance.

I had always been puzzled by Inigo's decision to open a gallery in Miami. To an outsider, it might seem like the place where it all went wrong for him, or at least where the cracks began to show. But I think to understand Inigo's story, it's necessary to begin at the end. In London, Inigo had largely been a private man; in Miami, where he moved in 2018, he became a very visible man, selling very visible things.

The oft-quoted line of Gertrude Stein's, that when she arrived in Los Angeles she found 'no there there' might as well have been written about Miami. Despite its high-rise skyline, its Art Deco hotels awash in pastels; despite the neon clamour of its beaches and the insistent hue and cry of music everywhere calling you to an after-party that never seems to end; despite all this, Miami has a sense of impermanence that is pervasive. Protected from the Atlantic only by the tidal prophylactic of Miami Beach barrier island, it is likely the whole city could be underwater within eighty years. The humidity hovers around 80 per cent almost all of the year, creating a climate that fosters strange beauty and stupid brutality; the whole glittering city seems to rest uncertainly on a skein of asphalt atop the swamp below, boiling over with vanquished ambition and sin.

The air on the morning of 12 October 2019 must have felt thick as a curtain. When Inigo leaned his head against the greenish tempered glass of the penthouse apartment he was viewing with his fiancée he felt no relief from the feeling that a crack which was opening beneath him would soon swallow him whole. Inigo had been in Miami on and off for about two years by this time. To others in the art world, opening a gallery there was an odd move, one which smacked a little of desperation. Miami is an art town for only a couple of weeks a year, when Art Basel Miami arrives in early December. There are a few major collectors in the city, but none of the major galleries consider it worthwhile having permanent spaces there; not even Larry Gagosian, the Genghis Khan of the art market, whose deep tan and shining helmet of silver hair are de rigueur among Miami's older men.

I was bemused when Inigo told me about his plan. Like me he'd always hated the heat, always preferred the cool nights of a London autumn. What I did know was this: the move to

Miami was something of a fresh start. While Inigo had spent the first years of his life in London and then called it home again from 2005, the majority of his business had been done with Americans and in the USA. For almost a decade he had criss-crossed the Atlantic on at least a monthly basis, staying in increasingly luxurious hotels in New York and Los Angeles, always turning left as he boarded the British Airways planes. His operation in London grew, but his American clientele – among them the billionaire oil trader Andy Hall, members of the WalMart-owning Walton family, and the hedge fund billionaire and owner of the New York Mets Steve Cohen – were always central to his business.

In London, Inigo was walking away from business relationships that had become fractious and a commercial environment which was confused by Brexit and a government plagued by indecision and inaction. He was also walking away from an almost decade-long relationship and a three-year-old daughter.

As well as a new domestic environment, Miami offered Inigo the prospect of new clients – fresh meat. Florida, and Miami in particular, has long been the hub used by wealthy South Americans to do business within the USA. Operating in countries like Brazil, where the monied class has grown exponentially since 2000, can be extremely tricky for art galleries: import duties can be as high as 35 per cent and sales tax for artworks is between 50 and 60 per cent. White Cube had tried in vain to make a success of a space in São Paulo and Inigo had seen the failure close-up. But Miami was the perfect place to sell expensive art to newly minted South American millionaire collectors.

At his London galleries, Inigo always liked to keep his circle of employees small – he knew all too well what ills could come from trusting too many people – and the opening of his Miami space was no different. On 8 December 2018 Inigo opened his first show. Timed to coincide with Art Basel Miami, the exhibition featured works by Avery Singer, Bridget Riley and Wade Guyton. As news spread among dealers and collectors at the fair and further afield, the consternation was the same. Inigo had done it again: exemplary works by three of the most sought-after art market stars of the moment gathered together for sale. Crowds of collectors flocked to Miami from Europe and South America and New York and LA.

Typically, however, Inigo was seldom to be found in his gallery during this time, leaving an assistant at the front desk to field the walk-ins and tyre-kickers. (Inigo had learned from years of experience that real clients seldom turn up unannounced and that, if they did, his absence was just as likely to intrigue as to annoy.) He knew that the hard work of procuring the artworks was done and that creating a sense of distant unavailability would be key to achieving the enormous prices he was asking. Instead, he saw friends and colleagues in town for the fair and did Pilates at the Vita Body Club around the corner. He sat at the bar of Joël Robuchon's restaurant, L'Atelier, drinking Gin Gimlets – ice-cold Monkey 47 and the juice of a whole lime – and waiting. But underneath this confident demeanour was simmering panic.

Inigo was fielding increasingly concerned emails from Daniel Tümpel and Loretta Würtenberger of Fine Art Partners (FAP) in Berlin, with whom he had been doing business for a couple of years by this point, and always at a sizeable profit for all concerned. FAP, whose suitably vague corporate motto is 'Providing professional services to the art world', essentially acts as a private bank and uses as collateral high-value artworks owned by dealers or collectors in exchange for high-risk, high-return financing. But a spate of recent deals which Inigo and FAP had entered into were taking longer to conclude than Tümpel and Würtenberger were comfortable with. Inigo placated them by reply, often apologising for the tardiness of his emails: the opening of the new gallery had taken up all of his attention lately. Now he could return to what he did best: being an art dealer.

The show over and a success, Inigo started to relax into his life in Miami. He took a trip to St Barts with a client for a week after the fair was over, flying back to London briefly in the run-up to Christmas. When I had lunch with him at Harry's Bar in Mayfair that month, he was his usual gregarious self. Afterwards we went bowling and laughed until it hurt. I have a black and white photograph we took in the photobooth at the bowling alley. In each of the four photos his face is different: one shows a buoyant and mischievous grin; in another he is sticking out his tongue at the camera. But in the other two his eyes are downcast, sad, as if he is taking a breath between pictures, stealing a moment to control his emotions.

Early in 2019, Inigo was back in Miami for the opening of his gallery's second exhibition, *Through the Alps*, a pairing of works by Rudolf Stingel and Franz West. Photos shared on the gallery's social media show that the opening was attended by Instagram influencers wearing fur collars and lamé dresses: perfect for a photo opportunity against the silver Stingel paintings. The ring-flash of the hired photographer bounced off champagne flutes and wide eyes and glittered cheekbones and iPhones held like prayerbooks, making everything look simultaneously expensive and cheap.

If you had been an onlooker that day, walking along 41st Street to an early dinner, this scene might have looked to you like success epitomised. But the cracks in Inigo's world were rapidly growing. In March, the son of a close friend and collaborator committed suicide in London. Inigo was distraught and sent me a message that read, 'Don't you ever do this to me. You call me first, OK?' I was in New Mexico at the time, driving solo across the southern USA, hoping eventually to visit Inigo in Miami, stopping at diners and motels and national parks and visiting land art installations like Robert Smithson's *Spiral Jetty*. In those vast expanses of desert and sky I had never felt more alone. A year before, when the depressive episode had landed me in a psychiatric ward, I had phoned Inigo repeatedly to no avail. This time, it was my turn to ignore his message.

As spring turned to summer, Inigo did his best to make everything appear normal. His inbox told a different story. As well as FAP, a company called Athena Art Finance was chasing missed payments in increasingly agitated terms. He later told me that his monthly interest payments to Athena were $150,000. I couldn't fathom that kind of pressure and wondered, not for the first time, if Inigo and I were made of very different stuff.

Still, even Inigo's hardened nerves were starting to fray. Over the next few months he did what he could to extricate himself from the mess he was in. The desperate measures that had long characterised his modus operandi were repeatedly failing him, however, and when he stood with his head against the sweating glass in Miami in early October, in his pocket, on his phone, was a list of the countries that have no extradition treaty with the USA. It was time to run.

In April and May of 2020, after his disappearance, Inigo sent me several emails containing folders full of documents and correspondence. I very quickly realised, as I looked through them, that along with the conversations we were having – conversations I now see were tantamount to confessions – what Inigo had sent me amounted to evidence. And specifically, it was evidence against him. At the time, Inigo and I were intending to collaborate on a magazine article which was to give his side of the story of his fraud that was being played out in the international press, and these emails and documents were provided by him to help me write about him, about his actions. What he sent me and what he told me was selective and our interviews were cut short by his arrest, but along with documents made available by the United States Attorney – along with my basic understanding of the world and the players involved – I feel I have been able to come to a picture of how this all happened.

I never asked Inigo to tell me his story, to send me the documentation – but I believe he hoped to get something in return: he wanted me to tell not just his side of the story, but his version of the truth. By the time I had read the documents in their entirety, however, any collaboration between him and me had become impossible. I had to go it alone. This was not an easy decision: I wrote this chapter after I'd written the rest of this book, partly because it was so difficult to get my head around what happened, but also because I was in denial (a place I spend rather too much time). I spent so much of the past two years wanting to believe Inigo's version of events, defending him to friends, feeling outrage at his treatment in the media: what did they know about this man who had been my friend for fifteen years? In the conversations he and I had, over months, he had put across a persuasive picture of a young man in over his head. I believed it wholly, and I was planning to write it.

Reading the emails and later the court documents and the lone, singular victim statement, I had to conclude what I believe no one could fail to: that these were not wholly the actions of a young man who got in too deep, but rather those of a charming and devious fraudster, too. I had been of a mind – of a desire – to believe that these were in a sense victimless crimes, that this was a case of a rich young man stealing from other rich people in some bathetic version of Robin Hood. It wasn't true.

What's so odd about Inigo having told me all he did with the intention that I write about it is that he clearly felt safe, or at least safe enough. Writing an article, after all, even if I had produced something as exculpatory as he wanted, would clearly have been a provocation to both his victims and law enforcement – an unnecessary act of bear-poking. When I think about it further, had he been actually as untouchable as he believed himself to be in Vanuatu and had I written and published a long article, it would likely have been me that the FBI – a force Inigo referred to in our conversations as 'the bogeyman', as if it weren't real – would have questioned, doubtless requisitioning the emails and documents I had been sent. And let me tell you now, I wouldn't stand up to interrogation well at all.

Nothing could diminish the affection I still somehow feel for Inigo. The stark truth of what he did has tested that feeling, however, as I'm sure it did for many of the people who knew, liked and admired him. How were we all so beguiled? At the time all of this was happening I had an inkling that something more had to be going on, that the money Inigo was making could not possibly be the proceeds of straightforward art dealing. Surely those people he was working closely with could sense this, too? Or perhaps, like me, the moral temperature of the art market made what they could see seem reasonable. Like the possibility of a utopia, people always want to believe in unlikely success even if its representation is often too good to be true.

We saw the signs, I more than most – the bombastic, generous displays of wealth; the smothering magnanimity; the increasingly frequent contact with solicitors and accountants; the interminable communication blackouts – but we ignored them. The more successful Inigo appeared to his clients, the more comfortable they felt around him (i.e. the less they felt like they might be marks and more like his financial and social peers). As if by magic, Inigo suddenly started flying on private planes and paying for dinners that cost more than a month's salary; he rented extravagant villas in Ibiza or the Hamptons, holidaying with clients who were far wealthier than him, his exuberant financial peacocking helping to put them at their ease. He had become one of them, one of the tribe, and no one suspects an attack from within.

These things were not a secret, but the full truth was inconvenient, because in its acknowledgement would be our partial complicity. It would mean the dream wasn't true. As Inigo later said to me, 'No one makes that much money that quickly in the art world. It's not possible, it's never been done, and never will be done . . . A lot of people knew, and thought that I would land the trick.' But sometimes things are only obvious when you know them, and people always want as much of everything as they can get.

When Inigo told me this, in the spring of 2020, it felt like a plausible part of the narrative that he'd been spinning, that of a young man in over his head. Reading it almost three years later, however, I can see that it is an attempt to dilute his guilt, to pass off the weight of his moral responsibility to be carried by some anonymous others. It feels to me quite inconceivable that 'a lot of people knew'; certainly none of those people have come forward. Indeed, it hurts me even now to realise that not only did he take me for a fool time after time, but that I allowed myself to be so taken in, so shamefully duped. It has made me question not only the nature of our long friendship, but my relationships with other people – good people, those whose motives and actions are irreproachable. To have spent so long in the realm of mendacity can have the effect of destabilising reality. And, like so much when it comes to fraud, illusion can lead to delusion. Inigo may well have believed what he was saying, but I can find no evidence to support it.

As I tried to understand the mess of deals that led to Inigo's downfall it struck me that in their opacity they appear to point to something larger. The manic complexity of Inigo's scheme now seems to me analogous to the art market as a whole – deliberate, wilful obscurity as a modus operandi. It's a multi-level illusion, one in which ordinary materials are elevated in cultural and financial status and vast sums are generated by a self-selecting few adhering to a set of unwritten conventions and rules that benefit only them and that work to keep the club as small as possible. And at the exalted level Inigo was operating, discretion is the art market's gravitational force; it is a celebration of capitalism at its most secretive and unregulated. Inigo and his clients knew this and they revelled in it, in its dark pools of liquidity and its tax-free hidey holes. What they didn't know or expect, however, was that Inigo was not only taking full advantage of the art market, but of them as well.

But no dance goes on for ever and eventually Inigo ran out of moves. What follows is what I have come to understand as the downfall of my friend. It's by no means the totality of his crimes and misdeeds (there are enough stories to fill a whole book and perhaps Inigo will write his own account of his time in the art market), but I hope the events detailed here will give a picture not merely of the scale of what Inigo did, but of how he managed to keep doing it for so long – and how he almost got away with it.

To get to grips with what Inigo did, we have to start with Jay Jopling. His and Inigo's business relationship started well:

Modern Collections made good money for them both (and would continue to do so for the next four years). The basic arrangement was that Jopling would finance the deals and the running of the gallery and Inigo would take a commission (usually somewhere between 15 and 20 per cent of profits) when he sold an artwork. And Inigo was selling *a lot* of art and turning it around fast, so to begin with everyone was happy.

Emails I have seen from 2012, 2013 and 2014 present a jovial picture of their relationship, almost like those between a father and his son who has joined the family business and is doing rather better than the father had anticipated. In other emails they joke back and forth about the quality of paintings, and Jopling asks Inigo why he had made negative comments on Instagram about the artist Christian Rosa, who was at the time a White Cube artist. Despite the fact that their business relationship was hardly a secret – to the point that Jopling was identified as Inigo's backer in an *Art Newspaper* article from 2011 about the opening of Modern Collections entitled 'Too Much Too Young?' – Jopling attempted to erect a Chinese wall of sorts by writing to Inigo to say that it would be good if they were seen bidding against each other for the same painting. Jopling was saved in Inigo's phone as 'X X'.

Mostly, though, the emails I've seen from that period consist of Inigo telling Jopling about deals he'd done on their behalf and how much money he'd made for them both. Jopling is sternly congratulatory, but there is genuine, understandable pride there beneath his stiff English tone. He had taken a punt on this young man and his instinct was paying off – and this game's all about instinct. Even by late 2013, when, as other emails show, their business relationship had already undergone some restructuring, the relationship was still generally cheery.

But at some point, something went wrong. The folders and

folders of email chains that Inigo sent me – some of them going on for hundreds of pages – are an almost seismographic map of a relationship falling apart. Gone is the witty, unstructured repartee, replaced by formal language set out in regimented paragraphs. Emails are no longer replied briefly and rapidly, but are now delayed by days, sometimes weeks. Even without knowing any of the parties involved, you would be able to tell that something had shifted.

As I understand it, both from conversations with Inigo and from an interstitial reading of their correspondence at the time, the schism was to do with money: Inigo felt he wasn't making enough and Jopling thought Inigo was making too much. Jopling denies any knowledge of Inigo's criminal activity. In a statement he said, 'I am aware of the serious allegations made against Mr. Inigo Philbrick. It has hurt and saddened me to learn that Mr. Philbrick, whom I respected and whose early career I supported, has not only betrayed my trust but, it appears, that of many others. We are privileged in our industry to work closely with the artists and art that we love. I am enormously disappointed that Mr. Philbrick appears to have abused this position of privilege. I was shocked to discover the allegations of serious wrongdoing by Mr. Philbrick in U.S. media reports in October 2019. At the earliest possible opportunity, I applied for an injunction against Mr. Philbrick to protect my interests.'

At the moment that Inigo and Jopling's relationship was faltering, Inigo and Robert Newland were introduced to each other, and began colluding behind Jopling's back with amazing speed. By the autumn of 2014 they were both in regular contact with a solicitor at a West End firm. This solicitor was engaged to help extricate them both from their roles at Modern Collections, although he had a limited remit and there is no evidence to suggest that he was complicit in or aware of any criminal activity. After what appears to have been their initial meeting, the solicitor sent Robert and Inigo a hand-drawn 'schematic summary of the (complex) contractual arrangements to which [Inigo is] subject'. The document looks like a treasure map with Inigo ('IP') and Jopling ('JJ') at opposite ends of the trail.

Despite best attempts at a legal separation of their business interests, Inigo and Jopling still owned wholly and in part around fifteen artworks. These works were the crux of the matter: they represented tens of millions of dollars. As the months went on – and these renegotiations in the commercial relationship between Inigo and Jopling continued in one form or another, until October 2019, when Inigo's frauds came to light and he fled – it was the joint ownership of these works that, as Inigo told me, came to be the significant bond still connecting the two men financially. There were also lengthy disputes about who should pay for renovations and the rent on Inigo's premises on Davies Street. Inigo felt that until the works had been sold, he would be unable to free himself from an increasingly difficult relationship with his former mentor. By the middle of 2016 there remained two significant artworks that the men co-owned; the rest were stock they felt happy to liquidate at auction.

The two paintings were typical of the kinds of artworks that Inigo had made his name trading: big, expensive, abstract paintings by big, abstract, expensive white men: a Wade Guyton and a Christopher Wool. As per their standard arrangement, Jopling had provided the financial backing to buy the paintings. Inigo didn't have the funds to buy Jopling out but he needed his permission in order to sell them. Because both the Guyton and the Wool were also part-owned by other parties (Andre Sakhai and Sasha Pesko respectively), Inigo told me he was worried that Jopling would go behind his back to sell the works and cut him out of the sales commission due to him. While Inigo's claim does, like all the best lies, contain a believable kernel of truth – dealers do routinely cut each other out – he supplied me with no evidence to suggest that Jopling routinely cut out business partners and I must therefore assume that this was pure conjecture, or perhaps paranoia, on Inigo's part.

Part-owned? I hear you ask. Most people will sensibly assume that if you buy a painting you own the painting, but among art dealers (and so-called collectors) at this level, owning a part share in a valuable artwork is fairly common. Mainly it's a way of mitigating risk; if you buy a painting for $1 million and then immediately sell a half share on the understanding that you'll split the profit when the work sells, sure, you're going to make less profit but you've also got half the purchase price back, in cash, and you can therefore have more fingers in more pies. But if there's a point where art dealing stops having anything to do with art, this is it. When you're dealing in shares in things which cannot be split up, you're just trading and it makes no difference what it was being traded. This is no longer dealing in abstract art, it's dealing in abstractions of art.

Inigo often told me that he had difficulty persuading Jopling to sell artworks they co-owned, saying, 'It was always the problem with Jay that it wasn't even about finding a buyer, it was about convincing him that at the same moment that you had a buyer, that we were right to sell.' And so Inigo began to work deals back to front, first telling Jopling that he had sold something, getting his sign-off, and only then going out to find a buyer. Through this Inigo saw a way to sever the bond with Jopling once and for all, as well as to gain control of the two contested paintings. In late 2016 Inigo told Jopling that he had sold their joint remaining one-third share in the Wool, along with the half-share of the Guyton owned by Modern Collections, to an anonymous client for a total of around $4.5 million (the US government's sentencing memorandum gives a lower figure of $3.5 million). The anonymous client didn't exist, but Inigo now had physical control of both paintings. Of the many moments in Inigo's story that could be considered his Rubicon crossing, I believe this was the most clear-cut. Over the years, there may have been many instances of illegality and devious practice, but the creation of a fake client was the beginning of a protracted fraud that had no endgame and no exit.

This wasn't a perfect solution, by any means: as Inigo told it, Andre Sakhai, his other partner in the Guyton, was happy to own the painting with him indefinitely, which was helpful, but Sasha Pesko, the British-Serbian financier who was the third partner in the Wool, repeatedly blocked sales of the painting at what Inigo considered solid market prices; and he was equally unwilling to pay Inigo out at that price for his share of the work.

In his telling of this story, Inigo paints this scenario – Jopling thinking the artworks have been sold to a third party, with Inigo unable to divest himself of them – as 'an impossible situation' for him. He didn't have the funds to pay Jopling the proceeds from the fake deal, but neither was he able to persuade Pesko that they should sell at a level that would have allowed him to do so. But, he told me stoically, 'I had to start somewhere. If you're going to unpick a knot, you gotta get a piece of rope between your teeth and start unpicking it at some point. You can't just stare at the knot.'

It was in part, Inigo told me, a way for him to show Jopling that he had clients whom Jopling didn't know or have access to, a way to persuade him that he could do deals without needing his oversight and permission. Inigo also apparently felt it was necessary to fabricate a buyer because, in the past, he said, when he had made big sales, Jopling would often approach those buyers after the fact in an attempt to do business with them directly, thereby cutting out his protégé. Inigo recounted to me an instance when he sold a Wade Guyton painting to a major client of his, and Jopling invited her to lunch. 'We were supposed to be business partners,' Inigo told me, 'and even when we were most joined at the hip, and I'm doing great deals for [Jopling], he knows that he makes more money selling her White Cube stuff than he does having me sell her stuff that we own together. And he's too greedy to stop doing that.' Inigo supplied no evidence to support this somewhat dog-ate-my-homework claim, and indeed it feels to me now like a rather obvious attempt at projection.

By the following summer, Jopling was becoming under-standably frustrated. When the 'sale' went through, he had transferred physical control of the artworks to Inigo: they were in Inigo's storage and could only be released with his (non-existent) client's sign-off. As the months wore on and no payment arrived, Jopling grew more and more impatient. Inigo reassured him, saying that the buyer was locked in a legal dispute that would be resolved soon and that he would then be able to make payment in full. This did not placate Jopling for long. On behalf of his anonymous client, Inigo paid out around $1 million to Jopling in order to secure the deal; the remaining funds were due further down the line once his client's supposed legal dispute had been settled. This is not unusual in the art market, where payment terms can be very long and deadlines missed do not automatically result in cancelled deals; the buyer pool for artworks at this level is exceedingly small and inti-mate and a dealer who develops a reputation for being overly zealous about punctual payment will live to regret it. Liquidity is *always* the core concern of the mega-rich and you'd do well not to forget it.

Eventually, however, the $1 million wasn't enough and, in August 2017, Jopling demanded not only to know the identity of the client but to be put in contact with them directly.

Relations were by this point so bad between Inigo and Jopling that Rob was writing draft emails for Inigo to send to Jopling, even penning an email to announce the birth of Inigo's child in April 2017. Rob was a remarkable mimic of Inigo's written voice and many of the emails between Inigo and his victims were, at least in part, drafted by Rob. At times he even went as far as to pre-choreograph meetings, advising Inigo not to be 'too cool' when he first meets an art finance executive. Inigo and Rob were clearly worried that Jopling and his staff suspected something. Inigo wrote to one of Jopling's staff, 'I think I understand Jay's concern – to put it in words, he has a worry that I'm going to abscond with these works somehow or that he won't receive payment.' But Inigo and Robert didn't panic. Instead, they doubled down.

Looking at the dates that this was happening – the summer of 2017 – I am surprised to realise that I was with Inigo around this time. He had rented an enormous surgical villa on a clifftop in Ibiza for the month of August and had invited me to stay with him for a few days. Pesko was there with his girlfriend and Sakhai was staying nearby. If he was stressed, he didn't show it. There were long lunches and late nights at DC-10, and all the while Inigo was calling Jopling's bluff. He was putting flesh on bones; he was giving his anonymous client a name: Martin Herrero.

Before he would reveal the name of his non-existent buyer, however, Inigo did something bold: he asked Jopling and his colleagues at White Cube to sign non-disclosure agreements.

To ask someone to sign a legal document promising not to reveal the name of someone whom you have just conjured out of thin air takes a certain kind of gumption.

Over the next year, Robert and Inigo corresponded with Jopling using the email address martinherrero1810@gmail.com (the addition of 1810, the date that marks the beginning of the Argentinian war of independence, was perhaps a dig at Jopling, whose father was a cabinet minister in Thatcher's government during the Falklands conflict). Inigo didn't send me any of the emails between Martin and Jopling, but traces of their content are discernible in Jopling's emails to Inigo. Martin was clearly sympathetic to Jopling's plight but, for obvious reasons, equivocal as to when he would make payment. At the beginning of 2018, Jopling wrote to Inigo in a tone that was confrontational, bordering on accusatory. The previous October Inigo had told Jopling that Martin (Inigo always refers to him by his first name, underscoring their familiarity, perhaps in the hope that it would burnish any vestige of trust still remaining in his relationship with Jopling) was willing to pay a further $1.3 million towards the amount owing, but by January 2018 the funds had still not materialised. Six months later, Martin hadn't paid any more towards his debt but had been offering to pay Jopling with art, some of which Inigo owned with Pesko. Inigo's aim here was clearly to use his creditors to pay each other off. None of these deals came to fruition.

While all this was going on, Inigo was using the Wool in his control to raise yet more money. (Though it is not unusual in the art market for dealers or collectors to raise capital secured against artworks they own, it is far from standard practice to do so with artworks you do not own wholly and without the knowledge of your partners.) In June 2017 he sold it to Guzzini Properties Ltd, a company controlled by the billionaire property tycoon brothers David and Simon Reuben, but effectively run by Simon's daughter, Lisa, of whom more later. About a year later, Inigo bought the painting back for $2 million. He also later sold a further 25 per cent of the painting to Pesko for $3 million and by March 2019, Pesko had physical control of the painting. I assume, but don't know, that Sakhai ended up controlling the Guyton. Jopling is still owed $1.95 million by 'Martin', money he is unlikely ever to see.

When I asked Inigo how long this went on for, he paused and sighed deeply. 'Years,' he said disconsolately. 'Years.' I heard shame in that pause.

Freedom is something we all crave, but it often comes at a price. As his longed-for separation from Jopling slowly began to come into focus, Inigo needed to look for external investment in order to grow his business. This was when his problems really began. There were, Inigo told me, many reasons for his wish to part ways with Jopling. Initially it was simply that Inigo felt that the original arrangement was financially restrictive to his business, but he also told me of a tendency of Jopling's to 'overnegotiate' (something Jopling admits to in an email from 2015). In seeking out a new financial partner, Inigo wanted to find someone who would defer to his expertise and allow him more or less free rein while providing him with the cash to do big deals.

In 2013, Rob introduced Inigo to Daniel Tümpel and Loretta Würtenberger, the husband and wife founders of Fine Art Partners. Tümpel, who has a background as an investment banker at Morgan Stanley and whose father was a widely respected Rembrandt scholar, is, from the images I have seen online, a tall, lean man with a shaved head and a smile that feels milliseconds away from becoming sinister. His wife, a former judge, has the glamorous aspect of a Hitchcockian heroine. Together they own a castle whose grounds they have turned into a sculpture park. In conversation, Inigo referred to them as 'The Germans', which always made me think of the *Fawlty Towers* episode of the same name.

The arrangement was fairly straightforward and not uncommon in the art market: Inigo would find artworks to buy in which he thought there was a decent profit. FAP would front 70 per cent of the purchase price and after Inigo had sold the work, he and FAP would split the profit in various fairly complex ways according to several different contracts. They did their first deal together in 2014. According to Tümpel's victim statement – the only one submitted to the court by any of the people Inigo defrauded – Inigo told them he had sold the work, a piece by Danh Võ , before they had even sent him their share of the purchase price. Tümpel goes on to write that he had subsequently seen bank statements that showed that the 'sale never took place and he paid our alleged profit share out of other funds to make us believe that he was a talented and successful art dealer. This was his investment in this relationship with us. Unfortunately, we took the bait and believed him.'

Over the next five years, Inigo and Robert would do twenty or so big money deals with FAP, many of them legitimate. The frustrations and rebuttals evident in the emails I have seen between Inigo, Robert and FAP are familiar ones. Payments to FAP are frequently late, delayed by forces beyond Inigo's control – beyond anyone's control. Each time, however, Inigo does a majestic job of deescalating the situation: theirs is a storm that they must weather together and he is the only helmsman to steer the ship through these roiling, murky waters. As Inigo told me, his job as an art dealer was 'managing expectations and changing realities'.

In an email from early 2019, Inigo wrote at length to Tümpel and Würtenberger lamenting the struggle he was having extracting funds owed to him (and by extension to FAP) by a man he referred to only as 'Leonid', that is, the Russian businessman Leonid Friedland, whose Mercury Group own Phillips auction house. (Inigo referred to this as 'herding Russians'.) 'I am well aware,' Inigo wrote, 'that the biggest frustration in our relationship comes from stress about money, and that this has been compounded recently by dealing with Leonid, who over the course of my career has been one of my most consistent clients, but also certainly the most aggravating. I am doing everything in my power to collect the funds still due to us, including using other clients' business as a lever in our favor and I'm expecting the next instalment imminently . . . We do such good work together and it is so important that we work together as a team.' Inigo then went on to mention a painting he referred to as 'our Stingel Picasso'.

This is a painting by Rudolf Stingel *of* Picasso, though the painting's actually called (or not called) *Untitled*. And it's a stunner. Almost two and a half metres high by almost two metres across, the canvas is imposing, to say the least, and that's before you factor in ol' Pablo's imperious, what's-this-on-the-sole-of-my-shoe leer. With his rumpled double-breaster and his smouldering cigarette and eyes, he looks more like a captain of industry than an artist. As a painting, it seems to mark a zenith of a sort. Stingel started painting photorealist works in 2005, beginning with one of his gallerist, Paula Cooper. For the portrait of Picasso, Stingel worked from an unpublished photograph of the artist given to him by Picasso's family. It's a taunting bit of trivia because, although the painting itself looks like a photograph, you realise you've *still* not seen the original, only Stingel's interpretation. When he made the painting, Stingel was the same age as Picasso was when the photo was taken. It's a portrait of a portrait, a memento mori of artistic genius, a reminder, perhaps, that talent fades but art will outlast us all.

This next bit is fiendishly financially complicated, so for clarity the headlines are these: Inigo had physical control (but not controlling ownership) of the Rudolf Stingel painting of Picasso from around the beginning of 2016 until May 2019. Over this period, he had numerous partners to whom he sold shares of this painting. Some of them knew that there were other people involved and were happy about it; some had no idea. In total, Inigo sold around 220 per cent of the painting, which is, of course, 120 per cent more painting than existed.

Anyway, here come the numbers.

In January 2016 Inigo sold 50 per cent of the painting to Sasha Pesko for $3.35 million and shortly thereafter he also sold it to FAP, with FAP agreeing to a price tag of $7.1 million and a resale target price of $9 million. FAP paid Inigo $2.485 million, 35 per cent of the purchase price, agreeing to remit the remaining 65 per cent when the painting was resold. Inigo informed FAP that there was another investor in the painting who owned a half share and provided them with a handwritten note, which he said came from the other investor, agreeing to FAP's involvement. The name was redacted, so FAP had no idea who it was – and Pesko had no idea there was another investor in the painting at all.

Fast-forward eighteen months and Inigo sells the painting again – this time to Lisa Reuben (via Guzzini Properties Ltd, the company controlled by *her* father; 'the problem with Lisa', Inigo told me, 'was that Lisa liked to sit at the table, but really it was her dad sitting at the table'), who buys it, along with two other artworks including yet another Christopher Wool painting, for $6 million. In reality, the deal with Reuben was actually a loan and the paintings collateral; Inigo had a year in which either to sell the paintings or pay Reuben a figure of $599k. After a year of this, Inigo re-upped the loan and paid Reuben the $599k, but he knew it couldn't go on like this. The only way he could pay back the $6 million was to sell the works, which was obviously a problem because Reuben was one of three people who believed they owned the Stingel, and was one of two (the other being Pesko, who also owned part of one of the other paintings, another Wool, in the Reuben loan collateral pool) who thought they had physical control of the work in their storage. At this point, as later court documents would state, 'Pesko, FAP, and Guzzini paid or agreed to pay the defendant more than $15 million total for the Stingel Picasso, and they were unaware of each other's respective claims'. That is the simplest possible account of what was going on: no fraud is constructed to be understood and this one was taking place within a world obsessed with secrecy. It's not surprising that pretty well everyone involved lost track of it.

Up until now, this story has just been about big numbers and plutocrats, but in order to free himself of this self-created mess, Inigo needed to get creative. There was, he told me, already some 'mistrust' in the relationship between him and Pesko, and so it was decided that the works they co-owned, including the Wool, should be put into joint storage in Switzerland. But Reuben also thought she owned the Wool in question and so quite reasonably wanted to have it in her storage elsewhere in Switzerland. So how do you make the same painting be in two different warehouses at the same time? Simple: you place a blank canvas of appropriate dimensions into a crate and send it to the warehouse where the new owner is expecting to take delivery. Because these guys aren't buying art, not really – they are making money – they don't open the boxes.

How Inigo managed to substitute the real painting for the blank canvas he didn't get around to telling me, saying at the time that this was merely a 'tributary' to the main narrative. There were countless missed stories like this, so many anecdotal antics on the horizon of our conversations, that I wish those calls had gone on for years. With trust between Inigo and Pesko somewhat restored, Pesko asked him what he would take for the Stingel Picasso. Sensing a way out, Inigo quoted a bullish price; Pesko, Inigo told me, always felt more comfortable owning things outright, but didn't agree with Inigo's assessment that the painting was worth $10–15 million. They agreed to show the painting to Christie's. Inigo had to put his money where his mouth was: not for the first time, a potential way out had become a dead end.

As Inigo relayed to FAP, the auction house was incredibly enthusiastic about the painting. Writing in February of 2019, he told Tümpel and Würtenberger that '[Christie's], and increasingly I, feel there is an opportunity in May to set a new world auction record for the artist with the painting . . . I have a very strong belief that our painting could completely reset the Stingel market.' Christie's, Inigo told me, were so keen that they immediately asked Inigo if he would like them to talk to possibly guarantors, thinking that they may be able to secure a guarantee of $8 million or more. (A large, greyscale self-portrait by Stingel had sold for $10.5 million in 2017, then the auction record for the artist.)

A guarantee is exactly what it sounds like: you put your artwork up for auction at, say, $1–2 million, but whatever happens – even if the lot doesn't sell – the auction house *guarantees* you, say, $1.5 million. After that they own the work and it's their problem. Auction houses began offering guarantees for estates when wary executors became worried that their one chance to maximise value might be ruined by events out of their control like a yachting accident or these peoples' worst fear: the instigation of a wealth tax. But when the contemporary art market really started to boom in the late 1990s, auction houses also began to offer guarantees to consignors of really prestigious artworks. Then everyone wanted a guarantee (a reserve was no longer enough) before they handed over their artworks and the houses couldn't keep up with the demand, so they came up with something clever called a third-party guarantee. Third-party guarantees are when someone outside the auction house – a dealer like Inigo, say – takes on the role of guarantor. In this instance, if the same $1–2 million lot doesn't sell but Inigo has guaranteed it at $1.5 million, he buys the painting. But if the lot sells for $2.5 million, Inigo and the auction house split the upside. And yes, I know what you're thinking, and yes, it is basically gambling. Almost all of this is gambling, and that's partly what makes it so much fun for those involved.

But for all his bullishness, Inigo was hesitant about pricing. He'd been involved so deeply and for so long in the Stingel market that, he told me, he could feel it plateauing. As he wrote to FAP, 'My experience with auction tells me powerfully that if we put the painting at 8–12m (which C[hristie]'s are willing to do) it sells towards the low end of the estimate, but that if we allow the market to have more leeway with the picture then we can see a result in the teens.'

Inigo's plan was for Christie's to give the painting a lower estimate range; instead of the $8–12 million that would seem fitting for a painting of this stature, he wanted them to price it less aggressively. Just like when you see something priced at $4.99 your brain focusses on the 4, not the .99's proximity to 5, Inigo surmised that a lower estimate would generate more bids. 'If it looks cheap in the room,' he figured, 'there's going to be really good interest.' They settled on $5–7 million. Reuben, who had physical possession of the painting, was the official consignor, while Inigo got Pesko to release his blank canvas in a box to Inigo having shown him a fake draft contract from Christie's.

As the weeks rolled on, Pesko became increasingly excited by the deal and was also intimating to Inigo that he might like to bid on the painting himself. But FAP were wary, writing to Inigo, 'With regard to the Picasso: we would only agree to consign it to Christies if we would get a guarantee well above our purchase price to reflect the long holding period. I think a selling price should be at least 12 mln USD.' This put Inigo in an awkward position: not only did Pesko believe that he and Inigo were calling the shots, but he had already entered into an agreement with Christie's whose terms FAP would not accept. FAP told Inigo they would only accede to consign the Picasso if Christie's gave them a guarantee of $9 million.

After what I imagine must have been a torturous night of the soul, Inigo went all in, telling FAP that Christie's had agreed to a guarantee at $9 million, later providing them with a copy of a consignment agreement detailing this. In the email confirming the guarantee, Inigo doubled down on his and Christie's enthusiasm: 'I've consigned many major works to auctions both on behalf of clients and from my own inventory, I've never seen so much excitement. Let's now hope that the timing of the sale and the marketing are enough to take us the distance we want it to.' The agreement was fake, as was the guarantee.

As Inigo told me all this I couldn't help remembering a piece of video art he had introduced me to years before. In the piece, *Six Colorful Inside Jobs*, the artist John Baldessari is filmed from above as, over six days, he paints and repaints a room proceeding through the colour spectrum, finally painting himself into the corner before exiting through a hidden door. If it came off, the auction would be Inigo's hidden door. Over lunch in the run-up to the auction, Pesko told Inigo he would bid to $7 million, maybe even a little higher. At around this level Inigo was sure he could pay everyone out. It was a big roll of the dice, but he was in a corner and there was nothing for it: he needed everything to go his way on the night or he'd be bust.

In the end Pesko authorised Inigo to bid up to $6.5 million. If the Stingel Picasso sold at this level, Pesko would effectively be buying Inigo out of his share in the painting; if it sold for more, the two would split the upside and Inigo would be able to pay off Reuben and FAP. Christie's sent the painting on a whistle-stop tour of key places to drum up interest: Los Angeles, San Diego, London and Hong Kong, and Pesko, according to Inigo, was becoming more and more excited, deciding to come to New York for the auction. While on the face of it the numbers looked like they wouldn't work for Inigo, from documents I have seen, it is possible to see that both the deal he did with Christie's and the structure of his arrangement with FAP (as well as some additional subterfuge along the way) would have allowed him to slither his way out of his mess had the bid gone to $6.5 million. The consignment deal with the auction house was enormously generous to Inigo, paying him a sliding scale of the buyer's premium (what the buyer pays to the auctioneer) to the extent that, at the lower estimate range, Christie's wouldn't have earned anything at all. This is known as an 'enhanced hammer' deal. Inigo informed FAP about the enhanced hammer deal, but misled them as to the percentage. And, as he would later tell me by email, 'The peculiarities of the deal with the Germans allowed [that] a good result would fulfil the repayment of all funds necessary to exit the transaction.'

There were, however, a few moves Inigo still needed to make

before the day itself. Christie's knew that Inigo had an ownership stake in the painting and so wouldn't allow him to bid
on Pesko's behalf; Inigo therefore enlisted his friend the dealer
Stellan Holm to bid for Pesko, although Inigo never showed
me any evidence that Pesko was aware of this arrangement
and there is no suggestion Holm was aware of Inigo's stage
management. Inigo was also in almost daily contact with his
specialist contacts at Christie's to monitor the level of interest
in the painting and, with a few days to go until the auction,
they were still telling him that they had 'good, but not amazing,
interest'.

On the day of the auction, Christie's told Inigo that, besides
Holm bidding on behalf of Pesko, they had only one or two
other people registered to bid on the Stingel. This wouldn't be
a problem if at least two (though preferably all three) were keen
as mustard, but Christie's told him that one of the two was not
particularly motivated; that it was a collector who had registered to bid merely to protect the artist's market. (Inigo told me
he knew this bidder to be the billionaire François Pinault, whose
company Artémis owns Christie's, as well as Gucci and other
luxury brands.) The other, the auction house claimed, could be
a serious contender for the lot, but it took Inigo almost no time
to find out that this bidder was his friend the collector Laurent
Asscher, who he knew was not intending to buy the painting.
Suddenly, his plan was collapsing like a cake in a rainstorm.

Even a year after the fact, when Inigo recounted this to me
from his desert island hideaway, I could hear the change in his
voice. His smooth, assured tone became minutely constricted,
his sighs deeper, as if his body were stuck in that saleroom back
in Rockefeller Center with the world closing in on him. Hours
before the auction, Inigo scrambled to formulate a new plan.
'So,' he told me, 'I turn to my trusty pal Damian Delahunty.'

Delahunty had had a gallery one door down from the original Modern Collections on Mount Street when I first worked there and I remember him being unfriendly to the point of rudeness. Inigo and I would sneer at the artworks he showed – Warhol prints and celebrity photographers' African holiday snaps. I was bemused, years later, when he and Inigo became apparently friendly collaborators. Nevertheless, on the day of the auction, Inigo thought he was a guy he could rely on to help him out of a sticky spot. He called Delahunty, asking him if he would bid up the Stingel; Delahunty readily agreed. While this is Inigo's account and he never provided me with any proof that Delahunty had agreed to act as a proxy bidder in this auction, Inigo used regularly to tell me about his collaborations with Delahunty, or 'DD' as he called him. At this stage in events, according to his own account, Inigo was back in control. He had two guys who were doing his bidding (literally and figuratively): surely nothing could possibly go wrong.

As he related all this to me, Inigo breathed a sigh of relief. 'Everything's lined up,' he told me. 'I've got a guy who actually wants the painting at a number that actually works for me for the whole deal; I've got an underbidder who's a solid underbidder – you know, Christie's will take his bid at that level, no problem; and I've danced out of this devilish jam.'

Jussi Pylkkänen has a plummy voice and the round, rosy face of a gentleman farmer. His suits, though, are urbane and sombre, rendering him a mere silhouette against the wildly expensive artworks he sells with his gavel. On the night of 16 May 2019, Pylkkänen climbed the podium at Christie's New York with ineffable smoothness. He wore a mauve tie that shimmered like an oil spill. The room in front of him was packed. But he didn't smile. There was business ahead.

Just to be in that room must have been intoxicating. In the YouTube video of the sale Inigo isn't immediately visible in the crowd; apart from a moment when a young woman turns heads as she strides up the aisle to claim her seat, there is very little to see in the footage of audience, let alone the skyboxes where the really exclusive folks sit. (Just when you think you've made it in this world, it turns out there's always another rung up the ladder.)

The sale starts out slowly. Two James Rosenquists, a Jean Dubuffet and a Wayne Thiebaud sell within or below estimate and without fanfare. The atmosphere in the room is flat. Many of the audience must have turned their thoughts to dinner. Until, that is, we come to the Robert Rauschenberg. It's a peach of a painting; a rhapsodic bric-a-brac mix of American iconography from JFK to Coca-Cola to a bald eagle. The bidding *starts* at $38 million and from there it just runs and runs. Time and again, Pylkkänen shrugs off another million; he laughs benevolently at the paltry half-million dollar increases. Be serious. He leans this way and then that like he's bucking a horse and his wrists flutter as he threatens to end the bidding, to bring it down with that sharp and final snap. He pauses theatrically: let the millions do the talking.

It's like watching a great sportsman at work. And for him it is sport, it has to be: these numbers are necessarily abstractions. How could they be otherwise? How can anyone really countenance these crazy numbers? After almost eleven minutes Pylkkänen's gavel comes down at $78 million. With fees, that's $88 million and change (the kind of change that could buy you a house or two). The room erupts in applause, perhaps born of relief: no one wants to be at the sale which smashes records for not smashing any records. This isn't modern-day New York, it's ancient fucking Rome.

The sale moves quickly on, with Pylkkänen trying to harness the momentum. A Jeff Koons balloon animal rabbit sells for a whisker over $91 million (more applause), but a little more than half an hour later the room has lost its pizzazz. All the while Inigo and Delahunty are exchanging messages, working out the game plan. A few lots before the Stingel comes up, Inigo told me, Delahunty suddenly goes quiet. Doesn't reply. Inigo doesn't panic, though, no sir. He assumes that Delahunty is on the line with his Christie's specialist. Inigo knows the woman Delahunty works with – there she is: Katharine Arnold, white jacket, blonde hair, red nails, diamond the size of an eye – and she's got her phone to her ear, her bidding hand in front of her mouth. It's going to be fine, it's going to be fine. Breathe.

Then comes the Stingel and Pylkkänen wastes not a moment. He's out of the gates and running. 'Lot number thirty-three is a Stingel of Picasso. 2012. Here he is, wonderful picture of 2012, and we start the bidding at four million. Four million, two hundred thousand for the Stingel. At four million, two hundred thousand, at four million two.' Pylkkänen pauses, leaning far to his right, his arm outstretched out towards the phone bank even though he's still reading from his commission bids on the lectern in front of him. Keep it going, Jussi, bring it home. 'Four million, five hundred thousand now. At four million five, not yours here,' he says with a dismissive wave to the phones. Then he leans to his left: 'At four million eight, not yours, Barrett.' Thanks for nothing, Barrett. 'At four million eight hundred thousand, looking for five.' Someone alerts him to a new bid. 'Five million with Adrien. At five million dollars and selling. At five million dollars.' Woah there! Selling?! Hold on a minute! Why so fast? Adrien's the guy on the phone with Pinault. He doesn't even want it. Give the thing a chance, why don't you! Give *me* a chance!

Pylkkänen looked forward into the room. Last chance. Did he see Inigo sitting there, his face barely holding it together? He leans forward and to a man on the aisle says: 'You coming in, sir?' The man demurs: 'Not this one.' And then suddenly from the back of the room, the cavalry: 'Five million, five hundred thousand new place.' That's gotta be Stellan Holm, reliable old Stellan, thank fuck for Stellan Holm, Stellan the cavalry. About fucking time. Now come on, Damian, baby, bring it home, this'll all be over soon. 'At five million five hundred thousand. Give me six.' Give him six! Give him six! 'For the Picasso. At five million five. The gentleman's bid, I have it. At five million five. Six will be next, Adrien, would you like it?' Of course he doesn't want it, you know he doesn't want it. Fuck Adrien. Fuck Pinault.

Katharine Arnold, Delahunty's specialist, raises her hand to half mast, flat out in front of her, steady, like a drunk with something to prove: hold the bid. Hold the fucking bid. She's not smiling, why's she not smiling? Her hand hangs there, big diamond ring shining big and bright like a promise. That's Damian's hand in mid-air like a goddamn emperor deciding the fate of a gladiator. Up! Up! Come on, bid, you bastard, bid! (Arnold is present and on the phone in the YouTube video of this sale, though Inigo provided me with no proof that it was Delahunty on the other end of the line and certainly there is no suggestion that Arnold or Delahunty were knowingly participating in Inigo's fraud scheme.)

In that moment time seems to buffer. Pylkkänen just keeps repeating the same thing. 'Five million five, in the sale-room and selling.' NOWNOWNOW! Bid, you fucker! Come on, Damian, you can do it. Do me this one, last solid. 'At five million, five hundred thousand.' Pylkkänen looks left to the hand, Delahunty's hand by extension, hovering still. 'You sure?'

Pylkkänen asks the hand. Nothing. No bid. No bid. Are you fucking kidding me, Damian? Where the hell are you? Raise that hand fucking now!

'At five-five, then, yours it is, at five million, five hundred thousand.' Pylkkänen checks back in with the room, swooping low to his right and making eye contact with someone in the audience. Don't do it, Jussi. Wait for Damian. He'll bid, he'll bid, I know he will. But then, with the campest of flourishes, the gavel raps down with a seismic crack. 'Yours, sir, at five-five.'

Pylkkänen moves swiftly on. The quiet of the room sounds like falling. Holm may have bought it, and Pesko may now own it, but the Stingel Picasso is Inigo's problem all over again.

Inigo left the saleroom with Pesko at his side, 'incandescent with anxiety about why he was the only person in the world who would want to pay five and a half [million]' for that painting. I can see them now in my mind's eye, striding up Sixth Avenue (both Inigo and Pesko are very much uptown guys), Inigo's mind spinning new excuses with each step, desperately looking for an emergency exit from his newly untenable position. As they walked, Pesko harangued Inigo, demanding to renegotiate their deal, but Inigo had more than Pesko to worry about.

The following day Inigo wrote to Tümpel and Würtenberger: 'Strange sale. Super-strong sale for blue-chip post-war things, but not great for a lot of others. [Christie's] were talking to me about a hammer price in excess of $10m, but one party flaked ... We were right to take [the $9m guarantee]'. A few days later, however, when Christie's posted the sale prices for the auction on their website, Tümpel and Würtenberger were confused to see that the painting was listed as having sold for

$6.5 million inclusive of fees. But this didn't faze Inigo and he reassured them that Christie's would have 'internal reasons' for not listing the guaranteed price. And they believed him; at this point, while Inigo may have been frustratingly late with payment and erratic in communication, his excuses, though sometimes elaborate to the point of farce, were somehow always credible. He'd always come good in the end, and together they'd made a lot of money.

Inigo sent Pesko an invoice for half of the sale price and fees so that he could buy Inigo out of his half of the painting. Pesko paid Inigo in full, and Inigo, via Stellan Holm, sent partial payment on to Christie's. Auction house payment terms are long – often ninety days or more – and so Inigo had some time to figure out his next move. But summer arrived and by the end of August FAP still had not received their due; Inigo claimed that he had received the funds from Christie's but blamed the delay on a third party with whom he had to settle up first. Over email and in meetings around this time, relations between Inigo and FAP were souring and becoming increasingly confrontational in nature.

By early September, Tümpel's and Würtenberger's frustration was turning into suspicion. They contacted Christie's directly, trying to get to the bottom of the late payment and the disparity between the $9 million they believed the painting had achieved and the $6.5 million listed on the auction house's website. Tümpel asked that Christie's not share their suspicions with Inigo, stating plainly that they could not exclude 'the possibility that Inigo is acting in a criminal manner'. A lawyer for Christie's, the almost perfectly named auction house employee Jason Pollack, soon confirmed their fears: 'Christie's did not guarantee the lot.' Two days later, after Tümpel had sent through the seller's agreement Inigo had provided them,

Pollack told FAP that he believed the seller's agreement to be 'a falsified document'. Pollack also revealed to FAP that Inigo had not been the consignor of the Stingel Picasso as he had led them to believe.

Tümpel and Würtenberger realised that they needed to act quickly. Inigo still had control of over $14 million-worth of art that they were invested in. They quietly lawyered up and requested that the artworks be released and placed into joint storage. Soon after this, Inigo stopped corresponding with them; perhaps it didn't seem to matter anymore. Over the next month, both Pesko and Guzzini (the Reubens' company) came forward claiming to own the Stingel Picasso. Inigo confessed his crimes (or parts of them) to several of his major clients including Sakhai and Pesko. And then, in early October 2019, FAP filed a lawsuit against Inigo in a Miami court, prompting yet more people to come forward with conflicting ownership claims, a morass of money and art. Days later, Inigo ran.

I saw Inigo for the last time one wet Sunday afternoon in late April 2019 when he invited me to join him at his gym. He'd done this once before, when he was a member of the WASP-y Bath & Racquets Club in Mayfair, where we did precisely no exercise, preferring instead to drink Bloody Marys as a white-jacketed man brought us finger food. When you're very wealthy, even going to the gym has the sting taken out of it.

But this time his gym was the fitness centre of the Lanesborough hotel on Hyde Park Corner. I remember arriving there on the bus and thinking – not for the first time – who the hell is this guy? What thirty-four-year-old joins a gym in the basement of a five-star hotel located on an enormous roundabout in the middle of London? The answer is: no one, but Inigo did. I think perhaps part of the reason that Inigo was able to get away with the frauds he perpetuated for so long is because he made strange behaviour seem normal. The culture industries have long fostered successful oddballs and so when Inigo's behaviour morphed from eccentric to erratic and then from erratic to criminal, his clients – his victims – took a good while to cotton on. It was just Inigo being Inigo, they thought; his behaviour was priced in. The money had always materialised in the past.

In the year or so since I'd stopped working in the art market, I hadn't seen Inigo all that much. He moved between London, Miami and Ibiza and wherever else the deals took him; he always seemed to be somewhere *else*. On those rare occasions I did see him, he was often distracted to the point of rudeness and I found myself – yet again – questioning the viability of our friendship. On that Sunday afternoon at the Lanesborough, I stood around while Inigo ran on the treadmill – ran fast, as if he were being chased – and threw medicine balls at the floor with a wet, angry smacking sound. All the while, though, his attention was fixed on his phone and I realise now that he was in all likelihood working on the Stingel Picasso deal, piece by piece figuring out his escape, wriggling his way loose from the knots he had tied. When he was done working out he gave his phone to the receptionist so she could put it on charge and for the next hour or so we sat together in the steam room and talked. As the heat and the vapour swirled around us, a different man seemed to emerge. His anarchic humour and rapid-fire wit made brief cameos; it was a side of him I had all but forgotten.

To write about a friendship is to mourn its loss. Friendships aren't meant to undergo the kind of scrutiny to which I have subjected ours, if indeed there exists one still. Inigo wanted me to paint him as a talented young man who got caught up in something he couldn't control, but he cannot reasonably have expected me not to see, from the emails and documents he sent me, that that wasn't entirely the case.

Among the many glowing character references Inigo's defence team provided to the court, there is one by a young French art dealer, Ferdinand Gros. In his statement, Gros writes that Inigo was something of a mentor to him, as, in some ways, he was to me. He writes that 'it was difficult to conduct business with [Inigo], when I presented some opportunities, he was always a little shady and keeping me away. Which often got me confused as on the one hand he wanted me around but on the other kept me out of the business side. As soon as his crimes came to light, I understood he was trying to protect me by keeping me out. He could have taken advantage of me in a million ways but did not.' According to the US attorney's sentencing report, email evidence shows that in November 2017 Inigo tried to sell Gros a 1976 artwork by Donald Judd. The deal didn't happen when Gros's client passed on the work. Inigo had already sold the work to FAP the previous February, and pledged it as collateral to Athena Art Finance.

12

In January 2022, when I began to write this chapter, I hadn't been to New York for almost four years. The world was in the grip of the Covid-19 pandemic, this time in the form of the Omicron variant, and international travel was severely restricted. I had had no contact with Inigo since the previous summer and knew little of his life in the New York jail where press reports told me he was being held.

As I was pondering how to engage with this part of Inigo's story, what with the physical and communication obstacles I was facing, I was having regular Zoom calls with my godfather John Fordham, the jazz critic on the *Guardian*. At the time, he had just done a phone interview with the saxophonist Sonny Rollins to mark the sixtieth anniversary of his album *The Bridge*. The record resulted from a year when, having no space of his own in which to practise, Rollins spent up to sixteen hours a day playing alone on the Williamsburg Bridge. John told me that in order to write his piece, he had spent long hours using Google Street View, trying to locate the spots where Rollins had told him he'd stood, buffeted by wind and rain and the constant onslaught of automobiles and subway cars, playing his saxophone high above the East river.

Over the subsequent days and weeks, I too spent hours navigating the streets of New York by way of Google Street View. I walked around and around the jail I knew Inigo was being held in and wondered whether the images I was seeing had been taken since he'd arrived there, whether or not the photographs I was seeing contained, as it were, my friend. (I later read an interview with Martin Amis, who had moved into an apartment building that overlooked the prison, and realised what an Amis-esque character Inigo had become, a transatlantic figure of financial frivolity, not unlike John Self in *Money*. For years I had given Inigo Amis first editions for his birthday; I wondered whether Amis had followed Inigo's case in the media.) I did a deep dive into prison blogs and personal accounts of former inmates and prison consultants who offer advice to newly incarcerated felons and their families. As my research-in-the-age-of-Covid went on, as I watched on YouTube a brief speech introducing Supreme Court justice Ruth Bader Ginsburg by the judge who would be trying Inigo and spoke to a friend who had lived for a time in Guam, asking her to tell me about the airport and the courthouse. I felt ever more distant from Inigo, as if I were playing a video game in which he was a character I was pursuing, always just out of sight, scurrying away around a pixellated corner. He had been reduced to an idea, one which I have spent three years trying to imagine into something more.

At the moment Inigo was snatched from the street in Port Vila, Vanuatu, on the afternoon of Friday 12 June 2020, I don't imagine he had any idea where he was being taken or by whom. The men who took him did not read him his rights; at that moment he had none. He had no passport with him and only a little money in the local currency. With the strong hands of two Vanuatuan police gripping his arms, he was taken from the car into which he had been bundled and walked towards a waiting Gulfstream jet.

Vanuatu has a reputation, so one former lawyer told me at the time of Inigo's arrest, as being 'a sunny place for shady people' – a phrase originally coined by the novelist Somerset Maugham about the French Riviera. Its main attraction for Inigo was that it has no extradition treaty with the United States. He told me that the statute of limitations on the crimes of which he was accused (crimes which to me he never denied) was five years. What with the pandemic raging and the future of the (art) world looking uncertain at best, he was happy to wait out the time on his desert island. The country has no income tax and you can effectively buy citizenship for $150,000, a snip since a Vanuatu passport, given the nation's French and British colonial past, will allow its bearer visa-free travel throughout Europe, a boon for wealthy Asians wanting to do business there. However, as one Chinese citizenship agent told the BBC, as few as one in ten of his clients visit Vanuatu after receiving their passport. The policy is deeply unpopular among resident Vanuatuans.

No country wants to be seen as corrupt, however, and so on Wednesday, 9 June 2020, when Jeffrey Markson, Director of the Vanuatu Immigration Services (VIS), received an arrest warrant for Inigo from the American authorities via the US Embassy in Papua New Guinea, the decision was likely a simple one. I googled Markson, wanting to see the face of the man who had orchestrated Inigo's capture. I found photographs of an athletic, unsmiling man often sporting brightly coloured shirts. I can imagine that he would have wanted to be seen as acting with propriety in the matter; his is the department which has garnered much of the local criticism in the cash for citizenship scandal. Requests like this from the FBI aren't frequent occurrences, however. Big decisions like this would need to be signed off by higher-ups.

In contrast with Markson's dour online presence, Ishmael

Kalsakau, Vanuatu's then Minister for Internal Affairs, who was elected Prime Minister in 2022, looks to be a cheery-faced man with bushy, impudent eyebrows. But when Markson came to him with the FBI arrest warrant and told him about the crimes of which Inigo was accused, he had little choice but to hand him over to the US authorities. His fate was sealed.

When the call came, in the afternoon of 12 June 2020, I was exactly where half the world was at that moment: on a sofa, wondering what I was going to do with my Friday night in the middle of a pandemic lockdown. London was closed for business and I couldn't go to work. My days were a perpetual Wednesday; little distinguished one day from the other.

I didn't recognise the number, though I knew the +678 dialling code to be Vanuatu. The voice, however, was unmistakably that of Inigo's fiancée: crystalline, imperious, worked, like a tuning fork. That day, however, I heard another side to that voice, its corollary: fragile, fearful. 'They've got Inigo,' she said. 'They took him. Snatched him in the street. I don't know where, where they're taking him. I watched them put him on a plane. And now he's gone. I don't know what to do!'

I felt myself plummet, felt the sofa envelop me as I sank into it. Adrenaline pricked at the back of my neck. 'Oh my god,' was all I could force out. Inigo and I had been due to speak earlier that day, but when I'd called him a few hours previously the line had rung out. Now I imagined Inigo's phone in the hands of some law enforcement officer, my name and the time of my call being carefully noted down. 'Did any of them say anything?' I asked her, panic rising in my chest.

'No. He hasn't got anything with him, no money, no passport. I saw them take his phone. It was local police, I think. The people on the plane were FBI.'

'Where are you now?' I asked, mainly for something to say.

'I'm back at the house. I'm trying to get a flight but I don't know where to. I don't know where they're taking him. It's a nightmare.'

As the initial shock dissipated, my mind turned to self-preservation. At that time, I had already begun writing the article Inigo and I had planned and was in negotiations with a major international magazine about its publication. I wasn't willing to give up on the work I'd done or the opportunity it represented. 'For better or worse,' Inigo had said to me, 'I have a little star power just now. I'm hoping some of that might rub off on you. Good for both of us.' He was right, of course. But generosity in the right hands, as I have come to realise, can be its own form of power.

Inigo had shared with me thousands of emails and documents. Reading them, I felt like I was in possession of the Pentagon Papers of the art world. While these documents do not exonerate Inigo, they paint a picture of a world in which some of his actions – now widely decried – are common practice, even encouraged. I had known Inigo for almost fifteen years, but much of his career – his extraordinary early success, his sudden wealth – had been a mystery, even to me. It was a thrill to spend hours reading through these documents, a strange experience that felt at once voyeuristic and deeply satisfying. As I read on, I realised that I had been handed not just a key to understanding Inigo's career, but the man himself, and by extension a greater understanding of the strange friendship we had shared for fifteen years. Since his disappearance, I had spent long hours thinking about our friendship and had more questions than answers. But these were questions I would no longer be able to put to Inigo. I would have to find answers for them myself.

Despite our conversations and the documentary evidence he'd sent me, however, I knew I didn't have anything like the full picture – of Inigo's alleged crimes, let alone our friendship. In the months and years after his arrest, I was in the odd position of having to rely on the media for news of my friend (reading an article about him in *The New York Times* entitled 'The Talented Mr. Philbrick' was a particularly surreal moment) and of combing through court documents in search of the complete story. But no headline, no cache of documents, could tell the whole truth and so in these pages I have tried not just to fill in the gaps, but to paint a picture of a man I knew (or thought I knew) for almost half my life. Along the way, I have had to engage in some armchair detective work, scouring the streets of Miami and Port Vila on Google Street View, laid out like a digital Pompeii, and reconstructing Inigo's last hours as a free man by way of media reports and art world gossip.

Inigo was in Vanuatu only on a tourist visa. This was the flaw in his plan. Mere visitors to Vanuatu, it turns out, do not benefit from the diplomatic protections that arise from the lack of a US extradition agreement. Had Inigo attained resident status – a process he told me he had begun – the FBI would have found it a much trickier task to rend him as they did; as it was, the whole process took less than forty-eight hours.

On the morning of 11 June, according to reports on Artnet, as Inigo went about his day, Kalsakau signed the removal order and handed it to Markson. From that moment, Inigo was no longer welcome in Vanuatu: without his knowledge, he had been diplomatically expelled. He was on borrowed time.

That same morning, according to media reports, Markson met with members of the Vanuatu police force. Officers were detailed to begin following Inigo and to communicate his whereabouts back to VIS. Markson communicated with the FBI and

US marshals, who told him they would be sending agents and a plane the following day: Friday, 12 June. In their eyes, Inigo had run before. They were determined that he shouldn't be able to do so again.

The next day – the Friday – broke foggily and the haze sat low and heavy on Efate island; even early in the morning the heat was dense. As Inigo was waking up and going about his last morning in Vanuatu, FBI agents and US marshals 4,000 miles away in Guam were readying the Gulfstream jet. Around 11 a.m., it took off, bearing south-west for Bauerfield International Airport, flying at over 600 mph.

Inigo was arrested at just after 3 p.m. The cars holding him and his fiancée pushed their way slowly through the heavy Friday afternoon traffic, the drivers leaning on their horns until they managed to leave the busy market street. As they picked up speed on the highway, I can imagine that Inigo looked out at the water, out over Fatumaru Bay. He was always remarkable for his calm head in adverse situations.

The federal agents touched down at 3.50 p.m. and waited. Only the pilot left the plane, making what few checks he deemed necessary as the jet cooled on the runway. The agents stayed on board. This wasn't their jurisdiction and they weren't going to do anything to jeopardise their operation. As the high whine of the twin jet engines at the back of the plane seemed to sigh as they came to rest, the agents remained in their seats and looked out of the windows, biding their time.

The two cars arrived at the airport shortly after 4 p.m. and Inigo was escorted across the tarmac. As they approached the plane, the first of two agents came tentatively down the steps of the jet, navy polo shirt tucked sharply into his ironed khakis. Behind him, photographs show his colleague wearing a bullet-proof vest, a baseball cap and some lilac-coloured latex gloves. On the tarmac, he patted Inigo down. His phone and the cash from his pockets were placed in evidence bags. The agents exchanged some perfunctory words of thanks with the Vanuatuan police, signed some paperwork, and led Inigo on to the plane where they read him his rights.

Within half an hour, the jet had taken off again, climbing high and fast, the ground – and with it Inigo's old life – plummeting away beneath it.

The unofficial motto of Guam, an island of just over 200 square miles in Micronesia, and the westernmost territory of the United States, is 'Where America's Day Begins'. By the time the Gulfstream jet that brought Inigo to Guam – more specifically to its capital, Hagåtña – had landed, his day was ending. On the plane, FBI agents had told him that he was being charged with one count of wire fraud and one count of aggravated identity theft. He talked to the agents and was apparently eager to help them. I can imagine that he also tried to enjoy the flight, likely the last private jet he would ever take. Inigo was never one to make a bad situation worse by worrying; it wouldn't help, after all.

A few hours later, Inigo was led off the plane into the steamy Guam evening. Around him, the sound of American voices and the sight of American flags atop the terminal building and American licence plates on the cars driving towards him must have brought it all starkly home. He might have been 8,000 miles from New York, but he was already in its legal grasp.

Back in New York, where it was still the morning, Assistant United States Attorneys Jessica Feinstein and Cecilia Vogel would have woken up to the news that Inigo was in custody. For months now they had been trying to understand what he'd done, had been combing through documents and emails between Inigo and his associates, the people he was accused of having defrauded. The deals were baroque: one company selling to another and then back again for seemingly no reason; dizzying amounts of money changing hands without record of goods ever being exchanged. Feinstein, according to her LinkedIn profile, had studied art history at Yale and Oxford Universities before studying law at Stanford; none of that could have prepared her fully for the complexity of this case.

Despite Inigo's confidence that there were no ongoing investigations into him, federal authorities had, it later transpired, been aware of Inigo's deeds since the previous October when news of FAP's lawsuit in Florida broke. Back then it was only a civil matter, but as more and more detail emerged it became impossible to ignore. According to court records, in early 2020 an investigation was officially opened by the FBI's Art Crime Team, led by Special Agent Christopher McKeogh.

McKeogh is not a government-issue kind of guy. In photographs, he has the suave good looks and debonair appearance of a college professor whose students have a crush on him. He has two Master's degrees in physics and at one time taught science at a university. He wears his hair medium long so that he would occasionally have to push it out of his eyes as he speaks. His mostly dark blue suits are better cut than the boxy jackets and flappy trousers one has come to expect from Hollywood portrayals of federal agents. You couldn't imagine him pulling a Glock from under all that midnight gabardine.

McKeogh has worked in the FBI Art Crime Team for almost a decade and in that time he has tracked down over 4,000 objects, caught an infamous forger of Jackson Pollock paintings and reunited the violinist Roman Totenberg's daughter with his Stradivarius thirty-five years after it was stolen. The art market, McKeogh says, 'provides an opportunity for people to move money in a way that they can't with other commodities'. And when it comes to wrongdoing in the world of fine art, 'The proof is usually in the documents.' In Inigo's case, by the time he, Vogel and Feinstein filed their complaint with a federal judge, they were certain it was.

Along with FAP, other victims had by this time come forward and provided reams of documents and bank records as well as emails, texts and WhatsApp communications. Everything Inigo had done: it was all there in black and white. It's odd for me to think about these agents and lawyers poring over many of the same documents that I would go on to possess, albeit from Inigo rather than his victims. We had much of the same evidence, but were looking for different things. I realise now that it wasn't until after Inigo's arrest that I began to believe his guilt in real world terms; until then, I think I was working under the assumption that what he had done was par for the course in the lofty upper levels of the art market. After a friendship that had started when we were no more than boys, I realised that I was still in the active mode of looking for him, rather than seeing him as the sum of his parts. At that point, I still hadn't read the documents.

The US District Court in downtown Hagåtña looks out over the ocean, over a white sandy beach. If you were to stand on its steps, you would see, in the near distance, the glinting blue waves breaking white on a reef. After that there is only the profound nothingness of the water and the air. With its darkly mirrored windows and granite portico the colour of dried blood, the building has the wiped-clean look of a desert golf motel.

Inigo spent the weekend in a jail cell. On the Monday he was finally provided with a change of clothes and a local lawyer.

The jail was populated largely with men and women – whole families, Inigo later told me – who had become embroiled in Guam's crystal meth epidemic. Around him, Inigo's cellmates detoxed as they awaited trial, their bodies wracked with fever as they contemplated their uncertain futures.

On Tuesday 16 June, Inigo appeared before the court. There, Inigo waived his right to an identity hearing (they'd got the right Inigo Philbrick) and consented not to apply for bail in Guam upon the understanding that he be transferred to the Southern District of New York within a month (if he'd applied for and been granted bail in Guam, he would likely have had to remain there for an indefinite period). The initial hearing date was set for 15 July 2020.

From Guam, Inigo later told me, he was flown to a prison in Honolulu and then to an Immigration and Customs Enforcement (ICE) centre in Nevada. After that, Inigo spent Independence Day in Grady County Jail in Chickasha, Oklahoma, a facility made famous as the place where Joe 'The Tiger King' Exotic had been held. Inigo was in Grady County for just two weeks but there he had access to a pay-per-message email system called Jail Mail, proudly provided by a company called Smart Communications, and when he emailed me from there was the first time I had heard from Inigo since his arrest. His mood was distinctly chipper as he recounted to me in typo-ridden emails (the keyboards were metal and bolted down to prevent them being used as weapons; the keys, he explained, were sticky) tales of his daily life behind bars.

I was relieved to read that he was being well treated by his fellow inmates. 'You meet better people here than you do in a five star hotel, and it's telling,' he told me. He had met an old con artist who'd tried to convince him that he'd booked Diana Ross to play the O2 Arena in London the day he was due to be released and who also informed Inigo that Australia is in Europe, 'actually a fairly widely held belief here'. Many of the incarcerated at Grady County were, he told me, illegal immigrants. 'Only in this country do we enforce our hospitality.' I wondered how long this hospitality would be enforced on Inigo, how long his cheery demeanour would last. I knew I'd be a basket case.

Less than a year before this, Inigo had lived a charmed life. He enjoyed the best food, wine, clothes and beds that money could buy. Much has been made in the press of his love for expensive wine and restaurants, but I knew him as a man who was just as happy at a good pizza joint or a roadside taco stop as in a Mayfair restaurant with a sommelier. Nonetheless, adjusting to his new gastronomic reality was a shock. The food in prison, he told me, was 'diabolical', but he was learning to improvise: he added crunch to a chicken breast with crushed jalapeño-flavoured Snyder's pretzels and had apparently received acclaim for his signature dish, 'black pepper blistered ramen . . . opening the individual servings of pepper is the skilled part of that on[e]'.

According to prison blogs and the incarceration consultants, prison days are long days: the liturgical life of the locked-in is eighteen waking hours of nothing much at all. Inigo told me that he read a lot – mainly thrillers and romance novels with raunchy equestrian or class-defying plots – but some Ian McEwan and James Joyce, too. And, he wrote, 'under quite severe cell block pressure' he acquired a jailhouse tattoo from a man who 'makes a very reasonable living tattooing his fellow inmates with a homemade gun. Amazing engineering, and he's head to toe himself; his handiwork where his hands can work – the rest by other residents. Remarkable quality.'

These emails were a lifeline for me, buoying me up and

making me laugh in the way only Inigo could. They made me feel special, too, amid the strangeness of the situation. Inigo was always an outlier among my friends: I mean, who has friends like him? Friends who become millionaire wunderkinds in their twenties and then, in their thirties, get arrested by the FBI on an island in the South Pacific? For so long, the very extraordinary nature of my friendship with Inigo had seemed entirely unremarkable to me. It took his arrest for me to begin to see how others saw him.

Suddenly I was being contacted by people I hadn't spoken to in years. When I had left the art world two years before almost no one had said anything to me; no one called or wrote to commiserate, to enquire if I was all right. Now, though, I was bombarded with messages – half intrigue, half self-concern – Inigo's notoriety conferring on me a tawdry but nonetheless thrilling newfound popularity. I see now that while I enjoyed the attention conferred on me as Inigo's confidant, what I truly liked was the sense that our friendship might really have been as significant to him as it had been to me. It wasn't until much later that I realised there likely weren't many other people who would take his calls.

Real friends are witnesses to each other's lives, not spectators. Nevertheless, I watched on as Inigo went from being a very visible man selling very visible things to no more than scammer, the wunderkind art dealer revealed as a liar and a cheat, a confidence man. It's an odd thing to start to see someone for who they really are. I thought I'd known him better than anyone else. It slowly became apparent that I knew him just as little as everyone.

While Inigo was born and spent the first few years of his life in London, he moved to West Fourth Street in Lower Manhattan when he was around five years old. He moved a few years later to Connecticut where he lived until he finished high school and returned to London for university. Despite this peripatetic life, New York always seemed the town that suited him best and where I think he felt most comfortable. The city's relentlessness, its straightforward ambition, were the perfect backdrop to Inigo's frenetic energy.

Returning on a JPATS (Justice Prisoner and Alien Transportation System) plane on 12 July – most are plain white MD-80s with a Stars and Stripes on the tail (an updated version of the one in the film *Con Air*) – was very far from the return to New York that Inigo might have imagined for himself when he fled to Vanuatu. Tray tables are removed lest they be used as weapons and each full flight carries fifteen US marshals, all armed with tasers. With the exception of Nicolas Cage in *Con Air*, no one has ever escaped from one of these flights.

On 13 July, Inigo went before a grand jury and was indicted on the charges of wire fraud and aggravated identity theft. To my surprise, he entered a plea of not guilty. The following day, at a bail hearing, Judge James L. Cott heard arguments from Cecilia Vogel and Inigo's lawyer, Peter Brill. Vogel, who like Inigo was in her mid-thirties at the time, and is a graduate of Harvard Law School, argued that Inigo was a flight risk. 'When he left,' Vogel stated, 'he abandoned his art galleries and abruptly stopped communicating with clients and lenders. He stopped responding to the legal process.' She went on to claim that Inigo had been a 'fugitive' in Vanuatu, that he had been 'under the impression that Vanuatu has no extradition treaty with the US' and that it would be 'difficult to apprehend him while he was there'. Vogel went on to tell the court that Inigo had also 'made several post-arrest statements that indicated his intent to flee'.

Brill pointed out that when Inigo had left the US for Vanuatu the previous year, he had had no notion that he was the subject of a criminal investigation. 'The way this arrest took place,' Brill argued, 'was designed so that he wasn't aware of one.' He also acknowledged that 'the cliché of the South Pacific island where no one can reach you is certainly not great optics'. Despite the fact that Inigo had travelled to Vanuatu under his own name and using his own passport (the same passport that he'd left behind on the island and which had since been cancelled); and despite the fact that he had never been convicted or accused of another crime and was by all accounts non-violent, the court denied him bail.

Inigo spent his first two weeks back in New York at the Metropolitan Correctional Center (MCC), the downtown brutalist facility that the *Los Angeles Times* has referred to as 'the Guantanamo of New York' and is infamous as the place where Jeffrey Epstein died. Before his transfer, and despite knowing whence he was bound, Inigo's mood was still good; he joked to me that he wondered if he would get 'the Epstein suite. Hopefully there's a plaque.' But Inigo wasn't destined to stay at MCC for long. Within a fortnight of his arrival there, he had been transferred to Metropolitan Detention Center (MDC), Brooklyn.

MDC is a nine-storey red-brick building that stands like a monolith and its weather-beaten facade gives it the clapped-out air of an Atlantic City casino. Although it was built in the early 1990s, and had been expanded to a capacity of around 1600 inmates by the turn of the century, its nondescript appearance gives it a sense of immovable always-thereness, as if it somehow preceded everything that surrounds it. At its main doors conical spotlights, along with the vertical letterbox windows, lend the entrance a distinctly Gotham-esque menace. This is architecture as deterrent, this is construction as threat.

Built as a response to overcrowding in the sclerotic Metropolitan Correctional Center, MDC Brooklyn is primarily a jail rather than a prison – a place where inmates, both male and female, await trial or sentencing rather than somewhere they serve lengthy terms. Those accused of violent crimes are housed together in two- or three-person cells and wear orange jumpsuits; inmates awaiting trial for non-aggressive offences wear khaki and are housed together in dorms of up to twenty people, sleeping on foam mattresses on yellow metal bunkbeds. Only the small number of permanent residents (around 300, who are kept on to service the building) have any regular access to outdoor space.

MDC Brooklyn came to prominent public notoriety in the winter of 2019 when, as parts of the US and Canada were in the grip of a polar vortex, the jail's heating and electricity systems failed. For over a week in late January and early February of that year, inmates were forced to endure freezing temperatures and were deprived of light. (Very little of the accommodation at MDC has natural light of any kind.) Inmates could be seen banging on windows, crying for help. Several of the jail's units went on hunger strike and staff retaliated by shutting off the valves to their cells' toilets so that human waste overflowed from toilet bowls mere inches from inmates' heads.

The living conditions in MDC, even before this, had been described as 'unconscionable' by a panel of federal judges; reading their report from the comfort of my home office, a room which had once been Inigo's bedroom, made me shudder with misplaced guilt. More recently, however, the jail's infamy has grown not due to conditions (which are still terrible), nor because of the numerous Covid-19 outbreaks which have occurred there, but because of the celebrity of its inhabitants.

Keith Raniere, the founder of the NXIVM (pronounced 'nex-oo-eem') sex cult and Allison Mack, the former *Smallville* star and high-level NXIVM member, were both detained at MDC before being sent on to federal prisons in Arizona and California respectively. The R & B singer R. Kelly was detained at MDC before and after being found guilty of child sexual abuse, kidnapping, racketeering and sex trafficking charges. While there, he shared a cell with a man named Brendan Hunt, whose lawyer sent them a booklet on yoga exercises to do in a confined space; Hunt turned the experience into a comic strip.

Most prominent among the celebrity inmates at MDC in recent years, however, has been Ghislaine Maxwell, the daughter of disgraced media tycoon Robert Maxwell and the erstwhile girlfriend of the paedophile financier Jeffrey Epstein. After her arrest on charges of sex trafficking minors in July 2020, Maxwell was repeatedly denied bail as a flight risk. During her eighteen-month-long pre-trial stay at MDC, she was apparently kept almost exclusively in self-isolation. She made repeated complaints about the conditions in which she was being held, telling of sleep deprivation and maggots in her food as well as physical and verbal abuse at the hands of her keepers, treatment which has apparently resulted in dramatic hair loss. In a written appeal, Maxwell's lawyers referred to her situation – that of someone subjected to such imprisonment with no criminal record or history of violent behaviour – as 'unwarranted, unrelenting, and utterly inappropriate'. Her family appealed to the United Nations, accusing the US legal authorities of blurring the 'narrow line between justice and revenge'.

When Inigo was first transferred to MDC, he was placed in a Security Housing Unit (SHU, aka 'The Shoe') – a single-person cell designed to prevent inmates from having any human contact. According to the Department for Justice Office for the Inspector General, the cells, which were modified in 2001 to house 9/11 detainees, are designed not for medical monitoring but 'to segregate inmates who have committed disciplinary infractions or who require administrative separation from the rest of the facility's population'. Inigo's food, which he told me was often served burnt, was delivered three times daily through a slot in the door. He was able to leave his cell for only occasional showers lasting no more than ten minutes. Pandemic restrictions meant that Brill could not visit him (visitors were in effect banned) and he and Inigo were restricted to discussing the case by video link or phone. In the facilities in which Inigo had previously been detained, this hadn't been a problem. In MDC, however, it became almost impossible.

At the end of July 2020, Brill complained to the courts about the conditions of Inigo's incarceration. In the six weeks since his arrest, Brill claimed, he and Inigo had 'not had a meaningful conversation of any length'. Guards told Brill that quarantined prisoners were 'not allowed video calls' and as such Brill had had to talk to Inigo on a phone which was 'given to him through the same slot in the door as his food, on a short cord'. Inigo had to 'kneel or crouch on the floor near the door'. There, Brill told the judge, 'his voice can be heard by fellow inmates and MDC personnel. There is no way to have a privileged conversation.' Brill told the judge that the effect of this treatment on Inigo had not only been 'detrimental on him', but 'may even rise to the level of a Constitutional violation'.

When I started to write this section of Inigo's story, I wrote the words 'Months passed'. Two words, twelve letters; futile, inadequate. Nothing of the loneliness of prison, nor the boredom, nor the sadness nor the yearning could possibly be contained in these or any other formulation of words. In the time since his arrest there have been many moments that I wished I could have shared with Inigo, things both personal and public: the release of the new *Fast and Furious* movie (we are both ardent fans of the franchise); my happiness in a new relationship; the birth of his child; the Damien Hirst show at the Newport Street Gallery; the reopening of Inigo's favourite restaurant, Bocca di Lupo. Perhaps the great irony of incarceration is that you must share everything – space, time, joy, food, misery, even loneliness – just not with the people you'd like to.

Much has been made about the Icarian nature of Inigo's demise. With no small amount of schadenfreude, the press enjoyed repeatedly reprinting the former United States Attorney Geoffrey S. Berman's snide remark that Inigo 'might have to trade in his jet-set life for a drab federal prison cell'. The intended moral behind this triumphalist comment is clear enough: the further you fall, the harder the impact. In the weeks after I read it, however, I found myself wondering if this can really be true. Terminal velocity for any human body, after all, is around 120 mph; it doesn't matter how much is in your bank account.

In June 2021, after Inigo had been in federal custody for a year, Cecilia Vogel wrote to the court asking for an adjournment 'because the parties are in discussions regarding a potential resolution of the case'. Then, in early August of the same year, Inigo parted ways with his attorney, Peter Brill, and instead engaged the services of Jeffrey Lichtman, a lawyer with a striking résumé. Before taking on Inigo as a client, Lichtman had previously represented the mafia boss John Gotti Jr, the drug kingpin Joaquín 'El Chapo' Guzmán, and the raw vegan chef-fraudster Sarma Melngailis (the subject of the Netflix documentary *Bad Vegan*), with whom he had had a concurrent, extra-marital sexual relationship.

At the end of August, Lichtman wrote to the court to request that a hearing scheduled for 14 September be postponed by sixty days. 'To briefly explain,' Lichtman wrote, 'we recently received extraordinarily voluminous discovery and are in the process of reviewing it with the defendant. The time we seek will permit the defendant and counsel an opportunity to digest the material and consider any pretrial motions.' The court granted the request and set the hearing for 18 November.

On that day, Inigo rode in a US marshal transport from MDC to the federal courthouse in Manhattan. If MDC is a building imbued with menace, then the Daniel Patrick Moynihan United States Courthouse, located downtown at 500 Pearl Street, is a solemn, haughty edifice, seemingly carved from the grey granite that is the very bedrock of Manhattan island. Its golden doors have a victorious glow to them, though perhaps that is because you seldom see the guilty speaking out in front of them on the nightly news.

For weeks in the run-up to 18 November there had been rumours that Inigo was intending to change his plea. There are any number of reasons why he might have done this. By this time Inigo had been behind bars for just shy of a year and a half, with little access to visitors or the outside world. Covid had put untold stresses on the already over-burdened US justice system and there was not yet a trial date set; one can imagine Inigo's desire to learn his fate and to face it head on. He was never one for stasis.

It might also be that once Lichtman had had a chance to review the discovery material he simply advised Inigo that he was unlikely to win and that a not guilty plea might in fact elongate his time behind bars if a jury came to the opposite conclusion. Add to that the 'voluminous discovery' and the incredibly complex nature of the deals Inigo had concocted and it would have meant a lengthy and expensive trial, both for him and for the US government.

Changing his plea might have brought advantages, too, beyond the mere expedition of the process. It might induce leniency in the judge when it came to sentencing, and almost certainly Lichtman would have asked for Inigo to be held in a minimum-security facility, somewhere he might have access to outdoor space and to work and visitors for the duration of his sentence. When it came to it the plea deal was struck and Inigo agreed not to appeal a sentence of under 151 months – twelve and a half years.

When Inigo arrived in Judge Sidney Stein's courtroom on that warm November day, his appearance would have shocked anyone who knew him or had seen his photo in the press. He wore a beige V-necked, prison-issue shirt and dark blue trousers. His mass of curly hair was free and wild and he was chained at his ankles. But his smile, that was still there, and as he sat down next to Lichtman, he turned to greet a friend in the front row, raising his eyebrows with delight. He acted like a man without a care in the world.

The courtroom was plush. The red medallioned carpets and reassuring wood panelling and decorative brass all around gave the room the feeling of a really top-of-the-line coffin. The face masks people wore contributed a visual hush to the whispered tones they spoke in, as if everything here were secret, proprietary. When Judge Stein came into the room everyone in the court rose and some adjusted their face masks, too, as if afraid of being told off.

Stein, who was appointed a federal judge in 1995, is a brisk, spry man in his late seventies. He has a full head of grey hair and a thin-lipped, inquisitive face, his brow often raised questioningly whether he is speaking or not. He can pull off a bow tie without a shred of irony. Though his speaking style can be circuitous, often reaching for historical comparison to further elucidate his point, he can also be remarkably blunt, saying, 'Speak to me' to a lawyer and then interrupting moments later with, 'Let me just continue.'

In pleading guilty, Inigo had also agreed to forfeit all traceable profits from the frauds he had perpetrated. At the bail hearing, Cecilia Vogel had claimed that $25 million was a 'conservative estimate' of the proceeds of Inigo's scheme. 'Conservative' was an understatement: in fact, the real number was just shy of $87 million, as the court would reveal.

By the time Inigo stood up that day in courtroom 23A, it had been just over two years since his disappearance in October 2019 and almost eighteen months since he had been in federal custody. In all that time he hadn't said a word publicly.

Stein began by asking Inigo to spell his name, how far he had gone in school, whether his mind was clear. The tone was somewhere between an arrest and that of someone inducting someone into a club or secret society.

'Mr Philbrick,' Stein continued, 'you heard Mr Lichtman a moment ago tell me that you wish to enter a plea of guilty to the charge in count one against you. Is that true, sir, do you wish to enter a plea of guilty?'

'Yes, I do,' Inigo replied. Stein went on to explain Inigo's constitutional rights were he to plead not guilty; that he would be presumed innocent; that there would be a jury of twelve people from the court's jurisdiction; that he would have the right to see and hear witnesses against him; that he would have the right to testify.

'Do you understand,' Stein then asked, 'that by entering a plea of guilty today, you're giving up every one of those rights?'

'Yes, sir.'

Stein turned to Cecilia Vogel, seated alongside Jessica Fein-stein and Christopher McKeogh, and asked, 'Why don't you set forth the elements of Count One that the government would have to prove to a jury beyond a reasonable doubt for that jury to convict Mr Philbrick of Count One?'

Vogel set out that the government would show that Inigo 'wilfully participated in a scheme to defraud or to obtain money or property by materially false or fraudulent pretences, representations or promises with knowledge of its fraudulent nature'. Vogel went on to say that she would have to prove that Inigo had 'acted with the intent to defraud' and that the crimes alleged had been committed in the Southern District of New York and that money had crossed state lines.

Vogel sat down and Stein turned to Inigo and asked, 'Do you understand that the elements the government just set forth would have to be proven beyond a reasonable doubt?'

'Yes,' Inigo replied, 'I do.'

Stein then asked if Inigo understood that the maximum term of imprisonment he could face would be twenty years; that he would have to pay restitution to the injured parties; that, even after serving his sentence, he would be liable to be on supervised release for up to three years; that he would no longer be able to vote, to hold public office, to serve on a jury, or to own a gun. He told Inigo that parole in federal cases had been abolished and that, if given a custodial sentence, he would serve all the years of any term handed down.

'Yes, Your Honour,' came Inigo's reply, again and again.

Stein then took Inigo and the court through the terms of his plea agreement: he would forfeit $86,672,790 traceable to his crimes; he would give up *Untitled* (1998) by Christopher Wool and *Untitled* (2018) by Wade Guyton; he agreed not to appeal any sentence handed down that would be less than 151 months.

'Yes, Your Honour.'

Stein instructed Inigo to tell the court, in his own words, what he did. 'From or in about 2016,' Inigo began, reading from a piece of paper on the table in front of him, 'up to and including November 2019, within the Southern District of New York and elsewhere, I knowingly engaged in a scheme for obtaining money and property by false pretences, representations and promises which was transmitted in interstate and foreign commerce.

'Specifically, I made material misrepresentations and omissions to art collectors, investors and lenders to access art and obtain sales proceeds, funding and loans. I also knowingly misrepresented the ownership of certain artworks, for example, by selling a total of more than 100 percent ownership in artworks to multiple individuals and entities without their knowledge, and by selling artworks and/or using artworks as collateral on loans without the knowledge of co-owners and without disclosing the ownership interest of third parties to buyers and lenders.

'In furtherance of this scheme, I made phone calls and sent emails from the UK to Manhattan. I knew that my actions were wrong and illegal.'

The courtroom fell quiet for a moment. And then, almost as an afterthought, Stein began again. 'Mr Philbrick, let me ask you this. Sometimes defendants don't know the answer to it. Sometimes they know it, but can't articulate it. Sometimes they know the answer. Why did you do this?'

'For money, Your Honour,' Inigo replied.

'That simple?'

'That simple.'

When I read these words, I must admit I smiled. While the honesty was admirable and the lack of contrition typical, I smiled because it felt to me as if Inigo were intentionally gifting me the last lines to this story, a final flurry of panache. It had been a collaboration, after all.

I thought I would find answers, thought I would come to understand him and our friendship, and by extension a great swath of my own life. But only those people who want to be known will ever be understood. Sometimes an inventory is the best we can hope for. D. H. Lawrence called it 'the leavings of a life'. It's done now.

I have tried to paint a portrait of the Inigo I knew rather than the Inigo I know now. In so doing, I have come to wonder if he ever really knew himself. I am ashamed to realise that I was duped longer than anyone else.

I came to see that the act of writing this book had been not simply an attempt at understanding the art market and my time in it, but also of Inigo himself and the friendship which more than any other had shaped, even defined, my adult life. Inigo ultimately evaded me, his chimeric unknowability not unlike the world that had brought us together. As I have written about our friendship I have been struck by the inadequacy of language to describe platonic relationships; that lexicon is geared towards romance. There should be more than one word for love; there should be more than one word for loss.

CODA

On 23 May 2022, the day that Inigo was due to be sentenced in New York, I was on holiday with my girlfriend on the Greek island of Milos. We arrived in the late morning on a crowded ferry from Athens. Seasick and nauseous from the boat's fumes, we sat for an hour or so in a bar in the port drinking cold beer.

Inigo's sentencing hearing had been moved twice already so it didn't feel unlikely that it might be moved again. In the shade, on my phone, I checked Inigo's court docket online and refreshed the various art news sites that had most closely covered his case. There was nothing to indicate it would move, but until that moment I had not registered the hour of his sentencing: 3 p.m. EST; 11 p.m. in Greece.

That night, I tried to stay awake, but two days of travel from London had taken their toll and I fell asleep early, lulled by the insistent shushing of the air-conditioning unit above the bed. At 3 a.m. I awoke freezing but resisted the urge to check my phone charging on a chair within reach of the bed. I turned off the air con and fell into a deep sleep. I dreamt that Inigo had been released, sentenced only to time served. I saw him vindicated in front of the courthouse, lit by camera flashes in a blaze of tabloid glamour.

For months I'd been anxious to know Inigo's fate. In the time since I'd started writing this book, I'd received vituperative emails from Inigo's mother and fiancée. Inigo himself wrote to me directly only to say that he had heard I was selling out our friendship, a claim I refuted, a claim I still refute. Later, he told his fiancée things – things meant to hurt and ridicule me – which she aimed at me in emails. Inigo has never asked me not to write this book but I had come to wonder whether I would have had the courage to write it were he not imprisoned. When I read that he had been handed a sentence of seven years, I felt relief.

I sat alone on the terrace of the guesthouse where we were staying and watched the sun come up and listened to the island coming to life. The cloudless sky moved through red to purple into a rich, beguiling blue. Fishing boats made their way hesitantly out of harbour and close at hand I could hear my girlfriend stirring in our room and other guests in bleary-eyed conversation at the beginning of a new day.

Writing is by nature a solitary pursuit and the writing of a memoir doubly so; it is to experience the solitude of living one's life twice over. Not long after Inigo's arrest, I set up a Google Alert for him. Each email bearing his name seemed to underscore his absence further. It is perhaps fitting that in this most extreme of absences, I have felt Inigo's presence the most acutely. He had been almost constantly in my thoughts. The seven years he received as punishment – five more in addition to the two he'd already served in MDC – seemed to put a sudden end to that, as if something had been severed.

Later that morning I began to receive messages and emails from people about Inigo's sentencing. The following day the *Guardian* published a piece entitled, '"He's sabotaged his entire life for greed": the $86m rise and fall of Inigo Philbrick'. One after another people sent it to me, sometimes with accompanying messages like 'I hope you're OK'; other times with no comment, just the link, like a mic-drop moment. The article was full of recycled facts and oversimplifications. In his absent presence, his story had become mine somehow, an intimate enmeshment of narratives and people like the accidental knots formed by the roots of old trees.

Four months later, Rob Newland was also charged with wire fraud. I had last seen him in November 2019 when I got off a bus in central London and stepped straight into his path. He told me he had had to part ways with Inigo earlier that year because things with him and Inigo had become untenable. He told me he was head of European sales for Hauser & Wirth. He gave me his card. A month or so later, after revelations about Inigo had continued to surface, I checked the gallery's website and could find no mention of him anywhere. Later, after Inigo's arrest, I looked him up again and found that he was head of sales at Superblue, a multinational purveyor of 'experiential art', whatever that means.

In September 2022 Rob pleaded guilty to one count of conspiracy to commit wire fraud. The US attorney's office said in a statement that Rob had helped Inigo to carry out 'a multi-year scheme to defraud various individuals and entities in order to finance Philbrick's art business'. I don't think that Rob was the voice behind the curtain, not quite; he didn't have it in him. But from what I witnessed, I believe he weaponised Inigo and his many charms and abilities, pressed the red button on what was perhaps a disaster waiting to happen. Inigo was far from innocent, but he also wasn't alone. In September 2023, Rob was sentenced to twenty months in prison.

Years ago, I met a young art critic (I'll call him James, which is a pseudonym) at a Frieze party in New York. We stood at the edge of a dance floor populated by sweating middle-aged men and gracefully attired younger women. The two groups acted on each other like opposite ends of a magnet and the whole scene had a regrettably primal feel to it. When I told James I worked in the secondary market, he rolled his eyes in knowing disdain. 'What a bunch of crooks,' he said.

James went on to tell me that he had once attended the engagement drinks of a woman with whom he had gone to college. They had seen each other infrequently since their college days, but he knew that she worked in sales for a major New York gallery; her betrothed, whom the art critic had not met, was a high-flying law enforcement official. As well as being in sales for a serious gallery, the young woman, as is not uncommon, was also the daughter of prominent art collectors. As such, not only was her employer present, but so too were the proprietors of a number of rival galleries.

As the evening wore on, James became emboldened by the open bar and as the party drew to a close, he introduced himself to his friend's fiancé. Dispensing quickly with pleasantries, James began haranguing the man, telling him an array of anecdotes about the dealers present, encouraging him to investigate them for the many rumoured illegalities. The fiancé smiled and nodded indulgently as James let off steam but when he finally came to a stop, he said simply, 'But, James, this is all just rich people stealing from other rich people. No one cares.'

Inigo's story tells us otherwise. Rich people care very much when people steal from them, no matter the thief's economic circumstances. And while a certain amount of financial malfeasance is priced in to our perception of the art market, there must occasionally be a blood-letting. Inigo was brash and young and had made too much money too quickly and spent it too loudly. He was a rotten apple, his arrest and prosecution told the world, and there's nothing more to see (at least not for a while). No one, of course, wants to acknowledge that the barrel itself is rotting.

And what would this matter anyway? No regulation has been proposed, no structural reforms. In 1988, in an interview with the *Village Voice*, Larry Gagosian was asked what he would change about the art market. '"That," he says with a touch of evil, "is like asking Dante what he would change about the structure of hell."' But people will always be who they are and Inigo was just doing what meteors do: burning with an awesome brightness before crashing down to earth.

As for me, I have largely wriggled my way free of the art world. I continue to be held in its gossipy, secretive thrall to some extent, and I go to the occasional gallery dinner when I'm asked; once in a while I travel to an art fair. Since I started writing this book, I haven't been working for Piers much, but I see him most weeks, get my fix of Lapsang and wisdom. Ben and I still walk into St James's most weeks, too; he to his gallery, me to the London Library.

I understand that, like Inigo, I have broken something by writing this book. It may not be something either of us can fix. This book and my happy life over the past few years is proof that even failed art dealers can have second chances. It is my sincere wish that Inigo should have one too.

ACKNOWLEDGEMENTS

It takes a village, or at least this book did. David Foster Wallace described the process of writing *The Pale King* (a book that eventually killed him) as like that of 'trying to carry a sheet of plywood in a windstorm'. I began to know a little of that feeling towards the end of writing this book but was so lucky to have Cecily Gayford and Shelley Wanger to help me carry it and eventually to make the incisive cuts that have improved this book far beyond my abilities. I know, too well, that good, caring, intelligent editors are hard to come by; my exceedingly good fortune was that two came along at once.

My agent, John Ash, is a man for whom I have run out of superlatives. His care and attention, but most of all his friendship during this whole process has been perhaps the finest thing to have happened to me in the writing of the book. I don't know that it would exist without him and he has made me a better writer with every conversation. Enormous thanks, too, to Emmie Francis, who introduced me to John and who I am proud to count not only as a great pal, but as godmother to Zola, the prettiest, grumpiest Jack Russell in London. Thank you to Patrick Walsh and Rebecca Sandell at PEW, who were instrumentally encouraging and helpful during the tricky midwifery of this book. Thanks, too, to Terry Wong-Lane for keeping the wolf at bay. At CAA, an enormous thank you to Daisy Meyrick, the finest translation agent in the business.

Despite a brief time spent working in publishing, long years ago, the world of books can be a murky one to navigate. My good friends Frank Wynne, James Roxburgh and Ravi Mirchandani have been kind and exemplary guides, drinking partners, late-night callers and early morning texters. James, in particular, is a man without whom my intellectual life would be a desert and the closest thing to a best friend that I care to have.

The art world may be murkier and even less navigable than publishing, but it too has its fair share of good eggs. Despite everything I have put him through over the years, Ben Hunter is still my companion in regular walks and a friend whom I value more with every step. Piers Townshend saved my life without trying and is the personification of Kipling's 'man of infinite-resource-and-sagacity'. Everyone should have a Piers in their life; I would be entirely at sea without him. My colleagues at Modern Collections, Simon Mitchell, Alex Hutchins and Olivia Paterson are a few of the people in the world who will understand what those strange days in Mayfair were like. Thank you for making them fun as well.

At Profile, Rebecca Gray, Kate McQuaid, Robert Greer, Dahmicca Wright, Jon Petre, and Georgina Difford have been not only encouraging, professional and bewilderingly efficient, but also kinder than I would ever have expected from colleagues. They have performed the weird magic of turning a scrappy Word document into the handsome book you hold in your hands. Copy editor supreme, Sally Holloway, performed an act of literary botoxing so fine that even the harshest light will not reveal my wrinkles. Steve Panton and Pete Dyer worked long and hard to make a cover that any gallery would be proud to show.

At Pantheon, hearty thanks to Lisa Kwan, who has not only been a faultless editorial assistant to Shelley, but has kindly sent me enough books to fill a small library. Thanks, too, to Lisa Lucas, whose weapons-grade enthusiasm is unrivalled in American publishing, and Sara Wood for her wonderful cover design.

Many friends read this book in manuscript and made the kind of insightful, honest comments that only the best readers can; others were there at the end of a phone or across a table with a pint exactly when I needed them. In no particular order, thanks to Sam Fletcher, Beth Jones, Martin Neild, Tessa Kerwood, Dolly Feaver, Drew Ackroyd, Henry Little, Orit Gat, Rhona O'Brien, Margaret Stead, Cecilia Campbell-Westlind, Christoper Page, Maria Garbutt-Lucero, Katie Hall and Peter Elliot. Especial thanks to Bobby and Betsy Bell, in whose cosy North Yorkshire cottage much of this book was written; and to Tim Bird, who lifted my spirits there when even the beauty of the landscape couldn't. For early support, many thanks to Charlie Brotherstone. To my redoubtable, extraordinary mother, who would never ever let me give up; and to my sister, Lily, whose eagle eye spotted solecisms and errors no one else saw: you are the cornerstones of my life.

And, finally, to Nadine, whom I love and owe more than I can put into words. For once in this book, I won't try.